Tammy

Every Day Is a Gift

Every Day Is a Gift

A Memoir

Senator
Tammy Duckworth

TWELVE

NEW YORK   BOSTON

Twelve
Hachette Book Group
1290 Avenue of the Americas, New York, NY 10104
twelvebooks.com
twitter.com/twelvebooks

First Edition: March 2021

Twelve is an imprint of Grand Central Publishing. The Twelve name and
logo are trademarks of Hachette Book Group, Inc.

The publisher is not responsible for websites (or their content) that are not owned
by the publisher.

The Hachette Speakers Bureau provides a wide range of authors for
speaking events. To find out more, go to www.hachettespeakersbureau.com
or call (866) 376-6591.

Library of Congress Control Number: 2020951068

ISBNs: 978-1-5387-1850-6 (hardcover), 978-1-5387-1849-0 (ebook),
978-1-5387-0604-6 (large-print edition), 978-1-5387-2121-6 (signed edition),
978-1-5387-2122-3 (B&N signed edition)

Printed in the United States of America

LSC-C

Printing 1, 2021

For my two beautiful girls, the joy in my world. Know that anything is possible, and that every day is a gift.

I will always place the mission first.
I will never accept defeat.
I will never quit.
I will never leave a fallen comrade.

—U.S. Army Warrior Ethos

Contents

Every Day Is
a Gift

Chapter 1

Half Child

Tammy, you're making the whole house shake!" My cousin stood in the main room of my aunt's house in Bangkok, arms folded, laughing at me. "You're stomping around like a big *farang*."

I had heard that word throughout my childhood in Thailand, along with other dismissive comments Thai kids would make to mixed-race kids like me. *Farang*, derived from *franc* or *française*, is the catch-all term Thais use to refer to a white person. But coming out of my cousin's mouth, it had a more pointed meaning of big, fat, clumsy... *different*. Born in 1968, the daughter of a six-foot-tall American dad and a five-foot-tall Thai Chinese mom, I was bigger than Thai girls my age—a fact my cousins teased me about every chance they got. Just walking through my aunt's wooden house, my footsteps falling more heavily than those of other girls, was enough to provoke a "joke" about my size.

My Thai cousins made it clear that they felt superior to me in other ways too. They'd tell me to stay out of the sun or I'd get even more freckles, which Thais considered blemishes. Any kind of spots were judged against the traditional Asian ideal of porcelain skin: If you're upper-class, you don't work outside, so your skin stays smooth and unmarked by the sun. My smattering of freckles

1

had nothing to do with working in the fields or anywhere else—I had them because my dad had them. But my cousins didn't care about that. They just liked finding another thing they could tease me about.

And then there was this classic: "Your dad smells like cheese!" Traditional Thai cuisine doesn't include cheese, and many Thais find the odor of it gag-inducing. When I was a kid, I did too. The first time my mom made me a cheeseburger, when I was about seven, I thought I was going to throw up. The smell of juicy burgers was completely overwhelmed by the sickening stench of gooey, slimy cheese. Even the texture was gross! As an adult, I did eventually develop a taste for cheese, and now good luck prying me away from a nice runny Camembert or a stinky Stilton. But as a kid who was self-conscious about being different, I felt embarrassed when my cousins would hold their noses and laugh about the way my dad supposedly smelled.

Being biracial in Thailand was complicated, especially in the 1970s, as the Vietnam War forever changed the calculus between Americans and Southeast Asians. Biracial children with *farang* fathers were looked down on as half children, and not just figuratively, as the word for "biracial" in Thai literally translates to "half child." Yet at the same time, some mixed-race people were seen as more beautiful, the result of an internationalization of white standards of attractiveness that was just starting to take hold. Pale skin, fair hair, blue eyes, aquiline nose—all of these were seen as markers of beauty. Of course, I didn't have any of those features myself. And neither did the many biracial kids whose fathers were Black U.S. servicemen, who unfortunately were treated even worse than those of us who had white fathers.

I was a mixture: I had a round face and an Asian nose, but double eyelids, sparing me the prospect of the now-ubiquitous double eyelid surgery. I also had dark brown, wavy hair rather than the glossy, straight black curtain my cousins had. Unlike theirs, my hair tended to frizz up in the humid tropical air. My mom would try to control it with braids and hair clips, until she finally just gave up and gave me short pixie haircuts instead.

I hated being teased and feeling different. But in other ways, I was very lucky. Unlike so many American men who fathered "half children" like me, my dad didn't abandon my mom, my little brother Tom, and me to fend for ourselves. He stayed and made us a family.

My dad, Frank Duckworth, grew up in Winchester, Virginia, a small town nestled in the Shenandoah Valley at the foot of the Blue Ridge Mountains. He never knew his father, Joseph Duckworth, who was killed in a motorcycle accident in 1929, just ten months after Frank was born. Suddenly left a widow at age eighteen, Frank's mother, Winnie, moved in with her parents, in a home they also shared with her two unmarried aunts. So my dad grew up in a household of four women and his grandfather, all of them struggling to survive in the dark years of the Great Depression.

Winchester is famous for three things. It was the town that changed hands the most during the Civil War, switching back and forth multiple times between the Union and Confederate sides. It's the hometown of country singer Patsy Cline, who was actually a classmate of my dad's at John Handley High School. And it's the self-proclaimed "Apple Capital" of the United States.

Surrounded by orchards, the town has celebrated the Shenandoah Apple Blossom Festival since 1924 with a big parade and the crowning of "Queen Shenandoah." Frank's mother and grandparents had no money, but like many of their Winchester neighbors, they had apple trees in their yard. So, during the Depression years, that was the one food the family always had plenty of. When my dad was hungry, which was often, they fed him every kind of apple product you can think of: apple pie, apple crisp, apple butter, apple juice, apple cider. Apples saved Dad during his childhood, but he ended up hating them. And he wasn't too keen on sticking around in the Apple Capital either, so at age fifteen he went to a local recruiter, lied about his age, and enlisted in the U.S. Marine Corps.

The Marines trained my dad to become a commo guy, setting up and wiring communications equipment. According to him, he spent the last few months of World War II in Okinawa, where his job was to run from foxhole to foxhole with a roll of wire on his back, linking up battlefield telephone systems. I can't confirm that he was actually there during the war, as what military paperwork we have of his doesn't reflect that. Then again, that paperwork is full of so many mistakes and erasures, even his birthdate was recorded differently on different documents. The one thing we do know is that early in his military career, he suffered a gash in his right arm, leaving him with an eight-inch-long scar that cut across his tattoo of the USMC anchor, globe, and eagle. He was awarded a Purple Heart, and for the rest of his life, my mom says, he was jolted awake by nightmares of being back in action.

The way my dad told it, after about five years of service, he left the Marine Corps and joined an Army program that helped enlisted troops finish college and become officers. He went to the University of Alabama for a year, but then was involuntarily recalled back to active duty, given a commission, and trained to be a signal officer. The Army sent him to France, where he spent much of the 1950s installing telephone lines and switches as part of the effort to rebuild Europe after the war. In the 1960s, as the U.S. ramped up its military involvement in Vietnam, he received orders to northern Thailand, where thousands of U.S. troops were sent in support of Air Force squadrons flying missions into the war zone. And that's where he fell in love—not only with my mother, but with life in Southeast Asia.

My mom, Lamai, was in her midtwenties at the time and working in a souvenir shop she owned with her brother. Running a shop came naturally to them, as their parents had been shopkeepers in Chaozhou, China, in the early part of the twentieth century. But in the late 1930s, as Mao Tse-tung gained power, their parents feared that the rise of communism would lead to discrimination, or worse, for capitalists like them. So they sold their shop, converted their cash to gold, and set out for Thailand—by train, by foot, by boat, any way they could get there. When they left China, they had two children. One more would be born on the journey, and my mom, the youngest, was born in 1941 after the family finally made it to Thailand.

Mom and her family were among many thousands of Chinese who immigrated to Thailand as Mao consolidated his power. They were broke by the time they arrived, but grateful to be in a country that translates, in the Thai language, as "free land." Although my mom is ethnically Chinese and her first language is Teochew, the dialect spoken in Chaozhou, not only does she think of herself as Thai, she has no desire to go to China—even for a visit. Once, when I asked if she wanted to see the Great Wall, she said, "Tammy, it is a wall of sorrow. There are bodies of slaves in the wall. Why would I want to visit that?" She and her family saw China as a place where those with power practiced brutality and those without it suffered, and they were glad to have escaped.

But tragedy followed her family to Thailand. When my mom was a toddler, her mother went to a nearby river to wash out Mom's little chamber pot. The exact details are lost to time, but somehow she lost her balance, fell into the water, and drowned. Though my mom was just a child and obviously not at fault, the rest of the family blamed her for the death. From then on, her father and siblings mistreated her horribly. Her sisters beat her, and her father refused to pay for her schooling, so she found her way to cosmetology school. The only family member who wasn't cruel to her was her brother—the one with whom, in adulthood, she would end up opening the shop in the 1960s.

My dad used to go into that shop and poke around, looking at all the sundries and souvenirs. But he wasn't really interested in what Mom was selling; he was just interested in Mom. He would follow her around, chatting her up and trying to get her attention, but she apparently liked some other American serviceman who also used to come around. There were thousands of them in northern Thailand in the 1960s, sent there as part of the war effort—young American men, very far from home, chasing, dating, and impregnating Thai women. My mom was wary of getting involved with a Soldier, though, knowing that most of them would leave at the end of their tours of service and never return.

She didn't know at first that my dad was a Soldier, because he never wore a uniform into her shop. At the time, he was serving in the U.S. Army Reserve, but his main job was working as a federal civilian employee of the Department of the Army. He told her he was a Soldier only after they started dating, and when she balked, he promised that he'd take care of not just her but her family too. That's how he won her over.

My mom agreed to marry him. The only problem was, my dad was already married.

I don't know much about his first wife, but he had three kids with her—two daughters they had together, and a stepdaughter from his wife's previous marriage. From what I could tell, when my dad fell in love with my mom, he simply decided he was done with that family. He flew home from Thailand to get divorced, then came right back to marry my mom. As a child, I was always a little bit haunted by the fact that Dad seemed to have abandoned his first family, which made me worry that one day he might just up and leave us too. My mom's sisters, who never missed a chance to belittle her, used to insist that he was going to do exactly that.

One of my first memories is from the early 1970s, when I was about three or four years old and my brother Tom was a toddler. My mom pulled me aside and told me that Dad was going away for a while. He'd gotten orders for a one-year Army tour of duty at Fort Sheridan, near Chicago, and instead of going with him, we would stay in Thailand. I'm not sure how she expected me to respond, but I jumped up and ran into the kitchen. I opened the cabinet under the sink to make sure we had enough rice to survive, in case Dad didn't come back, and was relieved to see a forty-pound bag there. "We have rice," I told my mom. "We will be okay."

"Don't be silly," she snapped, pushing me away from the cabinet. She felt bad that I was worried, and whenever Mom felt bad, her first response was usually anger. But she had to have been worried too, because there really was no guarantee that Dad would come back. And if he didn't, she would be stuck there, alone, raising two biracial children in a culture that rejected them.

In fact, discrimination against biracial kids was so ingrained in Thai culture that even the government officially exercised it. A few days after I was born, when my parents went to an office in Bangkok to register my birth, a bureaucrat there told them they weren't allowed to give me the name they had chosen. Dad wanted to name me Winnifred, after his mother, but the man behind the desk said he would only register me as a newborn if I had a Thai name. My parents argued with him, but he wouldn't budge. While I doubt he would have gone so far as to deny me a birth certificate, my mom decided it just wasn't worth the fight. She quickly chose Ladda—a common and nice enough Thai name, roughly the equivalent of being named Anna or Joan in America.

Discrimination is never good, but at least there was an upside to this particular instance: It saved me from being named Winnifred. Apologies to all the lovely Winnies out there, but it's just not the name for me. Neither is Ladda, really—but like most Thais, my mom decided to call me by a nickname rather than my given name. The name she chose was Tammy, and that's what I've always been called.

In the year that Dad was gone, we had to move in with my mom's eldest sister, and she spent the entire time criticizing my mom, telling her we'd never see him again. "This is what you get for marrying an American," my aunt would say. "You should have known better! He's never coming back." My cousins teased me about it too, saying, "Oh, look! Your *farang* father has abandoned you. Just like all the Americans do."

It was no wonder they believed that. We had all seen the homeless "half children" with round eyes and wavy hair begging for pocket change on the streets. And everyone knew about the orphanages full of biracial kids—children whose G.I. fathers had abandoned them, and whose Thai mothers either couldn't or wouldn't care for them. Many of these young mothers were shamed and wrongly accused as being prostitutes for having had sex with *farang*s, and some were pressured by their families to disown their children.

During the Vietnam War era, tens of thousands of Amerasian kids were born in countries like Vietnam, Laos, Cambodia, the Philippines, and Thailand. In Vietnam, they were derided as "children of the dust." In Thailand, as elsewhere in Southeast

Asia, they often ended up mired in poverty, lucky if they could find work as exotic decorations at restaurants, nightclubs, and strip joints. Sometimes strangers would offer young mothers money to "adopt" their "half children." Very few of these adoptions were aboveboard, and many such children were sold into a life of servitude. The worst outcomes were of countless children being sold into Southeast Asia's notorious sex trade and forced into sexual slavery.

One afternoon when I was less than a year old, my mom took me with her on a water taxi down the Chao Phraya River, which runs through central Bangkok. A man on the boat looked down at me and smiled. Then he turned to my mom and said, "She's so cute." My mom nodded, taking note of his expensive clothes, his southern Thai accent, and the fact that he appeared to be shaking. Suddenly the man blurted, "Twenty-five thousand baht!" He was offering to buy me, for the equivalent of about $1,200. He obviously thought she was raising me alone, probably desperate, and maybe even a prostitute. My mom reacted instantly and viscerally. "No!" she yelled, hugging me tightly and moving away from the man. "I'm not going to sell my baby!" She had a husband, and I had a father—but so many others did not, and sadly, men such as this one would have no trouble finding other young mothers and children to exploit.

For many such children, the wounds inflicted by their abandonment never healed. To this day, men and women my age contact my Senate office from Thailand, asking for help in finding long-lost fathers. People send me heartbreaking emails saying little more than "Can you help me find my father? His name was Sam. He was a Sergeant in the Army." Sometimes they'll have a piece of a uniform, or a long-abandoned Army footlocker, or an old black-and-white photo of a fresh-faced young American man posing with a smiling teenage Thai girl. It's heart-wrenching to have to tell them, "I'm sorry, but there were thousands of Sams like your father." I try to help when I can, but there are too many stories, too many children left behind, and too few answers to the questions that have burned in these people's souls for more than five decades.

Looking back now, I understand how desperate our situation would have been if my dad hadn't returned. My mom would have been young, abandoned with two Amerasian kids and no job, living at the mercy of her judgmental siblings. How long would it have been before we were out on the streets? I almost certainly wouldn't have been able to finish school, instead having to go to work in a factory or as a maid. I know my mom; she's tough. She wouldn't have abandoned Tom and me. But there would have been no other obvious path but to repeat her own early life in poverty with her two "half children."

Even as a child, I knew that without my dad, we had no future. And that scared me enough that when my aunt began berating my mom, I lashed out at her—which is not what little Asian kids do.

"He *is* coming back!" I yelled. "And you shouldn't talk about him like that. He paid for half the stuff in your house!" My aunt, infuriated that a child would dare speak to her like that, responded with a backhand to my face. She slapped me into submission while my mom stood by silently.

Mom didn't step in to pull me away from the beating; having been beaten all her life by this same sister, she knew that resisting would only prolong it. But after it was over, she pulled me close. "Don't do that again, Tammy," she said. She told me there was nothing she could do if my aunt hit me, because we were dependent on her for the roof over our heads. I was stung by the humiliation of feeling so powerless, but I could tell that my mom was grateful I had stood up for her. I also knew that I would never, ever let myself get into a situation where I had to stand by and watch someone innocent being beaten. I would act, even if it wasn't the smartest thing for self-preservation.

That was a long year for all of us, but at the end of it my dad did come back, just as he'd promised. He loved my mom, my brother, and me—but we weren't the only reason he returned. As I would come to understand later, my dad also loved the version of himself that he could be in Thailand.

In the States, Frank Duckworth would forever be just another regular joe, a lower-middle-class guy eking out a paycheck in some American town. But in Asia, he was a strapping, six-foot, two-hundred-pound man who towered over most other men. And as discriminatory as Thai culture could be, there was respect for Americans. My dad had a wallet full of U.S. dollars and a Yankee swagger, and he loved feeling like the big man when he was in Thailand.

As the Vietnam War began drawing to a close, most of the American servicemen in Southeast Asia couldn't wait to get the hell out. But Dad sought out jobs that would keep him in the region, first in Thailand and then in other countries such as Cambodia, Indonesia, and Singapore. He didn't make as much money as he would have in the States, but the salary he got overseas as a foreigner was more than what locals made—another reason he felt like a big man.

Thanks to the skills he'd learned in the Army, he had no trouble finding work; there was always a need for communications experts who could set up telephone switchboards and lines, cable systems, and, later on, satellite dishes and radar stations. He also used the rifle skills he'd learned to build a network of upper-class Thai and Malay contacts by working as a pro at local shooting clubs and winning skeet and trap competitions. Dad was a world-class shooter, even earning a President's Hundred Tab, awarded to the top one hundred civilian and military marksmen each year. This just added to his big-man mystique, which in turn helped him land more job offers.

We lived a comfortable life in Bangkok, my dad earning enough to send me to kindergarten at Saint John's, a private Thai school. I learned to read and write in Thai and soon was reading everything I could get my hands on. My mom and I spoke Thai together, and although my dad usually spoke to me in English, I couldn't really speak it myself. So while I may not have looked like the delicate, lithe Thai girls I went to school with, I still came across as more Thai than American at that time.

Eager for me to fit in, my mom tried to compensate for my being half-white by signing me up for classes in traditional Thai dance. I would rather have been out playing ball, or at home sneaking one of Mom's Thai romance novels to read, but I gamely clomped around the dance studio, feeling like a giant among the Lilliputians, in hopes of pleasing her. I loved the beauty of Thai dance, even though I couldn't do it very well. Despite the attitudes of some Thais toward "half children" like myself, I felt proud of my Thai heritage. I still do.

As much as Mom tried to instill Thai-ness into my brother and me, my dad set out to create his own little mythical America in our home. Every Christmas he went crazy with J. C. Penney and Sears catalogues, sending away for decorations, ornaments, and gifts that would arrive, via the APO address Dad got as an overseas service-member, just in time for the holiday. We'd hang tinsel and large multicolored teardrop lights in the branches of scraggly pine trees that, to this day, I don't know how he tracked down in Thailand's tropical climate. Mom got into the holiday spirit too, dressing me up like a doll in itchy wool stockings, red-and-green plaid jumpers, and long-sleeve sweaters, despite Thailand's hundred-degree heat. And Dad always made sure that Tom and I had those little stockings made of red plastic webbing filled with sticky American candies, which never survived the trip to Asia without melting and resolidifying multiple times.

Decades later, during my wartime service in the equally hot (but distinctly less tropical) climate of Iraq, I would experience a pleasant bit of déjà vu when opening Christmas care packages sent by church groups in the States. I'd tear open a box and revel in the smell of butterscotch candy fused to peppermint drops, packed together with squishy globs of melted fruit jelly slices. It took me right back to my childhood in Bangkok all those years ago.

But even as my dad tried to create a Little America for us, I suspect there was another, darker reason he preferred keeping us in Southeast Asia. Dad's family history stretched back to before the American Revolution, and his roots in Winchester ran deep. Like many Virginia families, his was split down a historical fault line, with some of his relatives having fought for the North in the Civil War, and many others having fought for the South. My dad never seemed to reconcile his family's Confederate history with the fact that he had biracial children.

And although it's difficult to imagine now, at the time my parents met, they couldn't have legally married in Virginia. It wasn't until June 1967, when the Supreme Court decided *Loving v. Virginia*, that people of different races were allowed to marry there—and even then, prejudice and racism against such relationships lingered. I can only surmise that my dad felt more comfortable facing prejudice in another country than right in his own backyard.

As my mom soon found out, he even felt more comfortable taking his young family to a war zone than back to the United States.

Chapter 2

Country Woods

In 1974, my dad took a job stringing telephone wires for a United Nations Development Programme project in Phnom Penh. At the time, Cambodia was embroiled in a violent civil war, with communist Khmer Rouge insurgents seizing territory controlled by the U.S.-backed Khmer Republic, mile by bloody mile. The fighting had been raging for nearly five years, a savage echo of the war going on just across the border in Vietnam.

The situation in Cambodia was dangerously unstable, but at age six, I had no idea about any of that. I loved living in Phnom Penh. In Bangkok, we'd had a small apartment, but here we had a multistory house with a garden. Because we were a UN family, we had security—a gate surrounding the house, with an armed soldier posted out front. I didn't understand that the guards' fully loaded rifles were more than just decoration, or that the threat of violence in the capital was real and ever present. I just liked playing with the soldiers and trying to learn enough words in the Khmer language to talk to them.

When I think back on our time in Cambodia, I think of drives down wide boulevards lined with mango trees and bougainvillea flowers. I remember the smell of French boules, crusty and golden, their interiors fragrant with warm, yeasty, deliciously doughy bread. Whenever Mom would take Tom and me to the market, she had to buy two or three at a time, because we would tear into them as soon as we got to the car, devouring an entire boule before the driver got us home. Phnom Penh was colorful and fun, and the people at the market always seemed so friendly.

But then, I remember another scene. My mom and I were in the car, heading to market, and suddenly she grabbed me and shoved me headfirst down to the floorboard. She yelled at the driver to turn around, and I lay there confused, my face flat against the mat and Mom's hand pressed to the back of my head to keep me from looking up. A bomb had exploded in the market just minutes earlier, and she was desperately trying to protect me from seeing the blood and body parts scattered among the stalls. The driver floored it, and we raced straight back to the house.

Somehow, I still wasn't scared, even as the bombings inched closer and closer to our home. My parents used to take Tom and me to the roof so we could see the bombs drop over the river and the flares soaring into the sky. "Look, Tammy," my dad would say. "Look at the pretty fireworks." I believed they were fireworks, so when I'd hear the sounds of explosions and see the rockets lighting up the sky, I never felt scared.

Dad also brought us to the airfield to see the C-130 planes that sometimes ferried him to Laos and Thailand for work. A couple of times, he brought us along for rides to Bangkok, to see our relatives. My mom wasn't keen on this, but to me, there was nothing cooler than sitting in the back of one of these big planes, looking out of the lowered tailgate, and seeing jungles, rivers, and villages whiz by below. I couldn't have imagined then that one day, thirty years later, I'd be piloting my own aircraft over palm groves and villages not so different from these.

In later years, when I asked my mom about our family's experiences in Cambodia, she would describe this time as a difficult one. While my memories are of colorful street scenes and fresh bread, hers are of being mostly confined to our gated home as the fighting closed in on the capital. It must have been incredibly stressful for her, worrying about the safety of her young children in a war zone that was only growing hotter. She also never knew if my dad would return home safely each night from his job sites across the city. Yet when most Americans started flooding out of Phnom Penh in early 1975, my dad insisted that we stay. He believed that there was no way the United States would allow Cambodia to fall to the Communists, and that any day, American troops would arrive to fight the Khmer Rouge.

"They're coming," he'd say. "You'll see." He was a firm believer in the domino theory, that if one country fell to communism, others would soon follow suit. The war in Vietnam had ground to a bloody stalemate, and if we couldn't defeat the Communists there, then surely we could—we had to!—erect a firewall in Cambodia. My dad trusted that the Americans would do everything they needed to do to hold the line in Southeast Asia. He refused to believe that our government would do anything less.

But as the fighting drew ever closer to our home, my dad finally realized that he couldn't keep us there anymore. So in early April of 1975, he got Mom, Tom, and me on the last commercial flight heading out of Phnom Penh. In my recollection, we just went to the airport and got on the plane. Years later, though, my mom told me that in the airport, we had to sit on the floor, our backs pressed to a wall, crouching below window height to avoid bullets that were flying overhead.

We made it safely to Bangkok, and shortly after that, my dad told my mom in a phone call that a bomb had blown up right outside our house. The explosion had sent shrapnel flying through a window and over the bed where he was sleeping, peppering the wall across the room. That same week, he was up a telephone pole, stringing wires with a Cambodian worker, and a rocket landed at the bottom of the pole. It didn't explode, thank God. But my dad realized that he too had to leave, or risk losing his life there.

Dad was evacuated in Operation Eagle Pull—the final wave of U.S. military transport planes to leave Phnom Penh, on April 12. By that date, the capital was surrounded by the Khmer Rouge, completely cut off from supplies and bombarded by endless waves of artillery fire. Five days later, on April 17, 1975, the Khmer Rouge stormed in, and Phnom Penh fell. We had made it out just in time.

From my family's safe haven in Bangkok, we watched TV news coverage of the chaos erupting across Indochina. Two weeks after Phnom Penh fell, Saigon did too, as North Vietnamese and Vietcong troops surged into the capital. And many of the Americans in Saigon did exactly what my dad had done, waiting until the last possible moment to get out.

At first, they evacuated in airplanes. But after the North Vietnamese Army launched bombing attacks on Tan Son Nhat Airport, the United States initiated the largest helicopter airlift in history, Operation Frequent Wind. In less than twenty-four hours, our helicopters evacuated more than 1,000 Americans and 5,000 Vietnamese from Saigon to U.S. aircraft carriers in the South China Sea.

On TV, I saw the famous image of people pushing their way up a ladder, trying to board a Huey perched on the roof of a Saigon building. Decades later, I would begin my own military service by learning to fly those same Huey helicopters, and much of my training—and the training of other pilots I'd fly with—would come from Vietnam War Veterans. Little did I know it then, but the tactical flying skills these helicopter pilots had learned in Vietnam would one day save my own life.

I also saw much more disturbing images, of rickety boats crammed with frightened people and their crying children. In the spring of 1975, tens of thousands of Vietnamese, some with nothing more than the clothes on their backs, clambered into fishing boats, trawlers, and sampans in hopes of making it to one of the many U.S. warships anchored off the coast. This was the first wave in what would become a nearly two-decade exodus of hundreds of thousands of "boat people" from Southeast Asia.

Watching these scenes as a seven-year-old child affected me, even though I was too young to fully take in what I was seeing. I understood that the United States was rescuing people with helicopters, and that the people who crowded onto those boats were looking to us for protection. I wasn't sure exactly what Communists were and why they wanted to do such terrible things, or even what those terrible things were. I just knew that we had been at war with them, and now they were winning and the Americans were leaving. The local people were desperate to go with the Americans, because they needed our help. This felt personal for me, because I was American and so was my dad. I was proud that we were the good guys, but also confused about why Americans couldn't save all those people.

Seeing those TV images of people crammed into boats in 1975 made a strong impression on me. But I also saw the plight of refugees in person. My dad got a job working with UN refugee programs, delivering aid to camps filled with Cambodian and Vietnamese people who'd managed to escape to Thailand. A couple of times he brought me along, so I could watch him deliver big bags of rice and boxes of medical supplies stamped with the American flag and see how people's faces lit up. Those moments intensified the pride I felt. From a child's perspective, this all seemed very simple: Americans were the ones who helped people in need, who opened their doors and took in refugees, who *cared*.

I had the same feeling when my dad took us to see the U.S. diplomats cutting ribbons to open new hospitals and schools in Bangkok. I would eagerly tell other people in the crowd that my dad was American, and because of that, *I* was American. I still had never been to the United States, and wouldn't get there for five more years. But these experiences marked the beginning of my deep feeling of patriotism for this country.

The following year, we moved to Indonesia. My dad had been hired to manage Country Woods Estates (now called Country-woods Residences), a gated housing development where wealthy expats could live with their families in a suburban-style setup. Country Woods had eighty or so houses, tree-lined streets, a big grassy field, and tennis and basketball courts, all of it spread over a few private acres in south Jakarta. It was pleasant inside, a tropical version of a small-town American neighborhood. But outside, it was surrounded by concrete block walls topped with broken glass and guarded 24/7.

There were no native Indonesians living there; it was mostly foreign oil company executives, businesspeople, and occasionally teachers from the international schools—although that only ever happened when both spouses worked, as Country Woods was too expensive on one teacher's salary. It was also too expensive for

Peace Corps folks, and it didn't take long before we started looking down our noses at expats like them, who were willing to live "on the economy," mixed in with locals. Living in Country Woods Estates made me feel special, maybe even a little snobby.

My dad did everything he could to turn Country Woods into a Beaver Cleaver–style neighborhood, and it was a great place to be a kid. Tom and I could ride our bikes all over the compound, play on multiple playgrounds without supervision, swim at the pool. When we were hungry, we could grab a hot dog, a Popsicle, or *nasi goreng* (a local rice dish topped with a fried egg and crispy shrimp puffed biscuit) at the general store or the pool clubhouse, and just charge it to our parents' account. On Halloween, all the kids trick-or-treated, and at Christmas we had a tree-lighting party for the whole community.

Dad pretty much ran the place. He set up a traffic management system and arranged for the compound to have its own water and electricity supplies. But the coolest thing he did was to wire all the houses to watch movies he'd play on a newfangled invention, the VCR. We had both the VHS and the more expensive Betamax versions, and after comparing the two, Dad proclaimed that Betamax would be the dominant format. He loved movies, especially John Wayne Westerns and war movies. He set it up so everybody in the whole compound could watch *Grease*, or *Close Encounters of the Third Kind*, or whatever World War II movie he felt like watching for the umpteenth time. People were amazed, and my dad loved it. At Country Woods, he was the big guy—the American hero—yet again.

He was also busy trying to turn Tom into a young version of an American hero. As the only son of a Southern American dad and Asian mom, Tom was the prized child. While I was expected to do chores and housework, he had no real responsibilities around the house. Dad spent hours teaching Tom the finer points of baseball, and all I could do was watch jealously, wishing I got half the attention my little brother did. This created a bitter sibling rivalry between us, which was a shame, because Tom was a smart and interesting kid.

Tom has always been able to fix anything. At age six, he took apart a radio and put it back together. He loved messing around with radio-controlled cars, and he even built one from scratch. Sometimes, when none of our friends were around, he and I would play with Legos together. We both were mechanically minded, so we'd spend hours creating elaborate buildings and structures.

Yet although Tom was obviously smart, he struggled academically. To my eyes, he wasn't applying himself, but Tom's response to challenges in school was to get really good at other pursuits—like making every all-star team in baseball, or building ever more complex electronics. I did the opposite, working my tail off trying to get good grades. I wanted so badly to make my dad proud, but no matter how hard I worked, he never seemed to notice. Tom never angled for Dad's attention the way I did—because he didn't have to. He always had it, just by virtue of being a boy.

With his knowledge of technology, his confident bluster, and his tendency to dismiss alternative opinions, Dad seemed all-knowing to me. It never occurred to me that he might not be right about everything; he would make a proclamation, and we all believed him. It's funny now to think about his absolute certainty that Betamax would conquer VHS. But as I would later realize, that declaration was just one example in a long string of bullshitting. My family would end up learning the hard way that Dad didn't always know what he was talking about.

I was eight years old when we moved to Country Woods, and fifteen when we left. This was the longest our family had ever stayed in one place, and I loved it. My best friend, Anna, lived down the street, and we used to bike all over, climbing trees and plucking sweet, crisp, pink mountain apples called *jambu* and spiny red rambutan fruits to snack on. I went to the Jakarta International School, where I learned to read and write in English. And a few years later, when I was twelve, my dad put me in the driver's seat of the Country Woods maintenance department's red Toyota pickup truck, then instructed me to drive back and forth across a dirt field at the back of the estate grounds. This served two purposes: teaching me how to drive a stick shift, and flattening the field so he could build a baseball diamond.

At least once a month, our whole family flew to Singapore. The corporate headquarters for Country Woods' parent company was there, and Dad had to go for meetings and to present reports. But these weren't boring old business trips—far from it. We all loved going to Singapore, which felt like the land of milk and honey.

An island nation perched at the southern tip of Malaysia, Singapore was super clean, had great stores, and best of all...it had a McDonald's. Tom and I would get so excited for Filet-O-Fish (the favorite sandwich for me and most of my Asian friends), fries, and milkshakes. At the supermarket, we could buy special treats like Pop-Tarts, which were near impossible to find in Jakarta—and when you could find them, they often had weevils or little wriggly worms in them. Even Mom would splurge in Singapore, treating herself to a bottle of nail polish or a lipstick. But our first stop always had to be Cold Storage, one of the two big supermarkets (the other was Fitzpatrick's).

Mom would pick out cuts of meat, which Cold Storage then put into deep freezers. During our three- or four-day visits, the meat would freeze solid, like bricks, and at the end of our trip we'd pick it up, pack it into cooler bags, and head straight to the airport.

We did this every visit, because although Mom bought most of our food in Jakarta, Dad refused to eat the local meat. He didn't trust its quality—which is not surprising, given the worms we found in the Pop-Tarts.

Dad didn't trust Indonesian dental care either, so he also took me to an orthodontist in Singapore. For a few years, every time we went, I'd have to drop in and get my retainer adjusted. But even that unpleasant chore didn't detract from the magical feeling of being there. It was just part of our routine, one of the things we did together, as a family, every month.

I felt incredibly lucky during these years. Despite my aunts' shrill fearmongering when I was little, our family had stayed together. My dad was strict and not very affectionate, but I looked up to him, as it seemed like he could do or fix just about anything. On Sundays, instead of going out right away to play with Anna, I'd sit cross-legged on the floor next to our leather couch, where Dad sat reading the Sunday edition of the *Straits Times*. Whenever he finished a section, he'd drop it to the floor beside me. I'd quickly read it, and then we'd discuss the week's news and comics.

I always looked forward to these mornings, sitting in our comfortable house, our bellies full of breakfast, enjoying the paper together. Although I was young, I was extremely aware of how different my life was from those of many other, less fortunate people I had seen in Thailand, Cambodia, and Indonesia. And I understood that it was my blood ties to faraway, mythical America that afforded me this privileged place in the world.

In 1980, when I was twelve, I finally got to visit the country I'd been dreaming of for so long. That summer, we took a three-week trip to the States, going to Hawaii; then San Francisco; then Washington, DC; and then the icing on the cake: Disney World! Weirdly enough, I don't remember tons of details from the trip.

I remember seeing hula dancers and swimming in Hawaii. And I remember my dad being pissed off because he lost our book of tickets to go on rides at Disney World and had to buy more. But the one memory that really stands out had to do with the American flag.

The United States had recently celebrated its bicentennial, and everywhere we went, there were clothes and towels and bandannas and even underwear made with Stars and Stripes designs. During our week in Hawaii, I saw a woman on the beach wearing an American flag bikini, and my mouth just fell open. Was this *legal*? Could you really make—and sell—any product you wanted out of the flag? This was completely unthinkable in the countries where I had grown up.

When I was a kid in Bangkok, I wore the kind of tube socks everybody wore in the '70s—white socks, over the calf, with three colored stripes at the top. One of the random color schemes was two red stripes with a blue stripe in the middle. But those were forbidden in Thailand, because they resembled the Thai flag. You might get a slap on the wrist for socks, but making underwear out of the flag? That would land you in jail. The Thai government took its symbols so seriously, you could be arrested if you stepped on baht currency, as it had a picture of King Bhumibol on it.

So walking around an American shopping mall and seeing Stars and Stripes boxer shorts and bras just blew my twelve-year-old mind. I kept looking around, waiting for the police to storm in and arrest everyone. And even though that didn't happen, I still couldn't believe that people actually bought this stuff and wore it. In public!

The degree of freedom Americans enjoyed to say, wear, and do whatever they wanted was shocking to me. I was used to places like Singapore, which kept tight controls on everything people did. Chewing gum was banned there—you could get fined if you were caught chewing it anywhere in the country. Spitting on the sidewalk could land you a $300 fine. If a male passenger flew into Paya Lebar Airport with long hair, the authorities would cut it *at the airport* before letting him into the country. And when I was in the eighth grade and the rock megaband KISS flew in to Singapore for a concert, the government actually made them wash off their stage makeup before allowing them to enter the country.

This was the strict environment I had grown up in, and it was what felt "normal" to me. So getting a glimpse of the freedoms Americans enjoyed was eye-popping. When you grow up with such freedoms, it's easy to take them for granted. But I saw everything through the eyes of an immigrant, even though I wasn't one. For all of these reasons, I realized from a young age what a privilege it was to be an American.

I was also very lucky that, unlike many others, I never had to find a way to prove that I was American. In 1982, when I was fourteen, President Reagan signed into law the Amerasian Immigration Act. This new law was aimed at allowing biracial children of U.S. servicemen—kids who were born in Korea, Vietnam, Laos, Cambodia, or Thailand since 1950, then abandoned by their fathers—to come to America. President Reagan called it "a major step of facing up to the moral responsibility which we can't ignore." He also said that "instead of saying 'welcome' to these children, we should say, 'Welcome home.'"

For the thousands of "half children" who'd suffered discrimination, poverty, and the psychic toll of abandonment, the Amerasian Immigration Act must have felt like the answer to a prayer. But now they had to find a way to prove they actually had American fathers. Anticipating this, the law decreed that in addition to "birth and baptismal certificates, local civil records, photographs of, and letters or proof of financial support from, a putative father," the attorney general would also consider "the physical appearance of the alien."

As soon as the law passed, U.S. embassies in Southeast Asia were overwhelmed by a rush of people trying to prove they had American fathers. And the "physical appearance" clause led to unbelievable scenes of Amerasian teenagers standing in front of U.S. consular officials, clutching faded war photos and pointing to their own wavy hair, light eyes, or freckled faces. I saw children, many no older than I was, frantically trying to claim their U.S. citizenship and passport—both of which I was fortunate enough to already have. Now, when I looked in a mirror, I saw that the freckles that had caused me such anguish in my childhood were actually a blessing. For many, freckles were the difference between life as a U.S. citizen or life in a refugee camp.

In so many ways, my life at that time seemed charmed. But in the spring of 1982, my dad lost his job. And that's when the trouble started.

Chapter 3

Cast Away

W e were all in Singapore, enjoying one of our monthly family trips, when Dad came back from a meeting with his boss. He told us to sit down on our hotel beds, as he had some news.

"Country Woods has been sold," he said—by one big multinational corporation to another. I stared at him in shock. What did this mean? Would we have to move? Was Dad getting fired?

"Don't worry," he quickly assured us. "Everyone's going to keep their jobs." He acted unconcerned, but I couldn't help but feel a tinge of worry. It was especially hard to get this news in Singapore, our family's happy place, which I knew we could afford to visit only because of Dad's job at Country Woods.

Dad insisted that if any employees did lose their jobs, he wouldn't be among them. He felt he had good reason to be confident, because he had spent the past seven years almost single-handedly improving Country Woods. When we first moved there in 1976, it was half empty and sort of run-down. Bit by bit, he fixed up every part of the property, from the houses to the grounds to the infrastructure. He made Country Woods the most desirable living space for expats in Jakarta, and now it was full of families who loved living in their little slice of America. The residents all knew him and appreciated his special touches that made it feel like home, and now there was even a waiting list of people wanting to move in.

But in the end, none of that mattered to the new owners. They knew they could hire an Indonesian manager for less than half of what they paid my dad, and they also wouldn't have to kick in for Tom's and my tuition at the Jakarta International School. Dad was very good at what he did, but he was expensive. So, within a few weeks of the handover, the company let him go. And he decided that instead of him trying to find another job in Jakarta, we should pack up and move to Singapore.

I was sad to leave Country Woods. It was an idyllic place for an active kid like me, and an island of stability after we'd spent the first part of my life moving from place to place. And although we'd loved our monthly trips to Singapore, it soon became obvious that making our home there would prove difficult. Dad didn't find a job right away, and the cost of living was a lot higher than in Jakarta. Pretty soon, money started to get tight.

My parents sent me to a tiny start-up school with only about a dozen students to finish out my eighth grade year. Dad kept applying for jobs, but nobody wanted to pay the higher salary needed to hire an American. He was weirdly unfazed by this, even though we were beginning to run out of money. "Everything's going to be fine," he'd say. "You'll see—there's a job right around the corner!"

This went on for a few months, until he finally found work at a shipping company. I don't know how much they paid him, but it was enough for my parents to afford the tuition for Tom at the Singapore American School and for me at the United World College of Southeast Asia, a British-style boarding school in Singapore.

It made no sense for me to go to boarding school in the same city where my family was living, but Dad had this idea that I ought to learn proper manners and etiquette, and the British school seemed like the place to do that.

Now that I was starting high school, I had a plan of my own. I decided that no matter how much work it took, I had to find a way to skip a grade. The reason had to do with Dad's first family, the one he'd abandoned all those years ago.

He didn't talk much about them, but every so often he'd make a revealing comment. I knew that the kids had been college age by the time he'd left the family. According to him, they had been opposed to the war in Vietnam, and as an Army officer serving the U.S. forces fighting there, he felt judged by them. But it was a particular detail about his stepdaughter Diana that stuck with me. Apparently, she was an exceptional student, so smart that she had skipped a grade in high school.

I first heard him talk about this when I brought home a report card in elementary school. I had done pretty well, making mostly A's, a few B's, and maybe a C in band, which was always my worst subject. (I had no rhythm but took up the flute because Dad said that was the proper instrument for a girl.) But I knew he'd be pleased about one fact. "Look, Dad," I said. "I got an A in math!" As usual, I was angling for his praise, though the most he'd ever say was "That's good, Tammy." But then I noticed his eyes were getting misty, and I felt my heart swell. He *was* proud of me! And then he said, in a voice choked with emotion, "You know, Diana always made straight A's." My mouth fell open. "She's got a photographic memory. She even skipped a grade."

Growing up, I knew that Tom, the only son, was my parents' golden child. As a girl, there was nothing I could do about that. But now, to my shock and horror, I realized that Dad had a stepdaughter that he felt prouder of than me. In his eyes, she was smart and special, and I was not. And that realization crushed me.

As he got older, my dad became very emotional about certain topics. In his later years, whenever he talked about President Reagan, or the Marine Corps, or Diana, he'd get a catch in his voice and tears in his eyes. He felt pride in them, and he wasn't afraid to show it. But he never once said he was proud of me. And that was the one thing I desperately wanted.

The sole positive comment he used to make about me was "Tammy's not the smartest kid, but she works the hardest." And he was right. I studied like crazy, often working through lunchtime. I was never afraid to put in hours of effort if that's what I had to do to excel. But I hated hearing him say that, because I thought of myself as a smart kid, and it hurt me that he didn't think so. "Keep up those grades," he'd say, "and one day you might be able to get into Duke. Like Diana."

It took me years to understand that Dad liked to create idealized versions of people and places. "The corn we used to eat in Virginia was *sooo* sweet," he'd tell us. "Sweeter than any corn in the world." He created his own mythologies, from the Beaver Cleaver neighborhood in Jakarta to the perfect Christmas (tree included), and even the vision of himself as the big man in Southeast Asia. I didn't realize it at the time, but Diana was one of his cherished mythological beings. Sure, she was real—and she really did go to Duke, as far as I know. But he idealized her into a perfect young person, creating an insurmountable goal for me—which, because of my nature, I never stopped trying to reach.

Dad was not only critical; sometimes he could be mean. When I was eight years old and wanted to take ballet classes, he made fun of my size, telling me I was too big. "You'll crush the boys trying to lift you, Tammy!" he said. "Why don't you join Girl Scouts instead?" He said this with a chuckle, but after years of hearing my cousins' comments about what a big lumbering girl I was, his words stabbed me right where it hurt.

I was angry when he signed me up for Girl Scouts instead of letting me take ballet, but there did end up being a silver lining. I loved all the camping and hiking and rough-and-tumble of it, and stayed all the way through to becoming a First Class Girl Scout (now called Gold Award Girl Scout, it's the equivalent of the boys' Eagle Scout rank). Even if I couldn't get straight A's like Diana, I was determined to excel at everything else I tried.

In hopes of making Dad proud, I turned to sports. I started playing volleyball and softball, and got really good at both, making junior varsity and then varsity teams. In high school, I took up the discus because my dad had been a champion high school discus thrower. He spent hours training me—the only time in my life that we ever spent any significant father-daughter time. I also took up umpiring, following in the footsteps of my dad, who was a certified baseball umpire. In Jakarta, he had put together a league with teams of expat kids, and when he needed more umpires, I volunteered. I was the only female ump, which felt pretty cool, but Dad never paid much attention to that; he just put me to work calling T-ball games.

Though Dad trained me in the discus and came to many of those meets, he never came to see me play softball or volleyball. But of course, he and Mom went to see every one of Tom's baseball games. While they fussed over Tom's uniform and drove him to the fields, I had to hitch rides with teammates and friends to get to my games.

My mom also treated me differently from Tom. She was incredibly strict about my clothes, not allowing me to wear shorts outside because it would be improper, even unseemly. When I had volleyball practice or games, she would make me wear long pants to the gym, change into shorts there, and then change back when it was time to come home. I had seen photos of Mom as a young woman, so I knew that in the '60s she had been quite fashionable and wore short dresses. But once she had a daughter of her own, she became obsessed with modesty and propriety.

"Tammy, you have to dress nice," she always said. "I don't want people to look down on us." Meanwhile, I was finally happy, thriving in sports thanks to a natural athletic ability I had only just discovered. I loved wearing my team uniforms, and couldn't have cared less about what these faceless "people" thought about how I looked.

Mom was also conservative in other ways. She was—and still is—a devoutly religious Buddhist, but this wasn't about that. She just wanted me to come across as a well-bred, proper young Thai lady. For years, I wasn't allowed to spend the night at my friends' houses, because she considered it inappropriate for me to sleep in the same house as a man I didn't know—meaning my friends' dads. Eventually, she did let me stay at my friend Allison Parson's house, because she liked and trusted Allison's mom. But that was a rare treat, even though my brother could of course spend the night with any friends he wanted.

My mom was the one who looked after us, made sure we were fed and had clothes to wear, and was generally present in our lives. But she didn't show love in the usual ways, through hugs or soothing words. When I was a kid, whenever I'd go to hug her in the kitchen, she would shove me away, saying, "I'm busy!" She was hard, and demanding, and obsessed with making sure we would never be poor and unable to finish formal schooling, as she had been. She was unavailable emotionally, but she found another way to pour her love into us.

Mom spent hours learning to cook amazing food. When there was a potluck or bake sale at school, her goal was to make the best dishes there. It wasn't easy to get all the ingredients she needed, but she found ways. She met a German chef who worked at one of the fancy hotels, and she bugged him to reveal the secrets of making great sauerkraut and schnitzel. She mastered German cooking, and then found a woman who could teach her how to make the best pies and cakes. How on earth my mom managed to locate cream cheese in Jakarta, I will never know, but she made (and still makes) a carrot cake with cream cheese frosting that's just unreal. When she saw how much I liked pizza, she learned how to make dough from scratch, and then would bug the German chef for some of his mozzarella. She heard that the classic pizza has anchovies, so she always made sure to track some down. Thanks to my mom's tireless efforts, I love anchovy pizza to this day. (Don't judge me. It's yummy.)

My dad's idea of parenting was discussing the latest stories in the *Jakarta Post* or the *Straits Times* with us or coaching us in sports. I toiled for hours trying to learn the skills he thought I should master. When I started driving, he told me, "You should know how to change a tire and put oil in a car," so I wasted no time learning to do that. For years after, my friends would ask for my help fixing their flat tires. I was everybody's personal AAA.

At the time, I didn't think of myself as craving my dad's approval, but looking back it's obvious how much I did. I wanted him to be proud of me, but I could never seem to achieve that. So, if the only way I could get him to pay attention to me was to learn to change a tire, then that's what I'd do. It's possible he did feel proud but refused to say so out of stubbornness or a desire to motivate me. Whatever the case, I was constantly pushing myself to be better, smarter, and stronger—forever chasing a goal that remained tantalizingly out of reach.

Yet I did manage to reach one goal I was obsessed with. I managed to skip the ninth grade, sort of, thanks to moving from the British-style United World College of Southeast Asia to the Singapore American School. The grade levels of those systems don't match up, so after I finished eighth grade at a small American-style school, I entered the British system's equivalent of second-semester ninth grade. A year later, when I returned to the American school, I was able to skip ahead another half year and enter the eleventh grade. I may not have had a photographic memory, but I'd at least managed to match Diana in skipping a grade. Not that my dad noticed.

Sometime during our first year in Singapore, Dad lost his shipping company job. After that, he couldn't seem to get hired. No matter how many positions he applied for, no matter how many interviews he managed to get, he was invariably told that he was overqualified, too expensive, or, at fifty-five, too old. Not all nations have the kind of employment antidiscrimination laws we have in the United States; in Southeast Asia, employers often included their desired gender, age, and even race for job candidates in their listings.

Once or twice, Dad landed short-term jobs, such as running a base camp for an oil exploration firm. But while these would tide us over for a little longer, nothing permanent ever came. My mom suggested we move to the States, but he refused. We thought he was being stubborn—and we were right—but what we didn't realize was that he was also afraid. After decades in Asia, he wasn't sure he'd be able to function back on American soil or compete in the American job market.

So, just as he'd done after being let go from Country Woods, he kept saying that everything was fine and he'd find work in no time. Living in Singapore was expensive, though, and our private school tuitions were draining my parents' bank accounts. Frustrated, my mom and I now started pleading with him to move us to the States. But Dad just wouldn't hear of it. He wanted to stay in Southeast Asia, and as before, he kept insisting that there was a perfect job for him just around the corner.

A little part of me knew that he was bullshitting, but there was no way I could say that out loud. In our house, the patriarchy ruled supreme: When we sat down to dinner, Dad got the first piece of chicken. Then Tom, as the son. Then me. Then Mom. My father was the king of our castle, not someone my mom—or God forbid, my brother or I—had standing to question. If Dad said we weren't moving to the States, then we weren't moving. Besides, none of us except him had ever lived there. He obviously knew more about it than we did, so what choice did we have but to trust what he was telling us?

Even so, I could sense my dad's growing desperation. And being the only other person in my family with sufficient English-language skills, I started helping him look for job postings in trade magazines and international newspapers. I would read through all of them, circling ads for positions in Tonga, or Oman, or the Philippines. "Oh, yeah," my dad would say, "I can definitely get this one! I'm perfectly qualified for it." We'd type up a cover letter and résumé, stick them in an envelope, and send it off, and then wait... and wait... for replies that never came.

Our family blew through tens of thousands of dollars during those years in Singapore. Finally, at the end of my junior year in 1984, we were so broke that my dad took me to the bank and told me to cash out my passbook savings account. It wasn't much, just about $300 I'd received as birthday and Christmas gifts. I handed the bills over to my dad, and that's what he used in part to help buy airplane tickets back to Bangkok. The cost of living was much cheaper in Thailand, and we had family there. We had to find a way to get back on our feet, and that was obviously no longer possible in Singapore.

In June 1984, my parents and brother flew to Thailand. But I didn't join them, as my high school track coach, Mr. Baker, had offered me a summer job as a counselor at a sleepaway camp in Malaysia. I saw my family off at Changi Airport, spent a final night in Singapore with one of my friends, then headed out the next morning with nothing but a small backpack.

At age sixteen, I made my way alone into Malaysia, traveling via bus and tuk-tuk (a motorized three-wheeled rickshaw) into the little port town of Mersing. In my pocket, I had the address of a general store that Mr. Baker had given me, and when I got there I told the shopkeeper in Bahasa Melayu (the Malay language, which is similar to Indonesian), "*Saya akan berkerja di Camp Castaway untuk Pak Baker*"—"I'm here to work at Camp Castaway for Mr. Baker." He led me to the Mersing jetty and put me on a fishing boat, which carried me to a tiny island in the South China Sea, where the camp was located.

Pulau Babi Besar, or Big Pig Island, was almost completely deserted. There was a small village on one end of the island, where a handful of Malay residents lived in tin-roofed houses while cows and chickens roamed the dirt roads. On the other end of the island was Camp Castaway, which consisted of one long house with a massive veranda facing the sea. As the camp's brochure put it, "There are no radios, TVs, video tapes, or junk food. Cash is useless on an island without a store." We were out in the jungle, miles from civilization—and I loved it.

At Camp Castaway, we taught the kids to fish, forage for tropical fruits, build shelters, and make fire without matches. The previous spring break, I had been a camper here, and when Mr. Baker had seen me trekking through the jungle in full Girl Scout mode, picking wild pineapples, digging up taro, gutting fish we'd caught, and cooking it for dinner, he'd said, "You need to come back next summer and work here." This was the opportunity of a lifetime, as far as I was concerned. I'd get to live off the land, tromp around in the jungle—and get paid $300 for the pleasure? Yes, please! I loved being a camp counselor, and when the summer was over, it was hard to leave—especially because instead of going home to Singapore, I'd be joining my family in a cramped apartment they were renting in Bangkok.

I took my $300 from Mr. Baker, found my way to the airport, and stopped at the duty-free shop to buy my dad cigarettes. I wanted to buy him his favorite kind, the "luxury" Dunhill brand in the shiny red-and-gold packaging. Back when we were making our monthly trips to Singapore, he'd send me running to the store to buy them while he had meetings with his bosses. Although we were broke now, I was flush with summer camp money, and I knew I could pick up a couple of cartons for my dad as a surprise. I hoped that having his status-symbol cigarettes might cheer him up—and also earn his praise for helping the family with my summer camp pay.

I flew alone to Bangkok, then made my way to my family's apartment, where I proudly handed my dad the cartons of cigarettes. "Hmm," he said. "Thank you." His indifference stung, but over the coming days, I felt a twinge of pride whenever I saw him open a pack and smoke one. I also handed over all the cash I'd made. It never occurred to me to keep the money for myself, even though Dad had *finally* managed to find another job, once again working with a company that was delivering goods to UN refugee camps. I started my senior year of high school at International School Bangkok, hoping that our family would finally be able to turn things around.

But those hopes were soon dashed. According to my mom, my dad uncovered some sort of corruption—either theft or kickbacks—among the officials managing the refugee camps. Once the officials realized what he knew, they threatened and bullied him into quitting his job. I can't confirm these details, but whatever the backstory, the result was that within a few weeks Dad was once again out of work. That meant we could no longer afford the little apartment my parents had rented, so we had to pack up our things yet again and take refuge with another of my mom's sisters.

By this point, we had moved so many times that each of us had whittled down everything we owned in the world to fit in one suitcase. To this day, I'm the world's best packer; I can fit anything into a suitcase now, because I *had to* then. During our last couple of years in Southeast Asia, we moved every couple of months. Some expat kids, like my brother Tom, grow up to hate all the traveling, but I was always happy to dash off anywhere with my single tightly packed suitcase.

Well, almost anywhere. I didn't relish going to my aunt's house. And neither did my parents.

Mom and Dad pulled us out of school, and the four of us moved into my youngest aunt's home in Bangkok, a little wooden house with no refrigerator and an Asian-style squat toilet. My dad seemed broken by this latest turn of events. He mostly stayed in an upstairs room, almost never coming down and showing his face, clearly ashamed of the fact that he couldn't support his family.

For the next month or so, my mom borrowed money from my uncle—the one who had been her partner in the souvenir shop—and my aunt made sure we were fed. She wasn't doing this out of the goodness of her heart, though, as we would learn. As "repayment" for helping us during this time, my aunt later stole a small plot of land that belonged to my mom, forging paperwork to suggest that it had been deeded to her.

My mom had scrimped and saved her own money to buy that land. It was her most valuable possession in the world, as by this time, she'd had to pawn all of her jewelry and expensive sewing machines. But it also meant much more to her than just its monetary value. That land was a symbol of something solid—a safety net, a piece of earth that she knew she could always return to. After a childhood spent in poverty, followed by an adulthood spent with my dad in rented apartments and houses, my mom wanted her own home. That land was the promise of a stable future, a reward for her hard work and determination to survive following her own mother's death. And her sister stole it right out from under her.

We were completely out of money. Dad had no job prospects, and he'd burned bridges when he reported the kickbacks at the refugee camps. My aunt wasn't willing to house and feed us forever, and even if she had been, my parents wouldn't have survived it. Our family was at a dead end, with no obvious way to get out. So, after years of begging, my dad at last agreed to return to the United States, the land of his birth—a place he hadn't lived in nearly twenty years. We'd have to borrow money to do it, from the only one of my mom's siblings who was still willing to help us—my uncle.

Yes! I was beyond thrilled that we were *finally* moving to the United States—to the country I'd dreamed about my whole life, a place where my dad would find work and our family could get back on track.

But my joy turned to shock when Mom said, "Tammy, I am not coming with you."

My uncle could afford to lend us money for three one-way air tickets to Honolulu, but he didn't have enough to buy Mom one too. And even if he had, she wasn't a U.S. citizen, so she didn't have the proper paperwork. Despite the fact that her husband and children were U.S. citizens, Mom would need a visa to live in the States, and we didn't even have a U.S. address yet for her to file an application.

So, in October 1984, my dad, my brother, and I packed up our suitcases one more time. We rode through Bangkok to Don Mueang International Airport, with my mother coming along to say goodbye. I couldn't believe we were actually leaving without her, but there she stood, shoving little bags of food into our hands and saying, "Do you have your passport? Do you have your jacket?" She hugged each of us, then turned to face me.

My mom and I always spoke Thai to each other (and still do); it was like our own secret language, since my dad didn't speak it very well. "Tammy, take care of your brother. Take care of your dad," she said in Thai. "You are in charge." I was only sixteen, but I knew she was right about this. My dad didn't cook, and he'd never really parented Tom and me in any significant way. If we were going to make it in Hawaii, I'd have to be the one to take care of us. As the eldest child and only daughter, that was my job—and I understood, even then, that it would remain my job into the years when my parents got older and my mom needed care herself. My sense of responsibility was always strong, and this would be my first real test of it.

At the last moment, just as we were about to board, my mom pressed a piece of paper into my hand. "This is your auntie's address," she said. And that was it, the only tie I would have to her for who knew how long. I jammed the paper into my pocket, pulled my mom into a tight hug, and then turned and headed to the gate.

Chapter 4

Booze Cruises and Buckets of Roses

We landed in Honolulu with a couple hundred dollars, no place to live, and no clue what to do next. At the airport, Dad bought a copy of the *Honolulu Advertiser* newspaper and we started to flip through it, looking for hotel ads. There was one for an inexpensive-looking place a couple of miles from Waikiki Beach, so Dad decided we would try there. He spent a precious dime calling from a pay phone, to make sure they had rooms available, and then we took a bus to our new temporary home.

After we checked in and unpacked our bags, Dad's self-confidence suddenly came roaring back.

"This is great!" he told Tom and me. "I'll get a job, make some money, and we'll get your mom over here. It's all going to work out." I was happy to see that old gleam in his eye, and despite the recent chaos, I believed what he was saying. I had always idolized my dad, and now that we'd made it through those rough years and were back in the States, I had no doubt he would find a job and make our family whole again.

It took only a few days for that bubble to burst. Two hundred bucks goes fast when you're feeding three people and living in a hotel, and by the end of our first week, we were already in panic mode.

"We've got to move out of the hotel," my dad said.

"To where?" I asked, fear and frustration rising in my chest. We couldn't just leave without any place to go. Did he think the three of us could just trundle off to sleep in a park somewhere?

Dad had no answer. So he did the only thing he could think of: He called the local American Legion. Founded in 1919, the American Legion is a membership organization for U.S. military Veterans, and one of its tenets is a "devotion to mutual helpfulness." Dad obviously hoped that we might be the recipients of some of that "helpfulness."

The person who answered Dad's call listened as he explained our situation, then told him to get a pencil and paper. "Write this down," he said, and rattled off a string of digits. "It's the phone number of a woman in the American Legion Auxiliary. She can help you. Good luck." Dad dialed the number, and the woman who picked up gave him an address and told him to come right over.

Too broke to take a cab, we rode the bus for what felt like an eternity. It was dark by the time we got off at a stop, and Dad, Tom, and I walked the rest of the way to the woman's house. When the door swung open, my brother and I shuffled in, my dad close behind. There weren't enough seats in the living room for all of us, so I plopped down on the floor beside the woman's La-Z-Boy chair. I heard it creak as she leaned down and asked me if I could guess how old she was. I shook my head.

"I'm ninety years old, how do you like that?" she asked.

My teenage brain couldn't take this in. So when I was born, sixteen years earlier...this woman was *already* ancient at seventy-four! There have been a couple of times in my life when I've felt unable to comprehend the reality I was facing—once with this old woman, and another much later, when I was serving in Iraq and first stepped out into the 125-degree heat of Baghdad. It's a confusing sensation, being unable to make your brain understand what your body is feeling. That day in Hawaii, I couldn't wrap my mind around the fact that my dad was telling this very old stranger that we were broke, had no place to live, and were on the brink of homelessness.

The woman—I truly wish I could remember her name—began ticking off tasks for my dad. "You need to go sign up for food stamps," she said. "And you need to get the kids enrolled in school. They have subsidized lunch programs, so that will help." When Dad told her we had been living in a hotel, she said, "No, no. You need to find yourselves an apartment." But of course, we had no cash to pay the first month's rent and the deposit, so what landlord would ever agree to rent to us? In one sickening instant, I understood how ordinary people became homeless: If you have no money, you can't get an apartment. If you don't have an apartment, you can't get a job. You fall into a cycle that, once it starts, is nearly impossible to climb out of. And I realized with a sudden and frightening clarity that my own family was close to falling in. I felt like throwing up, right there on this woman's living room floor.

That's the moment when this wonderful woman reached into her purse and pulled out a worn checkbook. As we held our breath, she made out a personal check to Frank Duckworth and then filled in the amount of $500. She carefully tore it out and handed it to my dad. "Use this for an apartment," she said. She gave him the name of a complex that might have vacancies, and advised him to get a job in a hotel until he could get back on his feet. "And first thing tomorrow," she said, "you need to go to the Department of

Human Services and sign up for food stamps." Then she gave him the address of that office too.

My dad nodded, either too stunned or too embarrassed to speak. So I stepped up. "Thank you so much," I said to the woman, putting my hands together in a Thai gesture called a *wai* and making a little curtsy like my mom had taught me. Then Tom, Dad, and I headed for the door.

We took the long bus ride back to our hotel, picked up our suitcases, and walked to the apartment complex the woman had suggested. These apartments were meant for short-term stays, pay-by-the-week places mostly rented by the working poor—the maids, bellhops, and gardeners who toiled for minimum wage in Honolulu's tourist-services industry. Dad cashed the check and put a couple hundred bucks down on a furnished studio apartment, and we carried our suitcases into our new home. The next morning, we walked to the Human Services office, where Dad signed us up for food stamps. Now we just needed to get enrolled in school, find Dad a job, and pray that the lifeline this woman had thrown us would be enough to keep us afloat.

Our apartment wasn't much bigger than a motel room. There were a couple of couches in the front, where Tom and I would sleep, and a small nook in the back just big enough for two twin beds, where my dad—and, we hoped, eventually my mom—would sleep. The tiny kitchen had a one-burner stove and a half-size fridge, and there was a single moldy bathroom. The whole place was crawling with cockroaches, which ran rampant in the warm, humid Honolulu climate. On most mornings, I would be jolted awake by the skittering of little legs across my skin, or by having a roach fall from the ceiling and smack me in the face. We tried everything we could think of, from spray to powder poison to glue traps, but even if we managed to get rid of them for a week or two, they'd eventually come back. So we quickly learned to keep food in either the refrigerator or a sealed container, or risk getting a very unpleasant surprise when reaching for something to eat.

A couch in a studio apartment was a far cry from my beloved pink bedroom with a queen bed at Country Woods—but at least it was a place we could call home. Dad enrolled us in school and showed us where to catch the bus, and now that we had food stamps coming in and a bit of cash left over from the woman's check, we could buy the bare necessities. We desperately needed Dad to find a job, though, because without any income, that money would run out soon—and food stamps wouldn't pay for clothes or medicine or roach poison. But at least for the moment, we were okay.

Not long after we moved in, the Thanksgiving holiday rolled around. We had a lot to be thankful for, of course, but I couldn't help missing my mom. I now understood that it might be months before we could afford to bring her to Hawaii, and it was hard not to compare this austere, lonely holiday with the good times we'd had in Country Woods, when we always had plenty of money and the family was together.

"Hey, let's splurge tonight," Dad said, sensing the gloom that had descended in our little apartment. "Let's go out for Thanksgiving dinner!"

The three of us walked down to Waikiki Beach, a gorgeous crescent of sand ringed by high-rise hotels, with views of the sun setting over the Pacific Ocean. Tourists from all over the world paid thousands of dollars for the pleasure of walking along this stretch of sand, drinking fruity cocktails and gorging on fresh-caught seafood in romantic beachside restaurants. We walked past bistros with fancy waiters and fresh flowers on the tables, then ducked into the Wailana Coffee House—the only place we could afford, with its early-bird special.

We slid into a booth, and Dad said grandly, "I'm going to have the turkey platter." Tom and I ordered the same, and we all devoured every bite. And while I do remember feeling thankful for that meal, in later years, whenever I passed by that café, I couldn't help but feel a twinge for the little family that was trying so hard to rescue itself on that long-ago Thanksgiving night.

I started taking senior-year classes at McKinley, a public high school perched on a lush green campus just a short walk from Ala Moana Beach. McKinley is historic, famous for being one of the oldest public schools west of the Mississippi, and also for its notable alumni, which include governors and U.S. senators as well as Hawaiian singer Benny Kalama and Dwayne "The Rock" Johnson, who started there the year after I graduated.

Senator Daniel Inouye, a World War II hero who became the highest-ranking Asian American in the U.S. government, also graduated from McKinley. I actually got to meet him during my senior year, when the principal took a group of us to his office. Senator Inouye was a role model for me, and I was completely starstruck to be meeting him. But what I remember most is awkwardly shaking his left hand, as he'd lost his right arm from a grenade wound suffered in the war. I was in awe of him, but I also couldn't take my eyes off his empty suit sleeve. And it's safe to say that at that moment, I never could have imagined that three decades later, I would serve in the same Senate chamber as he did—or that I too would have lost limbs in combat.

McKinley was famous and respected, but it was also underfunded. At the schools I'd attended in Jakarta and Singapore, most of the students came from wealthy families; at McKinley, my classmates were the sons and daughters of hotel maids, taxi drivers, and line cooks. Waves of new immigrants have come through the school for decades; when I was there, we called it Little Samoa because there were so many Samoan kids. Students have also called it Little Saigon and other nicknames, depending on which immigrant community was most represented at the time.

More than half of the students took advantage of subsidized meals, which cost 25 cents for breakfast and 25 cents for lunch. Tom and I did too, as my dad was still struggling to find work. He would spend whole days walking the streets of Honolulu, poking his fingers into public telephones in search of forgotten change, stooping to pick up stray nickels and dimes on the sidewalk, and collecting glass bottles to return for deposit. He'd also look out for those grocery carts that you had to put coins in to use, as sometimes people were too lazy to return them, and he could push them back and retrieve the dime deposit.

If Dad could scrabble together a dollar's worth of change, Tom and I could each get two hot meals the next day. And that's how I learned the value of always keeping an eye out for anything gleaming in my field of view. To this day, you should never get between me and any coins on the ground, because I'm not embarrassed to screech to a halt to pick up every penny in my path. More than once, I've run over a TSA agent's toes at the airport security checkpoint, zooming over to pick up loose change I spotted on the floor. Old habits die hard.

Without those subsidized meals, there's no way I would have finished high school. I'd have had to drop out to find a way to feed myself and my family—and who knows where I might have ended up. Is it any wonder that today I'm a vocal defender of social safety net programs? When I tell you that they work, it's not because I'm quoting from a study or reading a chart. I'm describing my existence as a sixteen-year-old struggling to survive. I believe in subsidized meals for students because they are what enabled me to get my high school diploma.

As my mom had anticipated, in her absence I ended up taking on her role in the family. I had to make sure that my dad's energy was focused on finding a job, so I did all the shopping, cooking, and cleaning. I washed our clothes in the tiny bathroom sink to avoid spending money at the laundromat. And I took care of Tom, making sure he got up, dressed, and out the door every morning. I became an expert at figuring out how to feed the three of us with the limited number of food stamps we got each month. At the little grocery store near our apartment, I would count out three brown one-dollar food stamps, then use them to buy a loaf of bread and a couple of packs of bologna. With those two items, I could make fifteen sandwiches, enough for Tom, Dad, and me to eat one each for dinner over the next five nights.

My brother and I relied on the meals offered at school, but there were times, particularly toward the end of each month, when our food stamps were running out, that I had to save some food to bring home for my dad. I'd get home and pull out a box of milk or an apple from my backpack, and lie to him that I'd mistakenly been given extra that day, or that I hadn't finished it because I wasn't hungry. And while Dad was grateful to have something to eat, I could see in his eyes how emotionally devastating it was to have to accept handouts from his teenage daughter. He knew I was lying, and I knew that he knew. But neither of us would ever admit that, because it would have destroyed the last shred of his dignity, and neither of us could bear for that to happen.

I didn't know it at the time, but for my dad, these moments were a painful flashback to his childhood in Winchester. Apples reminded him of those days during the Depression when he'd had to eat them to survive and grew to hate them; I never saw my dad eat an apple until I started bringing them home from school. I can't even imagine how he must have felt, having no choice but to eat this food that he hated—this reminder of earlier hardships—provided by his daughter. Yet whenever I brought one home, he ate it without a word of complaint.

Like my dad, my fourteen-year-old brother didn't complain about the hunger he must have been feeling—not that he would have said much to me, anyway. We had never been close, but as we got older, our differences grew even starker. My MO continued to be pushing myself, trying to excel at everything, trying to take care of everyone. Tom's was to blend in, not call attention to himself, and spend time focusing on what he liked.

Before dawn broke each morning, Tom would hurry down to the beach with a group of kids to catch some waves before school. Boogie-boarding and surfing might seem like high-end sports, but in Hawaii in the '80s, surf kids were some of the poorest kids around. You could always find a boogie board that some tourist had bought and then left behind when they returned home to the mainland. As long as you could get your hands on any kind of board, the waves were free. And out in the water, everyone was equal.

Tom loved being in the water, as he could focus on the waves and forget about his hunger pangs, his schoolwork, and his fears about the future. At the time, I thought he was lazy—that he didn't do enough homework and didn't care enough about school. But as an adult, I came to understand that the waves were his escape. I had no escape—or, more accurately, didn't allow myself time for one. I just worked myself to exhaustion so I could fall asleep faster, which kept me from lying awake worrying. I suppose that in some ways, sleep was my escape.

But if I thought that I was the only one of us worrying, I was wrong. It wasn't until years later that Tom told me that he too had brought home food and milk from his school meals, saving it to eat in the evenings. He said that one day, the box of milk he brought home burst open in his backpack, drenching his books and school supplies. That moment was his lowest point of misery in Hawaii, and I never even knew about it. I was trying so hard to make sure he and my dad were okay, I'm not sure I could have faced it if I'd known. Even learning about that incident as an adult, many years after the fact, nearly broke my heart.

As all this was going on, my dad continued to insist—as he always had—that a great new job was just around the corner. He kept applying for big, high-paying positions like manager of a housing compound or head of operations at a resort. No matter how broke we were, he wouldn't even consider taking any of the numerous minimum-wage jobs available in the tourism sector. "Don't worry!" he'd say. "You two just enjoy being kids. I've got this."

But ever since we had arrived in Honolulu, I'd felt like the only adult there. Tom really was just a kid, and my dad refused with childlike stubbornness to admit how bad our situation was. We needed Mom to come and help us climb out of the hole we were in, but every time I asked Dad about her, he said he hadn't sent for her yet. He was the big man, the provider, and he wanted to wait until we were on our feet before getting in touch. He couldn't stand having her find out that he was failing yet again.

As weeks, then months, went by, I knew my mom had to be out of her mind with worry. All she knew was that we had flown to Hawaii—she had no idea where we were living, what Dad was doing, or whether Tom and I were healthy and attending school. There was no way for her to get in touch with us, or even find us, for that matter. It was as if her husband and children had just disappeared across the ocean, never to be seen again.

One afternoon, I came home from school to find Dad waiting

with his usual song-and-dance routine about how he was applying for a big job and was just about to get it. And something inside me just snapped.

I had been hearing him say this for three long years and had always believed him. I'd bought into every single scheme, every single bet he placed. I loved and idolized my dad, and for the first fifteen years of my life, it was beyond my comprehension that he could actually fail. But after months of begging in vain for him to call my mom, or to apply for one of the ever-available entry-level jobs in Waikiki hotels, or at least let me get a job, I couldn't take it anymore. It *wasn't* going to work out. We *weren't* going to be okay. Dad was like a gambling addict, always thinking the big score was just within his grasp. And like a gambling addict, he kept rolling the dice, living in complete denial as our life savings dwindled away.

That's when I did the unthinkable.

"Stop it!" I yelled at him. "Just *stop it!* You *don't* have this! We are *not* okay!" Dad just stared at me. I had never in my life spoken back to him, much less screamed in fury. "You have to *get a job*," I pleaded. "And we need Mom!" How could he not see the truth of this? How could he continue to act as if our lives weren't hitting rock bottom? "We need *money*, Dad!" I said. "If you won't get a job, I will."

"Oh, no you won't!" he roared. "I will not allow it!"

"*You don't control me!*" I shouted back. "Stop telling me what to do. Stop acting like some kind of rooster strutting around the hen yard!" I'm not even sure where that rooster image came from, but I just couldn't take Dad's weird preening anymore, not while Tom and I were going to bed hungry every single night. "You can't order me around," I said. And that was the last straw for him. My father turned without a word and stalked back into the little nook where his bed was. He sat there stewing, probably unable to believe that the daughter who had spent a lifetime looking up to him was now, loudly and definitively, telling him off.

I knew he was mad, but I suspected he was also feeling another emotion: relief. Because he knew that now I was going to do exactly what I had said. I would go out and get a job, and start bringing in some money. True to form, we never discussed it, but that's what I did, the very next day.

That next morning, I marched down to Waikiki Beach and became the only member of our family with a paying job, passing out flyers to tourists for the minimum wage of $3.35 an hour. I had seen other young people doing this along the beach, and I knew I could get hired to do it. I had the look: long dark hair, vaguely ethnic features, young, pretty, and in shape—and wearing short shorts and a tight T-shirt. I got hired that day.

Each day after school I had track practice, and following that I would catch the city bus, which was free with my student ID. But instead of getting off at the stop near our apartment, I'd continue on to the beach, where I would spend the next four hours yelling, "Booze cruise! Booze cruise!" while handing out flyers with coupons attached. I had two sets of flyers. Whenever I saw a family walking by, I'd hand them a blue dinner-cruise flyer with pictures of yachts positioned in front of the famous Diamond Head volcanic cone. For the singles, couples, and frat boys visiting from the mainland, I'd hand out the purple booze-cruise flyers with pictures of orange mai tais and mugs of beer.

The guy who was my boss would hand me a stack of them, and I would write my assigned number on the corner of each flyer. That way, if anyone actually used one to buy a cruise, I'd get credit for it, plus a little extra pay—maybe a quarter per flyer. This was also how my boss ensured that we didn't just chuck all the flyers in the trash; if no tourists ever cashed in your coupons, you wouldn't keep the job for very long.

I spent hours working on Waikiki Beach, and developed a whole new group of friends there among the buskers and street people. I got to know the guy who walked around with a white cockatoo perched on his shoulder for tourists to photograph (one to five dollars a photo, depending on whether you wanted to hold the bird). I became friends with the ukulele players and singers, and the group of guys who did break dancing. Among those of us handing out flyers, there were a lot of young people who had made their way from the mainland, sleeping on the beach and trying to earn enough money to stay in Hawaii. There was also an older woman, a retired lady who was trying to pick up a little extra income. She had an amazing return on the expensive dinner cruises, perhaps because of her maternal vibe, which made people feel like they could trust her. Every single night, she cleaned up. She also became a sort of grandma to our group, looking out for everybody working on the streets.

And Dinner Cruise Grandma wasn't the only one who looked out for people. We all watched out for each other, especially on late nights when some of the drunk tourists might get up in your face. You never saw people move so fast as when some drunk asshole got in the face of a busker. There was a special, tight-knit community, almost like a family, of people working the beach, so not only was I making some money, I was actually having a pretty good time doing it. To this day, whenever I'm in Hawaii (usually in Pearl Harbor for Armed Services Committee work), if I can make it to Waikiki Beach, I always make sure to accept a few flyers and drop some cash into buskers' jars.

One evening in February, I was handing out flyers when a

stranger came up and said, "Hey, you want to make some extra money?" I mean, *yeah*. Who doesn't? But I was wary. "Doing what?" I asked.

"Selling roses," he said. "I'll give you a bucket of them, and you stand on a street corner and sell them to people in cars."

"Sure," I said. That didn't sound much different from handing out flyers, and with Valentine's Day coming up in a couple of weeks, I figured I could rake in some decent cash. People in Hawaii usually bought leis and tropical flowers from florists, lei stands, supermarkets, or 7-Elevens. But for Valentine's Day and Mother's Day, they specifically wanted roses. And that meant an opportunity for poor kids like me to make a few bucks.

The roses guy recruited three other girls, assigned us each to a different corner of the same busy intersection, and set us loose to sell as many as we could. I'd grab a handful of roses out of my battered plastic bucket, water dripping off the stems. As soon as the traffic light turned red and cars came to a stop, I'd hurry out in my flip-flops—or as we called them in local pidgin, "slippahs"—running between two rows of stopped cars, offering a handful to whoever would roll down a window. On a good night, I'd be able to sell all the flowers (at $1 each, or $10 for a dozen) in time for the guy to come back and refill my bucket. My cut was ten cents per rose, which meant that on a good night, I could make $20 or even up to $30. If I worked a whole Saturday or Sunday, I might make as much as $50 for an eight-hour day.

This was serious money. Twenty bucks meant my family could eat for a week. Fifty bucks meant we could pay our electric bill and repay some of the back rent we owed on the apartment. If I kept earning like this, I might even make enough to buy a dress and shoes for my high school graduation! I spent hours coughing from the exhaust fumes, dodging between cars when the traffic light turned green, and doing calculations in my head that made my heart beat faster with possibility. Every day that I was out in the sunshine, earning a little extra money, was a good day in paradise.

Hustling for cash became a way of life during my teenage years in Hawaii. During breaks from my shift handing out flyers, I'd put on my goggles and snorkel (scavenged from the tourist trash), jump into the ocean, and swim around looking for bills that had drifted out of stupid tourists' pockets. What kind of person is so wealthy they don't stop to take cash out of their pockets when they swim? I could usually find at least a one-dollar bill floating around, and every so often I'd find a five, or even a twenty. For a family that needed every penny, nickel, or dime we could find on the pavement, this was major income.

In addition to ocean cash, booze cruise flyers, and roses, there was one other way I made money. And this one really was a hustle.

Sometimes on a Saturday or Sunday afternoon, I would go down to the beach in my bikini and sarong, maybe with a plumeria flower stuck in my hair. I was super fit from running track, but I still managed to look like a mainland tourist's image of a delicate little Hawaiian girl (even though in reality, Native Hawaiian girls are of strong Polynesian stock and most look nothing like my half-Asian, half-white self). I would hang out near the beach volleyball nets, where one of the regular local guys would be waiting with a volleyball. We weren't really friends—we never hung out or even interacted beyond the volleyball pit. But they had seen me play, and on these days, we were there for the same thing.

Whenever a couple of tourist bros would start playing volley-ball, the local guys would casually join them. Then after a while, after some drinks, the tourists always wanted to challenge the locals to a match. "Us two versus two of you?" the tourists would ask. "Nah," the local guy would say, before taking a look around. "I'll take that girl, there." And he would point in my direction.

"Who, *me*?" I would squeak, then take a theatrical look around. "Sure! That sounds like fun!" As I walked to the net, asking, "How do you hit the ball, again?" the local guy would challenge the other guys to bet on the game. Of course, they always accepted. And then we would kick their asses to Diamond Head and back. I might have felt bad about taking these poor suckers' money, but then again, it's their fault for assuming a girl can't play, right?

Between my various hustles of volleyball, selling roses, and handing out flyers, I was able to earn enough money to pull our family back from the brink. But this level of activity wasn't sustainable for me. I wasn't getting enough sleep, and between running track, playing other sports, studying, and racing down to Waikiki to work for hours, I was overwhelmed. One afternoon during class, I started to feel woozy. The next thing I knew, I woke up sprawled on the filthy tile floor, watching in confusion as my classmates' shoes shuffled past. Apparently the bell rang just as I fainted, so the other students, being high school kids, were like, *Oh well, gotta get to my next class!*

We needed Mom. And if Dad wasn't going to get in touch with her, I knew I'd have to take care of that too. Fortunately, she had slipped me that piece of paper with my aunt's address on it, way back in October at the Bangkok airport. So I bought a postcard, carefully copied the address onto it, and wrote a note to my mom in my best third-grade-level Thai handwriting. I told her where we were living, and that we needed her to come.

When I dropped that postcard in a mailbox near school, I had no idea if it would reach her or not, or if she'd be able to come if it did. All I could do was hope...and wait.

Chapter 5

Surviving

Sixty-five hundred miles from our little apartment in Honolulu, my postcard finally landed at my aunt's house. She handed it over to my mom, and for the first time in six months, Mom had confirmation that we were alive and okay. She was not only relieved, she was excited. Because now, at long last, she knew where to find us.

I didn't know it at the time, but Mom's biggest fear was that if she didn't manage to reunite with us in Hawaii, Dad would move us to the mainland and she might never see us again. She was anxious to get to us, but unsurprisingly, she didn't have enough money for airfare. As soon as she got my postcard, she begged her middle sister to let her work as many hours as possible during the Chinese New Year rush at the small roast-duck store she owned. Mom worked for hours on end, saved every baht, and bought a one-way ticket to Hawaii as soon as she could swing it.

She arrived at Honolulu International Airport after nearly twenty-four hours of travel, and armed with the address I'd sent her, she was able to get a temporary tourist visa on the spot. In her best English, she asked how to find the taxi stand, and once there, she handed a driver the postcard I had sent and pointed at our address.

When she arrived, none of us were home. Tom and I were at school, and Dad had gone out either to look for work or to pick up spare change. So Mom took a seat in the office of the housing manager to await our return. After a while, she heard the manager, a guy named Bob, yell, "Hey, you—come look!" He was calling to my dad, who walked into the office, saw my mom, and according to her, turned pale as a ghost.

Dad didn't know I had sent Mom the postcard, because I was too angry, and also a little afraid, to tell him. Even if he had known, he probably still would have been shocked that she found us. Dad liked to think Mom was helpless without him—which couldn't have been further from the truth. He had always underestimated her, but now the tables were turned: She had found us and had come to save us. And he just stood there, speechless and ashamed, because there was no way to hide how badly he had failed.

I got home that evening, exhausted after a long day of school and handing out flyers at the beach. When I opened the door, there she was, standing in the kitchen with a pot of rice steaming on the stove. I looked at her, stunned—and then I collapsed onto the sofa and began to cry. Mom and I had a complicated relationship, certainly not one you'd call warm and fuzzy, so we didn't rush at each other to hug. But after a moment, she came over and put an arm around me. Then she said, "Okay, get up. Go wash your face and hands." This was her way of saying, "I love you."

Having Mom with us would take a huge weight off my shoulders. She was a fighter, and a survivor. Not only would she help us make enough money to get through this, she would look after Tom and me in ways my dad seemed incapable of doing. And she started right away. From the twenty-one bucks she'd arrived with, she peeled off a five-dollar bill to buy us dinner at McDonald's to celebrate—with each of us getting our own hamburger, a rare treat.

Almost immediately, Mom started finding ways to earn money. She would walk down to the Ala Moana Center, a huge open-air shopping mall near the beach, and collect aluminum cans in the parking lot. Bob the apartment manager introduced her to some couples with young children so she could pick up babysitting money while they worked the night shift as bartenders or waitresses. An excellent seamstress, she quickly found work doing alterations for cash at a touristy boutique shop. And she spent hours in the back nook of our apartment sewing labels into uniforms and making hula costumes for local dance troupes. At first, she didn't have a sewing machine, which meant that she spent days on end sitting on the floor, hunched over yards of fabric until her back ached, her eyes blurring from all the close-up needlework.

When she was a little girl, not even ten years old, my mom had gone to work as a child laborer, sewing hats in exchange for handfuls of coins. Now, after an adulthood spent in relative privilege, she was right back where she started—sewing for cash under the table in hopes of saving her family. Eventually she made enough money to buy a sewing machine for twenty-five bucks from the Salvation Army store, increasing her earning potential. She also lit into my dad for not having found work, shaming him into finally taking a job as a doorman at a department store, where he worked for tips.

My mom was dismayed at finding us in such a dire state. I grew to like our little apartment, but understandably, it wasn't her idea of home. And she could hear me getting up in the night to drink glass after glass of water, trying to quiet the gnawing hunger in my stomach. Soon enough, she was doing the same.

Mom was determined to scrape and claw our way to financial stability, no matter how many hours a day she had to toil at her sewing machine. In the meantime, she was grateful for the food stamps and subsidized meals that kept our family going.

Unfortunately, my dad decided that now that Mom was here and working, it was time for us to give up that assistance.

Almost as soon as my mom arrived, my dad went down to the Human Services office to report that she had joined us in Hawaii. The food stamps we'd been receiving were for a single parent with dependents, and now that both parents were here, he didn't feel right continuing to accept them. According to my mom, when Dad told that to the woman behind the counter, she urged him to reconsider. "Your wife has only just arrived," the woman said. "You can keep taking the food stamps for another couple of months, until she's settled." But Dad refused.

Maybe he thought it would be dishonest to keep receiving them. Or maybe he made the decision out of pride, to show that we didn't need them (though we definitely did). Maybe he did it to flex his patriarchal muscle, to show us he was still the head of the household and called the shots. Whatever the reason, giving up those benefits just meant that Mom and I would have to work that much harder. *After all this*, I thought, my resentment growing, *who are you trying to impress?*

Dad hated the idea of getting assistance of any kind. This was partly because of his ego, but also because of a strange notion that a lot of Veterans share—a feeling that if they accept aid for themselves, they're somehow taking it away from someone else. They see it like a chow line in a mess hall, where if they take too much food, there won't be anything left for the other guys to eat. But Veterans' benefits don't work like that; there's not a single pie that disappears if too many people take a piece. Unfortunately, too many Veterans don't understand this.

My dad recovered well from the arm wound he'd received as a Marine, but he had other disabilities relating to his time in the service. Throughout his life, he had problems with his kidneys, some of which resulted from a radiation therapy he'd received from military doctors in the 1950s and '60s. He had spots on his back where the radiation had burned his skin, and it also caused complications in his organs. Throughout my childhood, I remember Dad going into hospitals to get treatment for one or the other of his kidneys, which were both compromised.

But Dad always insisted, first to the Army and then to the Department of Veterans Affairs, that he had no disability. He didn't want the VA to give him any benefits that might "take away" something from other guys—even though he had fought for our country, had been wounded doing so, and was 100 percent entitled to them. He truly believed that whatever money the VA wanted to give him should be saved for someone else who needed it more.

When my dad died in 2005, we found out just how costly his actions were. By insistently denying himself disability benefits, he had set up a precedent that denied them to my mom in her widowhood. We applied for those benefits for her, but the VA informed us that since Dad had refused disability payments for all those years, she couldn't receive them. In his misguided attempt to protect his "guys," he helped no one and harmed his own family. "He was too honest," my eighty-year-old mom says now. "And too macho."

Since I entered government service, I've had this conversation with Veterans hundreds of times. I'll tell them, "Just apply for the benefits you deserve. If you decide you don't want them, you don't have to take them. But at least they'll be there for your spouse when you die."

Similarly, many Veterans are reluctant to stand up and be counted, which hinders our ability to properly care for them.

Here's just one example: When I was the director of the Illinois Department of Veterans' Affairs (IDVA), the national VA told us that there were 800,000 military Vets in our state. This was the number they planned to use to determine how many hospitals Illinois needed to care for its Veterans.

"No, we have way more than that," I responded. "We need more hospitals." But the national office insisted: 800,000 had enrolled for VA services, so that was the official number. Thousands upon thousands of Veterans simply never enrolled with the VA, many of them because they feared taking up resources other Vets might need. But once again, as with my dad, their misguided attempt to help was actually hurting.

How did the IDVA know there were more than 800,000 Veterans in Illinois? Because 1.2 million individuals had registered to receive special Veterans' license plates for their cars, and they'd been verified as Vets by the Illinois secretary of state. So, at a minimum, 400,000 Veterans in Illinois hadn't made themselves known to the national VA. And because the national office's numbers were so far off, we wouldn't have enough hospitals to serve them all.

After having spoken to so many Veterans over the years, I understand my dad's motivations a little bit better, because I've seen how common they are. I'm less angry at him for having turned down the food stamps and refusing VA help. As misguided as it was, this was his way of trying to give back and look out for his buddies.

But Mom would ultimately pay the price. She was forced to move when Dad died, because his incomplete benefits didn't provide enough money to cover her rent. At a time when she should have been mourning the husband she'd lost, she was instead sick with worry about losing her home.

*   *   *

After we stopped receiving food stamps, my mom started working even longer hours, taking on a third job and sewing later into the night. When she let me, I'd help her out by sewing hems and hook-and-eye fasteners. But those times were rare. She did almost everything herself so that I could focus on my schoolwork, get accepted into college, and escape this cycle our family was in.

Thanks to my mom's income, I was able to stop selling roses and just stick to handing out booze cruise flyers and my various side hustles. But between my jobs, studies, and sports teams, my last semester of high school was still a hectic race to the finish. I squeezed in as many activities as I could, and the one that I loved the most was working on the yearbook.

Mr. Nakamura, who taught graphic arts, was the yearbook advisor. He seemed like your stereotypical absentminded professor, always saying, "Ah, I'm sorry! I messed up the instructions—can you stay late after school so we can fix the layout?" My classmates and I would look at each other and roll our eyes. *Seriously?* What was with this guy? I'd had a lot of teachers in a lot of different schools over the years, but never one who screwed up as often as this one did. With the supreme confidence and self-determined superiority of sixteen-year-olds everywhere, I felt a little sorry for Mr. Nakamura, who was clearly out of his depth as a teacher.

On those nights that he kept us late, he'd always apologize, then dig a five- or ten-dollar bill out of his pocket and tell us to get some Taco Bell on the way home. There was a Taco Bell right behind our school, and back then two tacos were ninety-nine cents. So my friends and I would buy a pile of tacos and dig in, laughing as we talked about how, once again, our disorganized teacher couldn't keep his lessons straight.

It wasn't until much later, looking back on this time as an adult, that I realized all the students he kept late were food-stamp kids like me. Mr. Nakamura hadn't made any teaching mistakes. He had found a way to feed us without embarrassing us. And he did it on his meager public-school teacher's salary, never expecting repayment or even a thank-you, because he didn't want us to realize what he was doing.

When I think about what Mr. Nakamura did for us, I get choked up at his incredible generosity, and cringe at the attitude of my sixteen-year-old self. To this day, I am doggedly supportive of public school teachers—and I also still have a soft spot for Taco Bell, the luxury treat of my childhood.

After so many months of working, studying, sweating, and fighting to keep our family afloat, I finally made it to the end of my senior year. Along the way, I won a school contest to speak at the commencement ceremony, but I don't remember anything about that speech. There's only one scene I remember from that day, but it is burned into my memory.

As I walked across the stage and accepted my diploma from the principal, I was fine. But the moment I stepped down onto McKinley High's beautiful emerald-green lawn, I started bawling—and I couldn't stop. I walked to where my parents were sitting, tears and snot streaming down my face. Mom had made a lei for me, one of dozens she had made to sell at celebrations like these. She put it around my neck, and I just could not keep myself together. My friends were giving each other leis, hugging each other, and laughing as I sobbed. "Tammy, what's wrong?" they asked. "Aren't you happy?"

I *was* happy, but I was feeling so much more than that. I had been pushing a boulder up a mountain for so many months, huffing and puffing and terrified that it might be too heavy—that at any moment, my strength would give out and I'd be crushed under its weight. Finally, incredibly, I had made it to the top. I had earned my high school diploma, and no one could ever take that away from me. The relief, pride, happiness, and exhaustion I felt in that moment came out in that flood of tears. For the first time in forever, I could finally relax.

Of course, me being me, that didn't last for long. Having my precious diploma in hand, now I could focus on the next big step in my young life: going to college.

I knew that Dad's stepdaughter Diana—the one who'd skipped a grade—had gone to Duke University. But as much as I wanted to prove I could go there too, I didn't even apply. Duke was a fantastically expensive pipe dream, and even just applying there would cost money we couldn't afford.

Besides that, I doubted I could get in. Even though I had finished pretty high up in my class at McKinley, my GPA was about 3.8. I never managed to make straight A's, so I was never going to be the kid who got into the Ivy League or won the big scholarship. Much later, when I got to visit MIT and Harvard on a congressional trip, I called it my Tour of Schools I Wasn't Quite Smart Enough to Get Into. If I ever get rich, I'd like to set up a scholarship fund for merely above-average students—the kids who, like me, tried really hard, spent hours on homework, but always ended up with that B-plus rather than the A. Because grades are not the only indicator that a student has promise.

I ended up applying to only one school—the University of Hawaii. The tuition for state residents my freshman year was cheap, less than a thousand dollars a semester. And by staying in Honolulu, I could keep handing out flyers at Waikiki Beach until hopefully finding a job that would pay me more.

It wasn't until years later that I learned how my parents managed to pay for my freshman-year dorm room. On the days my mom worked at the boutique, she would leave the apartment early and walk there, rather than taking the bus. Dad did the same, walking to his doorman job and setting aside the bus fare. At sixty cents each way, my parents could save $2.40 per day. They'd put that money into an envelope, and by the end of the week, they had $12. They'd add in another $5 from their earnings, making $17—the amount they had to pay per week to reserve my dorm room by the August move-in date.

Then, one or both of them would walk the three miles from our neighborhood to the university to drop off the payment. My parents didn't have a bank account, so there was no way to write a check, and it wasn't safe to send cash through the mail. Not that they would have done that anyway—why pay good money for an envelope and stamp? At the time, postage for a letter cost twenty-two cents, which was almost enough to pay for a 25-cent subsidized breakfast or lunch for Tom or me. During those many months when we were still sticking our fingers into pay-telephone slots and keeping our eyes peeled for flashes of silver on the ground, it would have been a ridiculous extravagance to pay for postage stamps.

Over the summer of 1985, my parents continued to work and save every penny possible. When my mom landed a big job sewing costumes for a hālau hula dance troupe, she went into overdrive. These costumes weren't bikini tops and grass skirts; they were long ruffled skirts with multiple tiers, which meant multiple hems, each of which took hours to complete. I helped Mom when I could, but sewing those hems by hand was murderously boring and tedious, and doing them for even just an hour left me feeling catatonic. Mom, on the other hand, worked for hours on end. Watching her labor, her back aching and fingers bleeding, gave me great appreciation for all the workers who toil to make the cheap clothes and home goods we buy from overseas factories.

It also laid bare a simple truth about the working poor. My family never worked as hard as when we were living at the poverty line. The notion that the working poor don't need a living wage, or that they just need to work harder if they want to get ahead, is abhorrent. I can tell you from personal experience, that's not how life works—even though a whole lot of politicians who've never lived in poverty themselves seem to think it is.

Now that I'd finished high school, I was able to take a full-time job as a counselor for an organization that in the '80s was called the Association for Retarded Citizens and is now just called the Arc. All summer long, I taught life skills to adults with developmental disabilities during the day, then hurried down to Waikiki in the evening to hand out flyers.

That summer, our family cobbled together enough cash to buy airline tickets for Mom, Dad, and Tom to fly to Virginia. My dad had managed to land a job as a federal food inspector at a chicken processing plant in Woodstock, not far from his hometown of Winchester. He would start at a GS-4 pay scale, which at the time meant about $15,000 a year plus government benefits. For someone who'd spent years feeling like the big man, this probably didn't seem like much to brag about, but it was a lot more money than he was making working for tips as a doorman. After two decades of living across the Pacific Ocean, Dad was finally going home to Virginia.

His new job also meant that for the first time since we lived in Singapore, our family would have health insurance. During our time in Hawaii, we had no health or dental coverage at all. Like so many families, we just had to cross our fingers and hope that nobody got sick or seriously injured—and fortunately, none of us did. The only time I remember seeing a doctor was when I had to get a checkup for a waitressing job I applied for. In that instance, like so many women who need good low-cost medical care, I was saved by the local Planned Parenthood clinic, where I got my physical essentially for free.

Exhausted from endless hours of working just to make ends meet, Mom was excited for the move—mostly because she was relieved Dad finally had a better-paying job. And Dad had somehow made peace with returning to the place he'd eagerly left so many years before. But Tom, who was about to start his junior year of high school, was crushed. He had gotten so good at boogie-boarding, he was on the brink of getting sponsorship and turning pro at age fifteen. But he was too young to stay in Hawaii on his own.

My parents made plans to move at the end of August, just after I started college. It was a time of huge transition for all of us, but unfortunately for Tom, it meant his dream was ending—even as mine was just beginning.

When I walked into my new dorm room at the University of Hawaii's Frear Hall, I could hardly take in the luxury. There was an actual bed that I would get to sleep in. A closet with a little set of drawers that were all mine. A banged-up desk with a laminated surface. My mom ran her hand over the desk and murmured, "It's so clean. So nice." I don't know how many college freshmen look with awe and excitement at their dorm room furniture, but after months of sharing that studio apartment with three other people and sleeping on a living room couch, this semiprivate dorm room felt like Shangri-la.

I started crying, and then my mom did too. She wept because she could see how happy and excited I was, but also because this day marked an achievement for her too. She had done it—gotten one child out the door and into college. Watching me caress that closet door, she knew I was going to be okay.

Frear Hall was named after Mary Dillingham Frear, a writer and poet who was also Hawaii's First Lady, married to Governor Walter Frear—the territory's third governor after the United States overthrew the Hawaiian Kingdom's monarchy in 1893. A longtime regent of the University of Hawaii, she died in 1951 at the age of eighty, and the hall was built and named after her not long after. Her ghost was said to haunt the building, but that wasn't even the most colorful fact about it. My dorm's nickname was "Frigid Frear," also known as the "Virgin Vault," because in the mid-'80s, when most other dorms had gone coed, Frear was still women-only. It had a reputation as being uptight, with a curfew and a front desk where residents had to sign visitors in and out.

I loved living in Frigid Frear, and stayed there all four years of my time at U of H. If I felt like going to a party, I could walk to any of the coed dorms, which seemed to have ragers happening every other night. Then, whenever I'd had enough of all the shouting, drunk, and vomiting people, I could come back to my nice, clean, quiet dorm.

The mid-'80s was the era of Boone's Farm, campus keggers, and Bartles & Jaymes wine coolers. I tried drinking a couple of times, but after half a glass, I'd have trouble breathing and break out in hives. This was the dreaded "Asian flush"—a condition affecting about half of all East Asians and many Native Americans, in which a genetic variant makes it difficult for our bodies to metabolize alcohol. Basically, whenever I drink even a small amount, my body goes straight into alcohol poisoning, passing right by the "Go" of tipsy pleasure without collecting $200.

I've never been drunk, and never really even experienced a buzz.

It just wasn't worth all the swelling, itchiness, and respiratory distress. As my husband, Bryan, likes to say, the plus side is that I'm a cheap date (no bar tab!) and can always drive home. He claims that's why he married me.

I never tried smoking pot either, although a lot of my fellow high school and college students did. It's not just that I was straitlaced, although I was. I also never felt that curious about it. Weirdly enough, that decision came back to haunt me much later. When I woke up in agony at Walter Reed after losing my legs in Iraq, the doctors had a hard time figuring out how to lessen the unbearable pain I was in. My body was "narcotics naïve," meaning it didn't know how to react to the opioids the medical staff was giving me. The doctors asked Bryan about my drug history, and he said, "The strongest thing she's ever taken is Tylenol." Apparently none of them could believe it. Had I known in college that smoking a few joints might have helped me through that agony years later, you can bet I'd have lit one right up.

I developed special scavenger cooking skills to save money on takeout, using ingredients swiped from the dorm cafeteria and a contraband single-burner cooktop in my room. My specialty was tuna burgers made with salad-bar tuna, tomatoes, and onions, but I could cook up just about any random food scraps into a hot meal. This skill came in handy much later in Iraq, especially after KBR Inc. stopped serving hot chow to the troops because of a contract dispute with the Department of Defense. (The DoD, understandably, wanted to stop paying KBR thirty-eight dollars *per meal per troop*, a ridiculously inflated amount that could have bought us gourmet meals and champagne every night).

Several nights a week I worked as a waitress at a Thai restaurant called Keo II (sister restaurant to the Keo I in Waikiki), where in addition to making decent money, I was able to keep up my Thai language skills. I also took a work-study job, spending twenty hours a week working in the Department of Oceanography.

At the time, I wanted to become a marine biologist. I'd gotten the bug taking biology classes in high school, and being in Hawaii, marine biology and botany seemed like particularly cool and interesting areas of study. My plan was to work my way up through graduate school, get a PhD, and become a working scientist. But like so many grand plans in life, this one didn't take long to get derailed. As I got deeper into biology, chemistry, and physics classes, I quickly realized that I wasn't cut out to become the next Jacques Cousteau. Biochemistry in particular kicked my ass: Even though I got tutoring and pulled all-nighters studying, I barely managed to eke out a C. At the University of Hawaii, you had to have at least a B average in core classes to get into Marine Biology or Oceanography, so by my sophomore year, my dreams of marine biology had . . . sunk.

Meanwhile, in my political science classes, I was making straight A's. With all the moving around we'd done, and seeing up close the work my dad did with United Nations programs, I had developed a fascination with international affairs. I remembered watching the U.S. ambassador in Indonesia when I was about eight and thinking, *That's what I want to be when I grow up.*

Since then, I'd had a long-standing dream to become an ambassador someday, but of course, I had no idea how you were supposed to make that happen. It felt a bit like deciding to become an astronaut—a goal that was so far out of reach as to be practically unattainable. But I had at least heard about the Foreign Service exam, the test required for joining the U.S. State Department's diplomatic corps, so I decided to set my sights on that.

I switched my major to political science, and from that point on I absolutely loved my college experience. Yes, I worked hard, and when not in class I was laser-focused on making enough money to graduate with as little debt as possible. And my four years of undergrad were ramen-intensive, but whose college experience isn't? Every so often, I was able to treat myself to a pizza, and my enjoyment of it was enhanced by my pride at knowing that I was supporting myself while getting my college degree. Coming from nothing, this really felt like something.

But what should my next step be? I wasn't sure, so I started researching which graduate schools had the best international affairs programs. And I discovered an interesting fact about George Washington University in Washington, DC: At the time, it had the highest pass rate in the country for students taking the Foreign Service exam. Georgetown University also had a highly rated graduate program in international studies, so I applied to those two schools. When I got into George Washington, I decided that was where I'd go. Now I had a goal, and knew what I had to do to reach it—always my favorite position to be in. I still didn't know exactly how to get the ambassador job I had dreamed of, but this seemed like the right way to start.

But first, I would spend the summer with my parents in Woodstock, Virginia. And that's where I learned some fascinating history of my own family.

Chapter 6

"The Females at Advanced Camp Are All Fucked Up"

From the time my parents moved to Virginia in 1985, I spent every summer with them. I'd fly in from Hawaii with my jam-packed suitcase, settle into their little apartment in Woodstock, and work most days at a strip-mall pizza joint, trying to save up money for the next school year. On weekends, Dad liked to go for drives, sometimes taking us to his hometown of Winchester to see the house where he'd grown up and his alma mater, John Handley High School.

Dad was especially proud to be a Handley graduate. "Tammy, it's the most beautiful school you've ever seen." He described a stately redbrick building with a giant white-columned portico and an enormous flight of steps leading down to a lush green football field. "I'm telling you, it's even more impressive than the White House!" he'd say.

When I finally saw it for the first time, I was awestruck. For once, my dad wasn't exaggerating: Handley was gorgeous, like something out of a dream. Mom and I sat on that vast, tree-lined, emerald-green field and gaped at the magnificent neoclassical main building, which, a few years later, would be named by *Architectural Digest* the most beautiful public high school in Virginia. I tried to imagine what it must have felt like to go to a school like this—and have it be free! Only in the United States could a public school look this majestic and still be available to even the poorest kid. We spread out a picnic of my mom's Thai-style fried chicken with sweet chili dipping sauce and sticky rice and my dad's favorite liverwurst sandwich on soft white bread, and as we watched puffy clouds float by, the day felt perfect. After lunch, plucking about a dozen four-leaf clovers out of that beautiful lawn, I took it as a sign that luck was finally back on our side.

Dad, Mom, Tom, and I spent weekends exploring the back roads of Virginia. In the nearby Blue Ridge Mountains, we carried big empty jugs to collect spring water burbling out of the mountains ("the freshest, sweetest water you'll ever taste!"). We visited colonial towns and walked across Civil War battlefields. And because Dad had gotten into amateur genealogy and was tracing the history of his family, we spent a lot of time traipsing through cemeteries up in the hill country of Virginia and West Virginia.

I loved learning about our family's history. I already knew our forebears had fought on both sides in the Civil War. My dad found records showing that my great-great-great-great-great-grandfathers had actually fought in the Revolutionary War. In fact, my ancestors had served on this soil long before the United States was born. They had first sailed to the colonies way back in the mid-1600s, as indentured servants to a British lord. Their descendants fought in the French and Indian War in the mid-1700s—although we'll never know whether they served willingly or were "volunteered" by their lord.

Military service is the cornerstone of our family. My dad took a lot of pride in the fact that there has been a Duckworth serving in uniform during every major period of conflict in the history of the United States. We weren't always on the front lines, such as the years when my dad was stationed in Europe during the Korean conflict, but we have always answered the call should the nation need us.

Learning more about our family's military service had a profound effect on both Tom and me. Tom joined Junior ROTC at his high school in Woodstock, and eventually he would serve eight years in the Coast Guard. I already felt patriotic about the United States, but now I felt something deeper: a sense of responsibility for defending and safeguarding this nation. I too wanted to answer that call, and my plan was to do it by getting my master's at GW, passing the Foreign Service exam, and entering the State Department. Working as a diplomat would be my way of carrying on the family tradition.

While Dad reconstructed our family history, my mom began doing a little research of her own. After our family moved from Woodstock to Centreville, Virginia, she had started taking free English classes at the local public library, and at some point, she asked her English teacher for help contacting Dad's kids from his first marriage. Somehow, in those pre-Internet days, Mom and her teacher tracked down a phone number for the younger daughter, Hillary. Mom decided to give her a call, in hopes of clearing the air.

When Hillary answered, Mom identified herself as Frank Duckworth's wife. "I want to tell you that he is back in America," she said, "in case your family wants to talk to him." Mom wanted Hillary to understand that she never intended to keep Frank away from his children—and also make clear that she wasn't the reason Frank had divorced their mom.

I had grown up believing that Dad just up and left his first family, without any real reason or warning. That belief colored my entire childhood, instilling a deep-rooted fear that one day he might abandon us the same way. It was only recently, as I asked my mom questions while writing this book, that I learned what actually happened—and it was messier than I could have guessed.

When Dad was first stationed in Thailand in the mid-1960s, his wife remained stateside with their three kids—her daughter (Dad's stepdaughter) Diana, and their two girls together, Carol and Hillary. If what my dad told my mom was true, when he went home at the end of his tour of duty in Thailand, he found another man's cologne and toiletries in the bathroom. So not only was his wife having an affair, but it seemed like the guy had actually moved in. He also noticed that his wife had thrown out his favorite chair. When he asked her where he was supposed to sit, she told him, "You can go sit at the bus stop."

While going through my dad's papers recently, I found a copy of a letter he'd written to his ex-wife. In it, he writes that he harbors no ill will toward her, refers lovingly to his "three girls," and asks her to tell them he cares for them. He then says that now that they're over the age of eighteen, he feels he can move on with his new life, and he wishes them all well.

The letter was touching, but the fact that he never again spoke to those three girls, even as he professed to love them, felt like a gut punch. As a mom to my own two precious babies, I cannot imagine ever letting anything separate me from them. How could the man who created elaborate Christmases for Tom and me have simply walked away from his other children?

I don't have an answer to that, and never will.

I doubt that Dad's first family had any idea where he was until Mom called Hillary that day. She was trying to do the right thing, to offer a connection to him if they wanted one—and Hillary answered that yes, she would like to speak with him. But when Mom told Dad what she'd done and tried to give him Hillary's phone number, his response was brief and final.

"Nope," he said. "Not interested."

So Mom had to call Hillary back herself, to tell her that unfortunately, Dad was refusing to speak to her. And that's the last contact our two families have ever had.

My mom didn't tell me about any of this until years later, after Dad passed. Since then, I've always felt bad about it. For all my dad's bluster and bravado, he was not a brave man, and though it's not a nice thing to say about one's father, I think this was his most self-centered and cowardly act. After all those years, I wish he could have found it in himself to reconnect with his daughters. They didn't deserve to be abandoned like that. No one does.

In the fall of 1989, I enrolled at GW and moved to Washington, DC. This was my first time living on the mainland, and I felt like I was in a movie, walking past the White House, riding the Metro, even just buying hot dogs with sauerkraut from dirty-water-dog carts downtown (which I still love to do). This would also be my first time living through a real winter, so I popped into a discount store to buy some tights. I had hated wool tights when my mom made me wear them as a girl in Jakarta, but as soon as the air got chilly in DC, I loved them.

My master's studies were in international affairs, which was like geek paradise for me. I dove into my textbooks, exploring historical geopolitics. And outside the classroom, I was also getting a real-time education, as the world was undergoing huge political shifts.

The Soviet Union, with its shattered economy, was on the edge of collapse. The Chinese government was continuing its crackdown after massacring thousands of protestors on Tiananmen Square in June. In September, just as I started classes, South African president F. W. de Klerk declared that he would end apartheid and free Nelson Mandela. I devoured information about all these developments, trying to see them with the eye of a diplomat and mulling how they might affect American policy and security.

And then, on November 9, East Germany leader Egon Krenz announced that his government would open the Berlin Wall, allowing residents to travel freely to the West for the first time since 1956. But although he intended for people to apply for visas, with orderly travel to begin the following day, East Germans immediately rushed to the wall. They stormed checkpoints, climbed to the top of the wall, and began pounding at the concrete and tearing down that hated barrier between East and West.

Less than two weeks later, Czechoslovakian protestors launched what became known as the Velvet Revolution, a six-week peaceful overthrow of the Communist government. Suddenly, people all across Eastern Europe were flooding into train stations, desperate to reunite with loved ones they hadn't seen in years.

I watched all this on TV with my three grad-school housemates in our little rented town house in Washington, DC. Seeing those images, I recognized the desperation in people's eyes—the same desperation I'd seen watching refugees flooding out of Cambodia and Vietnamese "boat people" cramming into dinghies. It took me right back to memories of the Phnom Penh airport, where I was one of the lucky ones—an American with a ticket on the last plane out, while so many others sat surrounded by their belongings, fear and despair haunting their faces.

Around this time, I took a job working on a database for the U.S. Naval Institute (USNI), a nonprofit military association based in Annapolis, Maryland. Founded in 1873 by a group of Navy officers, it was intended as a place for people to debate naval strategies. In 1984, the USNI's Naval Institute Press paid an insurance salesman $5,000 for the right to publish a dense, complicated novel he'd just finished writing. No other publisher wanted the book, which was called *The Hunt for Red October*. Yep, the guy was Tom Clancy—and that deal made USNI rich.

Using the profits from the thousands of copies sold of that book, USNI hired a private company to compile a vast database of military strategy and technology called Periscope. I got hired to write about sensors, radars, and various communications systems, which was the perfect grad-school job for me. I liked doing research, and whenever I had a question about telecommunications or radar technology, I could just call up my dad and he'd talk me through whatever I didn't understand.

As my first year of grad school came to a close, USNI sold the database to a private company—which then proceeded to lay off a number of employees, including me. When I asked around for job leads, one of my military friends suggested I join the Reserve Officer Training Corps (ROTC) and go to Basic training for the summer.

"You've got nothing else to do," he said. "Why not?" I mulled it over for a bit and decided, *Yeah, why not?* It would be an interesting way to spend the summer, not to mention a physical and mental challenge. And I figured I could save some money, as the strict rules of Basic training meant no shopping, movies, or eating out.

Yeah, why not? And that's how I made the best decision of my life—a decision that started me down the path to my true calling.

GW didn't have an Army ROTC program, so I set up an appointment with the nearest one, at Georgetown University. "Go do Basic training," the officer there told me. "If you do well, you can join our program." Now I had a goal: to kick ass at the eight-week Basic Camp at Fort Knox.

Basic was just like you've seen it in the movies. A bunch of fresh-faced civilians clambered down off a gray military bus, where we immediately got screamed at by a buff Drill Sergeant (DS). The guys got their hair buzzed off, and the supply staff issued us uniforms—green "pickle suits" left over from Vietnam. Fifteen years after the end of that war, the Army was still trying to use up their surplus of those uniforms, so all us newbies had to wear them.

During the first week, I became very familiar with the phrase "Drop and give me twenty!"—usually shouted by a DS at the top of his or her lungs, instructing one (or all) of us to do twenty push-ups. Our days started at 0430 and were packed with grueling sessions of physical training: running, push-ups, sit-ups, road marching for miles with a fifty-pound rucksack. We dragged heavy loads for 250 meters, ran obstacle courses, and learned to rappel from a high tower.

I was pretty fit when I arrived in Kentucky, but Basic still kicked my ass. The DSs yelled at us day and night, getting right up in our faces, and more than once I locked myself into the latrine and cried from exhaustion. Everyone was sleep-deprived and tired all the time, because they pushed us to our physical limits in order to see who could continue to perform. The Army's goal was to tear us down hard, all the way to the foundation, so they could then build us back up to be warriors.

During those eight weeks, we learned how to be Soldiers. Each of us got an M16 rifle, along with training in how to properly hold it, take it apart, clean it, and put it back together. The DSs taught us to safeguard our weapons at all costs. They were always looking for an unsecured rifle, even if it was sitting on the ground right next to you. If a DS managed to swipe your rifle, you were in *big* trouble. "Drop and give me twenty" wouldn't even begin to cover it: You'd have to run laps around the training yard for hours, clean the latrines with a toothbrush, or be on guard duty at 0200 every morning for a week before you earned your rifle back.

One of our DSs must have been a former Marine, because he taught us the Marine Corps Rifleman's Creed. Learning these words, and understanding the powerful feeling behind them, made me feel like a Soldier for the first time. This wasn't a game. My life, and the lives of others, might someday depend on whether or not I maintained my equipment, and myself, in combat readiness.

I came to understand that when I was a Soldier, my rifle would become a part of my body, like a third arm. In the words of the Rifleman's Creed:

> *This is my rifle. There are many like it, but this one is mine.*
> *My rifle is my best friend. It is my life. I must master it as I*
>   *must master my life . . .*
> *I will keep my rifle clean and ready, even as I am clean and*
>   *ready.*
> *We will become part of each other . . .*

By week three, I was officially a goner: I fell for the Army like no one ever fell for the Army before. I loved the drills, the discipline, the camaraderie—all of it. The one time we were permitted to go to the base exchange, I used the opportunity to buy a cassette tape with all the cadences so I could lead the marches.

Tammy Duckworth

I knew the official ones…

The Army colors, the colors are blue
to show the world that we are true
The Army colors, the colors are white
to show the world that we will fight
The Army colors, the colors are red
to show the world the blood we've shed…

…the clean ones…

Saw an old lady running down the street,
Had a chute on her back, jump boots on her feet.
Said, "Hey, old lady, where you getting to?"
She said, "U.S. Army Airborne School."
"Whatcha doin' when you get there?"
"Jump from a plane, float through the air."
I said, "Hey, old lady, ain't you been told?
Airborne school's only for the young and the bold."
She said, "Hey, young punk, who you talkin' to?
I'm an instructor at Airborne School…"

…and the dirty ones…

A yellow bird with a yellow bill
was sitting on my windowsill
I lured him in with a piece of bread
and then I bashed his little head
The moral of the story's clear
to get a little head, you need some bread

...but I'm a terrible singer and have no rhythm, so they finally had to ask me to stop volunteering to lead cadences, because I always threw off my platoon. But that was the only part of the training I failed at. The rest of it I took to like a duck to water.

In addition to rifle marksmanship, we took classes in essential military skills such as first aid, hand-to-hand combat, and bayonet fighting. And then the instructors threw us into extreme experiences we might face in combat. The most intense was the tear gas exercise. We were given pro masks (protective masks, known to civilians as gas masks), then marched into a Nuclear, Biological, Chemical (NBC) chamber. One of the Sergeants set off a tear gas canister, and as the room filled with a pungent, choking cloud, they yelled at us to remove our masks and stand still until getting the order to march out of the chamber.

But the millisecond that gas hit people's lungs, they started gagging, retching, and freaking out. In a flash, my eyes were on fire and I couldn't draw a breath without searing pain flooding my throat and lungs. I was suffocating—but wanting to be a badass, I decided to drop and do push-ups, to prove how hard-core I was. As soon as I did, my entire squad did the same. This definitely impressed the DSs, who yelled for us to get out of the chamber ahead of the other groups. We were pretty proud of ourselves for that move, slapping each other on the back as we coughed and gagged, giant strands of snot rolling down our faces and dripping onto the fronts of our uniforms.

Along with all the physical exercises and weapons training, we also took classes in something called Core Army Values. This was where I began to understand what was special about serving in the Army. As the weeks went by, each cadet stopped thinking about himself or herself as "I," and instead began thinking of themselves as "we"—a team. In the Army, if one Soldier fails to complete a task, the whole platoon fails. We learned quickly to step up, help them out, and make sure every cadet succeeds, so that no one is left behind. We learned to trust and rely on each other, and to focus on something larger than ourselves.

Basic was grueling, but I loved it. And what I loved the most was discovering that the Army was a pure meritocracy. Every single cadet started from the same place, and every one of us was given the chance to show we could do the job well. Nobody in the Army cared that I was a poor, mixed-race girl. They didn't care where I'd grown up, what my parents did for a living, or what I had in my bank account (which was about fifty bucks). They only cared whether I was capable of completing my mission and willing to serve a cause greater than myself.

With each day of Basic, I became more willing—and more proud—to serve that cause.

I heard the guy's voice before I could see him. "The females at Advanced Camp," he said, "are *all fucked up.*"

It was the spring of 1991, and I was standing at attention with my fellow cadets in a WWII-era wooden military barracks at Fort Meade, Maryland. We were here for spring bivouac training, to help prepare us for Advanced Camp that summer. This was the most rigorous year of the program for the cadets in my ROTC class, and our scores at Advanced Camp would determine not only which jobs we'd get in the Army, but whether we'd get into the Officer Corps at all.

Anyone who scored three out of the possible five was on the bubble, at risk of being told "Thanks, but we don't need many Second Lieutenants this year, so we're only taking fours and fives." If that happened, then all your ROTC training would have been for nothing. If you scored a four or five, however, you were pretty much a lock at getting commissioned. And the higher your score, the more likely you were to get one of your top three wish-list branch assignments.

So I was taking this three-day spring bivouac seriously, trying to get ready for Advanced Camp. We had just been out in the field, marching in mud-caked boots and practicing rifle skills in the humid heat, and I was tired and dirty. All I wanted to do was clean my rifle, take my allowed five-minute shower, and hit the rack, but the fourth-year Military Science cadets (MS4s) who were training us were taking their sweet time before giving us the order to relax and clean our weapons.

As a graduate student, I was not only older than my fellow third-year cadets (MS3s), I was also older than most of the MS4s who were training us. I had reached my annoyance threshold for listening to them bark orders at me and drone on about what Advanced Camp was like. So I was especially unreceptive to hearing some frat-boy type make the absurd pronouncement that the female cadets at Advanced Camp were "all fucked up." I kept my face soldierly still, staring ahead into the middle distance, but my knuckles were white from gripping my M16 rifle, and my inner voice was screaming, *Misogynist assholes!*

And then the source of the pronouncement came into view: an MS4 with the name tag BOWLSBEY. I could feel him looking at me, but I kept my eyes forward, my face impassive. Even if I hadn't been standing at attention, there's no way I would have given this sexist jerk the pleasure of looking at him.

Finally, the MS4s allowed us to stand down and instructed us to begin cleaning our weapons. As I began rodding my rifle barrel, Cadet Bowlsbey strolled over. He sat down on the floor on the other side of my disassembled M16 and idly picked up and began cleaning the bolt carrier. He introduced himself, and apologized for the comment. Guess I hadn't hidden my irritation as well as I'd thought.

For the first time, I looked at Cadet Bowlsbey. He was handsome, with dark hair, a narrow face, and heavy eyebrows. But it was his hazel eyes that captivated me. He smiled at me, and my steely resolve just melted. It wasn't love at first sight, but I was definitely intrigued.

He started asking me questions—just getting-to-know-you stuff, like where I went to school and what I was studying. He told me he was prior enlisted, and that he'd served five years in the Army before enrolling at the University of Maryland. *He's like me*, I thought—older than the other cadets, in a different phase of life. Cadet Bowlsbey wasn't just an MS4 ROTC cadet; he was actually a helicopter crew chief in the Maryland National Guard, where he performed maintenance on the Cobra attack helicopter and the OH-58 Kiowa and OH-6 Cayuse ("Loach") scout observation helicopters.

By the time my weapon passed inspection, Cadet Bowlsbey had my phone number. He seemed different from those young, arrogant MS4s who'd been driving me crazy throughout training. So what was that "fucked up" comment about?

To this day, Bryan claims he's not the one who said it. He swears another cadet actually made the comment, though he does admit he agreed with it. (Somehow, he genuinely thinks that's better.) He also says that he could feel the heat of my glare on the back of his neck, and that's what made him turn around to see me with my white-knuckled death grip on my rifle.

Whoever made the comment, it led to my meeting the man who would become my husband, my rock-solid supporter through trials neither of us could have imagined, and the father of my children. Bryan is the reason why, after my helicopter was shot down in Iraq, I am able to walk again despite doctors' predictions. He was at my side every moment at Walter Reed hospital, and he bravely stood up to the medical team to save a part of my leg that I would need to walk.

Not bad for a "sexist jerk."

Over the coming months, Bryan and I spent hours talking on the phone. We couldn't really date, because during the week we attended different universities, and on the weekends either I was busy waitressing at a Chinese restaurant on Wisconsin Avenue, or he was away fulfilling his National Guard duty. As a helicopter crew chief, Bryan had to do additional training beyond the one weekend per month required of most National Guard troops, so he was often out of town.

But we did manage to squeeze in one date a few weeks after we met. Bryan came to pick me up, opening the car door for me like a gentleman. When he settled into the driver's seat and turned on the car, he was embarrassed when country music came blasting out of the cassette player. I didn't know this at the time, but Bryan felt self-conscious about the fact that he'd spent his life in small-town Maryland, while I was this exotic, multilingual woman who had lived all over the world. But as soon as I heard the song—"North to Alaska," by old-timey country music star Johnny Horton—I started singing along, off-key: "Where the river is windin'...big nuggets they're findin'..." Bryan burst out laughing.

"How do you know this song?" he asked.

"Oh, I grew up listening to Johnny Horton!" I said. "He's one of my dad's favorites." I might have seemed exotic to Bryan, but I was the daughter of a man from Winchester, after all.

A few weeks later, Bryan and I saw each other on another

ROTC bivouac. This time, the training included a prisoner of war scenario. The MS3s were tasked with capturing, searching, and interrogating MS4s who were posing as enemy combatants. So Bryan made sure that he would be among the cadets captured by my group.

As one of a handful of women among platoons of men, I made a point of never showing weakness. Some of the guys thought they could get away with stuff—that as a woman, I might be embarrassed or shy about getting up close and personal in physical scenarios. While posing as POWs, they would hide contraband in sensitive places, sticking fake grenades down their pants, to see if I was willing to go there. As they quickly learned, I was fine with frisking them wherever I needed to in order to get the job done, and I soon developed a reputation for being very aggressive in my searches.

Bryan thought it would be fun to hide candy bars all through his uniform as treats for me to find. (I know, this is the romance of my life, folks.) But I wasn't even thinking about that—I just did my job, eyes forward, pulling out a half dozen Snickers bars, thinking, *What the fuck is he doing with all these in his pants?* Instead of sneaking them for myself, as he had intended, I collected and catalogued all the candy bars as the POW's personal belongings. I don't even like Snickers, though of course he didn't know that. I may love my Taco Bell and Filet-O-Fish, but I am a chocolate snob. If you're going to give me chocolate, at least make it good, straight dark chocolate without all that nougat and caramel messing up the flavor.

By now, I was finishing up my second (and final) year of my master's program at GW. In addition to attending classes, writing my thesis, and fulfilling ROTC requirements, I had also taken a job at the Smithsonian. One of my professors had tipped me off about a fellowship for Asian American students there, and after I applied and won it, I went to work for Dr. Paul Taylor, a research anthropologist and curator at the National Museum of Natural History.

Dr. Taylor was an Indonesia specialist, and my job was helping him to prepare an exhibition called *Beyond the Java Sea*, collecting artifacts from different ethnic groups across the vast Indonesian archipelago. When I was done with my tasks, I could explore behind the stacks, peering into archive drawers at dinosaur bones, meteorite shards, fossils—all the cool stuff housed in the museum's vast collection. I also loved wandering around and talking to people as they did their work. "What dead thing are you looking at?" I'd ask, and get my own personal mini-lecture on *T. Rex* metatarsals or dire wolf skulls.

One afternoon, Dr. Taylor asked me what I was planning to do after finishing my master's. I told him I wanted to take the Foreign Service exam, and was hoping to work as a diplomat while serving in the Army Reserve.

"You should consider getting a PhD," he said. "With your interest in Southeast Asia and international affairs, you could get a job with the United Nations developing international aid programs." As he said this, I flashed back to that feeling of pride I had as a child, accompanying my dad as he brought aid to UN refugee camps in Thailand. Dr. Taylor was right—that would be the ideal combination of all my interests. But I had never considered pursuing a PhD. I mean, I cried with relief at getting my high school diploma, so I had already blown past expectations by getting my master's.

I liked Dr. Taylor and trusted his opinion, though, so I started applying to doctoral programs in the Washington, DC, area— GW, the University of Virginia, Georgetown, Johns Hopkins.

When I told him which schools I was considering, he said, "Oh, you should apply to Northern Illinois University too."

"I'm sorry," I said, "where?"

"NIU," he said. "In DeKalb, Illinois. They have one of the best Southeast Asian studies programs in the whole country."

Ummm, no, I thought. Why on earth would I go off to some small town in the Midwest, to a state I'd never been in except to make a connection at O'Hare Airport? I nodded and feigned interest, then changed the subject.

But Dr. Taylor was onto my game. As spring break approached, he brought up the subject again. "I'm going to give you some time off from work," he said. "Just drive up to NIU and have a look."

I obviously needed to be more blunt with him. "No, that's okay," I said. "I'm not really interested in going to school there." But to my surprise (and dismay), he wouldn't take no for an answer. He told me he'd set up meetings for me with professors so I could get a feel for NIU's interdisciplinary Southeast Asian studies program. He was so insistent that I finally just gave in. What could it hurt to have a little spring break road trip and check the place out?

So I got in my yellow Dodge Charger and set off on the twelve-hour drive to DeKalb. I cruised through Pennsylvania, Ohio, and Indiana, watching the landscape change from East Coast urban to Midwestern prairie. Pretty soon, I found myself surrounded by cornfields—rows and rows of leafy green stalks just beginning to poke up through the jet-black soil.

I can't explain it, but driving through those Illinois cornfields, I felt my whole body relax. They were lush and beautiful and weirdly comforting, like a place I knew in my bones. Every so often, I'd pass through a small town, and my heart would swell up at the sight of an old brick town hall, or a grassy central square surrounded by mom-and-pop stores and diners. The whole state felt warm, genuine, and welcoming.

My entire life, I had never known what to say when people asked me where I was from. Born in Thailand to a Thai Chinese mom and an American dad; growing up in Bangkok, Phnom Penh, Jakarta, Singapore; going to high school and college in Hawaii, then graduate school in DC—which of these places was my home? Were any of them? I'd tell people my dad's family had roots in Winchester, but even as he and I traipsed around the cemeteries with my ancestors' names on the graves, I never felt like Virginia was *my* home. Not having a simple answer to that question left me feeling unmoored. If I didn't know where I was from, how could I know who I was?

From the moment I drove into Illinois that day in 1991, I felt like I belonged there. The cornfields, the prairies, the people—all of it felt calming and familiar. For the first time in my life, I could finally take a deep, unencumbered breath.

So, I applied and got accepted to NIU. And finally, I was home.

It's incredible to think how a few random conversations can change the trajectory of your life. If my ROTC classmate at GW hadn't suggested I go to Basic Camp, I wouldn't have joined the Army— and would never have met Bryan. If Dr. Taylor hadn't insisted I check out NIU, I would never have ended up in Illinois, and would never have had the honor of making it my home and serving that great state in the U.S. House and Senate. These small moments, just pinpricks in time, marked the path I would follow as an adult.

I had seen a lot in my first twenty-three years of life. But nothing could prepare me for what was soon to come.

Chapter 7

Rotorhead

If you asked me today how I would describe myself, the first words out of my mouth would be "Soldier" and "helicopter pilot." Flying for the Army was more than the best job I ever had; it became my identity. It's who I am.

The strange part is, I didn't plan on becoming a helicopter pilot at all.

In the spring of 1991, all of us MS3s filled out our branch assignment requests, essentially an initial wish list for where we wanted to serve after being commissioned. Since I could speak multiple languages, I figured I'd probably end up in Military Intelligence. Or because I'd learned so much about sensors while working at the Naval Institute database, maybe I'd become a Signal Corps officer and work in telecommunications, like my dad.

Ultimately, the choice wouldn't really be mine, as the higher-ups make assignments according to the "needs of the Army." You can request whatever branch and position you want, but if the Army needs Infantry officers the year you're commissioned, you're going into the Infantry. If it needs Chemical Corps officers, guess what? You work on nuclear, biological, and chemical warfare! I decided I'd had quite enough of gas chambers, so I hoped like hell I wouldn't end up in the Chemical Corps.

"There are twenty-four branches available," our instructor told us. "Choose your top five. Have at it! But remember: You have to include at least two Combat Arms branches." The room went quiet as we all perused the paperwork.

Then the instructor said, "By the way, that goes for everybody but Duckworth. Obviously, females can't serve in combat. So, Duckworth, you can choose anything *except* the Combat Arms branches."

At that time, Army branches were grouped into three categories. Combat Arms were the "pointy end of the spear" guys. Their job was to wield weapons intended to kill the enemy—anything from rifles (Infantry) to tanks (Armor) to Howitzers (Artillery). The second category was Combat Support, with jobs in fields such as Communications (so Soldiers can talk to each other when they go to kill the bad guys), Military Intelligence (so they know who they're trying to kill and how best to do it), and Psychological Operations (so we can screw with the enemy's minds, making them easier to kill). The third category was the Combat Service Support folks, including Ordnance Corps, Finance Corps, and Acquisition Corps. Their job was to provide essential capabilities for troops on the ground in wartime.

After reading through the descriptions, I raised my hand. "Sir, are there *any* combat jobs for females?" I asked. "Aren't women allowed into combat as pilots?" I was under the impression that Army Aviation was open to women, and rumors were swirling that it might soon open some combat aviation jobs for females. That seemed like the best way for me to get into a combat position—and, of course, training as a pilot had its own allure too. But the officer punctured that particular bubble of hope.

"Nope," he said. "Women can't be combat pilots." Full stop.

I was disappointed. This seemed unfair, not just to the women, but especially to the men. If I was going to hold the same rank and receive the same pay, I wanted to face the same risks the guys had to face. I wanted to be a Soldier, not a "female Soldier." I reluctantly scanned the paperwork and started filling out my top five.

My first choice was Signal Corps, in honor of my dad. Second was Military Intelligence. Then…what else could I do in the Army? After you take out the Combat Arms branches, there aren't a whole lot of interesting positions left. My top five ended up including Ordnance Corps, which involves logistical support and procurement of ammunition, bombs, and other explosives. But I kept getting hung up on the instructor's answer. And while I hadn't originally been all that interested in Aviation, now I felt annoyed at the injustice of being denied.

Later that summer, I was musing aloud to Bryan about what branch I might get. "It's so stupid that I can't go into a Combat Arms branch," I said, still annoyed. Bryan asked what I meant, and I relayed what the ROTC instructor had told me.

Bryan made a face. "Technically, what the officer said was true," he said. "But he lied to you by omission."

He explained that while there weren't any "combat jobs" for women, there were two Combat Arms branches in which women could serve: Air Defense Artillery (ADA) and Aviation. So, even though women weren't allowed to fly Cobra attack helicopters in combat, we could fly Black Hawk Air Assault missions and medevac helicopters. And in ADA, even though women couldn't be Stinger missile commanders, we could be Patriot missile commanders—because Patriot missiles are a defensive weapon. Basically, women in the Army could serve in war zones as long as we weren't technically initiating the shooting. We were allowed to shoot back to defend, but we couldn't lead the actual "fight."

And by the way, how f'ed up is that?

I have no doubt that the Georgetown ROTC instructor didn't explain all this because he didn't want women applying for those jobs. The Army had only recently opened up even these limited positions to women, and a lot of the Combat Arms guys weren't happy about it. But equipped with this new knowledge, I went right back in and updated my list. And this time, I chose Aviation and Air Defense Artillery as my top two choices, followed by Signal Corps.

Now I was determined to be a Combat Arms officer, for two reasons. First was the principle of it: I didn't want to face fewer risks than the guys just because I was female. Second, in military service, there's a certain prestige in being a Combat Arms officer. If you look at who rises to the very top spots, such as Chiefs of Staff of the Army, Navy, or Air Force, they always have combat leadership tours of duty. I didn't want to be denied that opportunity.

In 1992, the top military brass was on the verge of allowing women to fly combat aircraft. I had never thought about becoming a pilot, but if Aviation was the one branch that would allow women to fight, then that was the branch I wanted.

I knew the competition to get accepted for flight training would be fierce. So I did a little research and discovered a backdoor way to lock in an Aviation slot. If I took a Reserves Forces commission, rather than going on active duty as a Second Lieutenant, the Reserve unit could sponsor me for flight school. I found one that would do that—the Bravo Second Battalion of the 228th Aviation Regiment—and so that's where I applied.

For those who haven't served, the differences between active duty, the Reserves, and the National Guard can be confusing.

Active duty forces are people for whom the military is their full-time, primary job. Reservists are part-timers who serve one weekend a month and two full weeks per year, and they usually have other jobs and careers. They're often called "weekend warriors," although that's slightly insulting, as it minimizes the extent of their commitment and hours spent on duty. Reservist pilots, for example, still have to complete the same minimum flight-training requirements to maintain their proficiency. So our "weekend warriors" often end up spending upward of ten hours per week on their military duties outside of those weekends, in addition to having full-time civilian careers. And if you're in a leadership position, such as Platoon Sergeant, First Sergeant, or company commander, you can count on having to commit as much as twenty extra hours of work per week, all unpaid, on top of your regular drill-weekend hours.

Reservists are further split into two branches: the National Guard and the regular Reserves. Both can be activated by the president whenever the country needs extra forces, most often in wartime. National Guard units can also be called up by governors to respond to tornados, flooding, riots—any kind of disaster for which the state needs helping hands or a military presence. So Guard units tend to be a little busier than the Reserve units.

When I applied to the Bravo 2/228th U.S. Army Reserve, they had an opening for my ideal position: platoon leader for a helicopter unit, which entailed assigning missions and aircraft to helicopter pilots. I'd have to interview for it, and also pass an aptitude test for flight school. But I didn't want to just *pass* that test. I wanted to *kill* it. So I bought a specialized study guide and started cramming a few hours each night after finishing up classwork for my PhD studies.

The test had multiple parts, including questions on flight

instrument comprehension, mechanical functions, and math. Some of these you could study for, but others, like visual perception, were really just ways of assessing innate ability. In one part of the test, you'd be shown a silhouette of an aircraft and have to determine from the angle whether it was coming at you or turning away. In another part, you had to look at an aircraft outline and determine its compass and artificial horizon headings. I did very well on these visual perception questions. Apparently my brain is just wired that way.

Another section of the test was background information, which the Army used to determine whether you had the right psychological makeup to be a pilot. There were questions like "Do you like to drive cars really fast?" and "Do you prefer to ride a motorcycle with or without a helmet?" There were no wrong answers on this part of the test, but the *preferred* answer was "I like to ride motorcycles but always with a helmet and other safety gear." The goal was to find people who were type A but not excessive risk takers— because a good pilot is confident, but not an idiot.

In order to be considered for flight school, you had to score at least a 90. I got a 133, which put me near the top of all test takers. So now I was set for flight school, except...there weren't any slots available. There were so many people wanting to get into Army Aviation, the expected wait time was a year or more. Having no choice but to hang tight until a slot opened, I kept on with my PhD studies. Bryan came to live with me in Illinois, taking the next step in our relationship. And one weekend a month, I did my Reserve duty, going to Glenview Naval Air Station.

I'd gotten the job as platoon leader for the helicopter unit, which meant that I was overseeing about twenty people, including some pilots who were Vietnam Veterans. At first, I wasn't sure how these experienced, older Vets would respond to having a young Asian woman in charge. But they loved shooting the shit about Vietnam and hearing me tell my dad's war stories. And they really flipped out when I told them that as a kid, I had lived in Cambodia in 1974. *Oh man, I was nineteen in '74!*, and *I used to fly over Cambodia!* The Vietnam Vets took me under their wing, literally: They would take me up in their helicopters, and one or two even gave me stick time—a big no-no before I'd had my flight training, but it bonded me to those guys forever.

The day after my commissioning in May 1992, the commander of my Reserve unit, Captain Robert Doehl, gave me some advice. "Whenever you get to flight school, you've got to study hard and get selected for Black Hawks," he told me.

I was confused. "But our unit only has Hueys and 58s," I said, referring to the Bell UH-1H and OH-58 Kiowa helicopters on the parking pads outside our hangar. "We don't even have any Black Hawks here."

"Doesn't matter," Captain Doehl said. "Hueys are going away. Black Hawks are the future of Army Aviation. If you want to fly helicopters, you gotta go Black Hawks." The Huey was a legendary helicopter, a favorite among pilots because it could do anything and would take unbelievable amounts of punishment. But the Sikorsky UH-60 Black Hawk was a newer, more powerful bird, a twin-engine helicopter while the Huey was single-engine.

I honestly didn't care which helicopter I got to fly, but I did want to fly for as long as possible. So I filed Captain Doehl's suggestion away, grateful for any advice I could get.

Knowing that it might be a year or more before any flight school slots opened up, I decided to follow another piece of advice from Captain Doehl. He'd told me about a little-known pre–flight school correspondence course that I could use to boost my test scores.

At the time, military members could take snail-mail correspondence courses through the military's distance-learning program, some of which gave you points toward your eventual retirement. I sent away for the Army Aviation Branch's pre–flight school course, and a couple of weeks later a package of yellow workbooks showed up in my mailbox. After reading through and doing the exercises, I filled out the test sheet in the back, tore it out, and mailed it in. If I passed, I'd get another set of workbooks in the mail the following week—and so on and so on, until I completed the whole course. It was tedious work, but each book was getting me another step closer to my goal.

Later that year, I got another great piece of advice from my Reserve unit's Operations Officer, First Lieutenant Pat Osowski. He told me I should make a habit of calling Army Aviation's flight school assignments manager at least once a week. Occasionally, someone who'd signed up for flight school dropped out, and the assignments manager would give the newly empty slot to whoever happened to call on that day. "But listen," Lieutenant Osowski told me, "she's been there for years. If you call her every week, she'll remember. And then she'll actually call you if a slot comes open." Apparently so many cadets had done this that a tradition had developed: Once you got to flight school, you sent her a dozen roses as thanks.

That was all I needed to hear. I started calling. And calling. And calling. "Hey, it's me again!" I'd say. "Got anything?" Or "Hey, I'm still here! Give me the word, I'm ready to go!" I made absolutely sure she knew who I was and how desperate I was for a slot. Then, one Friday in March 1993, I hit the jackpot. "Okay, we just got an opening," she said. "Can you get to Fort Rucker by Monday?"

"Yes, ma'am!" I practically shouted. *Yessss!* It was the middle of the semester, but I didn't care—I was raring to fly. I'd have to take a leave from my studies either way, as flight school required a year of full-time training. So I quickly made some calls, packed a single suitcase, kissed Bryan goodbye, and hopped into his red Honda Civic—I had sold my old yellow Charger to cover my college bills—for the fourteen-hour drive to Alabama.

From the moment I arrived in Fort Rucker, I started angling for the Black Hawk track. My first step was to talk to the Sergeant Major (SGM) in charge of assigning training slots for Reserve forces students. SGM is the highest rank an enlisted person can reach in the military, and like most of the men and women who attain that rank, this one was intimidating. Sitting behind an Army-issue gray metal desk, with piles of paperwork stacked in his inbox and a display of unit plaques and awards behind him, he seemed deeply uninterested in having some new, wet-behind-the-ears Second Lieutenant pestering him.

I got right to the point. "Sergeant Major, what do I need to do to get Black Hawks?"

He reluctantly looked up from his paperwork, then took a moment to size me up. "I've got one Black Hawk slot left this year for Reserve forces, and it's only March," he said. "I'm not gonna waste it on you this early." The Reserves get only a certain percentage of enrollment slots in flight school classes, as most slots go to active duty forces, and while there were plentiful slots for Hueys and 58s, there were far fewer for advanced aircraft such as Apaches and Black Hawks. Once that single slot was gone, that was it—bye-bye Black Hawks. The SGM turned his attention back to his paperwork, but I wasn't ready for the conversation to be over.

"Sergeant Major," I said, "I really want that slot. Just tell me what I have to do to get it." He didn't even bother to answer, just shaking his head to indicate the conversation was over. But just as I'd done with the assignments officer, I kept pressing. I went back again and again to see him. Whenever I had a free thirty minutes, or sometimes during lunch hour, I'd swing by his office and beg. To paraphrase the Rolling Stones, you can't always get what you want—but if you bug the crap out of the right people, you're more likely to get it.

"Sergeant Major, come on," I pleaded. "I really want Black Hawks. Just tell me what I've gotta do." He ignored me, as usual. "I'm going to camp out on your front lawn if I have to," I said. "*What do I gotta do?*"

"Fine," he finally snapped. "Get a hundred percent on your systems test and graduate number one in your class in instruments. If you do both those things, I'll *consider* it."

He probably thought there was a zero percent chance I could actually do both of those things. But he didn't know a simple fact about me: If there's something I really want, and you tell me what I have to do to get it, then I *will* do that thing. When the only obstacle is effort, then there is no obstacle, because I will move heaven and earth to get what I want, even if I have to do it one pebble at a time. My methods aren't the flashiest, but my dad had taught me to keep a goal in mind and my mom had taught me how to work hard, especially when short on resources. So I took the SGM's words to heart and set about trying to chip my way into Black Hawks.

The first part of flight school took place not in the air, but in the classroom. We memorized aircraft systems and mechanics, such as the parts of a jet engine and how it works. We studied hydraulics systems and aerodynamics, and air traffic rules and regulations. I had already learned the aerodynamic, weather, and air traffic rules in my correspondence course, but had yet to learn about mechanical engineering. So for me, these systems tests were the hardest and most frustrating—particularly because the Sergeant Major said I had to get 100 percent.

I took numerous tests on aircraft subsystems, and every time, I'd score between 95 and 99 percent. It was like my old report cards all over again—mostly A's, but never perfect. Whatever the subject, no matter how much I studied, I just couldn't seem to crack that ceiling. Jet Engines—98 percent. Hydraulics—96 percent. Transmission—98 percent. Arrrrrgggghhh! There was no way I'd score 100 percent on the all-encompassing systems final if I couldn't get a perfect score on the subsystem tests that made it up. There was no room for error, so I did the only thing I knew to do. I just kept studying.

Finally, it was the day of our systems test. I took my time, going over every answer to the one hundred multiple-choice questions until my eyes were swimming. When I handed in my answer sheet, I knew I'd done everything I could. Now all I could do was wait.

We took a lunch break while the instructor graded tests, and after about an hour, everybody filed back into the classroom. There was the usual joking and chitchat, and as I looked around, I saw that none of the other guys—and it was almost all guys, just one or two other women in my flight class of eighty—seemed to be anywhere near as stressed as I was about the results. As the assistants handed back our tests, the instructor said, "I'm disappointed in you guys. Only one perfect score. A lot of you were close, but only one person got a hundred percent." My heart sank, and the feelings of inadequacy I'd wrestled with since elementary school came flooding back. I knew that one perfect score wasn't mine, because it was *never* mine. I put my test facedown on the desk, and after taking a deep breath, I turned it over. There it was, the proof that I wasn't quite good enough, right there in red ink: 98 percent. I wanted to cry.

I skimmed down the page to find the two questions I got wrong, just to torment myself further. When I looked at the first one, I saw my answer was actually...correct. And when I looked at the other one, it was too. The instructor had marked them as wrong, but I *knew* my answers were right. I took another deep breath, then walked up to where he was sitting. "Sir," I said, "could you explain to me what's wrong about these two answers?"

A couple of guys were watching, and now they joined me at the front of the class. As the instructor looked at my answers, I blurted out why I thought they were actually correct. For an excruciating moment, he said nothing. Then he started to nod. "Yes," he said, "I can see how you'd get those answers from the way the questions are written." He then turned to the class and asked how many had selected the same answers I had for those two questions, and whether they were marked wrong. The two guys who'd joined me up front raised their hands—along with a half dozen others. "Okay, bring me your sheets," he said. And then, without even looking at me, he scribbled his initials next to my answers, crossed out that big red *98%*, and wrote *100%*.

"Congratulations, Duckworth," he said. *Yes!* I had done it! I had completed the first task for getting Black Hawks, and now I was having a hard time keeping myself from jumping up and down like a pogo stick. Instead, I said, "Thank you, sir," and walked back to my seat—but I couldn't resist high-fiving the two guys on the way.

Now it was time to focus on the second of my two tasks. By this point in the training, we were having classes every morning, then a quick lunch, and then we'd head out to the flight line for actual flight training. There were also flight simulators if you wanted to practice after hours, though by the time we completed all our assigned tasks, we had put in a full day. I didn't care. Every evening, I'd go straight to the flight simulators and put in another three hours of practice.

The flight simulators were exact replicas of Huey cockpits, mounted on a three-axis hydraulic system that moved the cockpit in all directions to simulate flying. The windows were painted, so you couldn't see anything outside; this was to make you learn how to fly based solely on what the instrument gauges told you about your aircraft and its location. There was also a mic and headset you could use to communicate with the cockpit operator, who was a civilian Army employee working a bank of simulators via a control panel.

"Flying" the simulator felt like piloting a real aircraft. So that's what I did, every single night.

Occasionally I'd see some of my classmates practicing too. In those days, you were allowed to bring civilians into the simulators—an indulgence intended for students who wanted to bring in their spouses to see what they were training for. Of course, the students immediately abused this system. Most of my class consisted of single guys, and they started bringing dates to the simulators to show off. The hilarious thing was that half the time, the women they'd meet at the Officers' Club or the local bars could fly the simulators better than they could.

One day, one of the cockpit operators pointed out a young woman who was there on a date. "See that girl?" he said. "She's a regular. She comes in with a new guy just about every flight class." He chuckled. "She pretends it's all new to her, but she can fly the hell out of these simulators." She might have been there just for the flying, but that was the exception, as some of the women from nearby towns like Dothan, Enterprise, and Ozark were looking for Army pilot husbands. From what I remember, at least two of my classmates ended up marrying women they met while at flight school.

While some of the guys were using the simulator as a seduction tool, I kept busy flying, over and over again, every permutation of every possible flight route or emergency scenario that might come up on the flight test. It was like getting ready for a driver's license test by driving every single road within a hundred-mile radius of your DMV, every night for three months. By the time our instruments test rolled around, I wanted there to be nothing the instructors could throw at me that I hadn't seen and done a hundred times already. All the extra practice paid off when I earned the top score of all students on the flight portion of the instrument exam—the second requirement that the Sergeant Major had given me.

Our class leader was a guy named Captain Baker. He was a big, tough guy, a tank commander in Desert Storm who'd decided after returning stateside that he wanted to switch to flying. When the instruments flight test scores were posted and everyone could see that mine was the highest, a few of the young frat-bro types started making comments. "Well, look at Duckworth," one of them said with a sneer. "Who gave you your flight test, Santa Claus?"

To my surprise, Captain Baker grabbed the guy by the shirt and pushed him up against the wall. "If you had been paying attention," he said in a low voice, "you would know that Duckworth has been flying three hours every night for the past three months. She's logged more hours than any of you punks, so shut the fuck up." Having a badass combat Veteran stand up for me like that just blew me away. I encountered plenty of sexist assholes during my time in the Army, but I also got to know plenty of really good guys like Captain Baker.

After the scores were posted, I went back to the Sergeant Major. "So..." I said. "I did what you asked."

105

"Dammit," he muttered, a half smile, half smirk on his face. "All right. It's yours."

In my flight school class of forty commissioned officers, only three of us got Black Hawks. Two guys took the two active duty slots, and I got the last Reservist one. I had busted my ass, but it was worth it. Because a few years later, when the Army moved its Aviation branch from the Reserves to the National Guard, only Black Hawk helicopter pilots got to make the switch and continue flying. If I hadn't followed Captain Doehl's advice, my Army Aviation career would have ended soon after it began.

About two months into flight school, we got to take what the Army calls a Nickel Ride, named after those kids' airplane rides outside grocery stores, which used to cost a nickel to "fly." This marked the first time students got to sit in the cockpit, at the controls, while a helicopter was in flight. The Nickel Ride was mostly symbolic, as the Instructor Pilot (IP) was actually flying the bird. But it was a hell of a lot of fun to be in the cockpit, in the air, getting a taste of what it would feel like to pilot a helicopter solo. At the end of the ride, per Army tradition, I gave the IP a nickel with my birth year on it. My flying career had begun.

There's a self-deprecating element to Army flying. We're not Air Force jet jocks. We're not Top Guns launching off aircraft carriers. We're rotorheads, journeymen, the grunt pilots of military aviation. We have a tradition of not letting our heads get too big— and the Nickel Ride is the start of that, the winking suggestion that anyone with a nickel can just hop on and ride.

Back in 1971, Harry Reasoner wrote a commentary for ABC News about helicopter pilots. I love this essay, as it captures essential truths about how we're different from other pilots:

The thing is, helicopters are different from planes. An airplane by its nature wants to fly, and if not interfered with too strongly by unusual events or by a deliberately incompetent pilot, it will fly. A helicopter does not want to fly. It is maintained in the air by a variety of forces and controls working in opposition to each other, and if there is any disturbance in this delicate balance the helicopter stops flying, immediately and disastrously.

There is no such thing as a gliding helicopter.

This is why being a helicopter pilot is so different from being an airplane pilot, and why, in general, airplane pilots are open, clear-eyed, buoyant extroverts, and helicopter pilots are brooders, introspective anticipators of trouble. They know if something bad has not happened, it is about to. (Harry Reasoner, ABC News Commentary, Feb. 16, 1971)

That "introspective anticipators of trouble" line describes me to a T. I mean, when I was a toddler, my first response to learning that my dad was going away for a year was to check under the sink for rice. I'm always looking for the fix for any possible problem, often long before it happens.

Helicopter pilots also have a dry sense of humor, and most of them are funny as hell. We'd hang all kinds of good-luck symbols in the cockpit, things like horseshoes, lucky rabbits' feet, or fuzzy dice, with my favorite being a little plastic hula girl. And there were many times in the cockpit—particularly in combat—when my fellow pilots and I would swap hilariously dirty stories and dark jokes to let off steam.

There was one joke in particular that I used throughout my Army career, to show new crews that despite being female and a commissioned officer, I was one of them. "Hey, what's the worst thing about being an atheist?" I'd ask casually, out of the blue, as we flew along. There'd be silence on the intercom, as the guys tried to figure out what the hell I was talking about and whether it pertained to our flight. When they were good and confused, I'd drop the punchline: "There's no one to talk to when you're getting a blow job." The joke always got a laugh, immediately lowering any tension in the aircraft. And I felt like it had official sanction, because Bryan is the one who taught it to me—and he had learned it from an Army aviator in his old Cobra unit who also happened to be a chaplain.

From the first time I went up in a helicopter, I couldn't believe this was something the Army would actually pay me to do. It's way too much fun to ever consider it work. We used to wear special "fun meter" patches on our flight suit sleeves, which we covered with the pen flap because they weren't regulation. The patch showed a little dial with green, yellow, orange, and red bands, and the indicator arrow was permanently pointed to red, or "Maximum Fun."

You might be familiar with the poem "High Flight" by John Gillespie Magee Jr., with the famous lines in which a pilot "slipped the surly bonds of Earth," and "put out my hand, and touched the face of God."

Well, flying a helicopter isn't that. It's not the graceful, soaring, silk-scarf-trailing-in-the-wind kind of flying. It's pure, heart-pounding adrenaline.

My husband enjoys flying gliders. He'll go out there and circle in the sky for three hours, going nowhere. For him, it's all about catching that thermal and drifting majestically in the sky. He loves it, but I think it sounds boring as hell. For me, flying is about charging into the sky, hitting my marks and checkpoints.

It's about strapping the bird onto my back and powering through the air, being in control of a ferocious, unforgiving machine. Bryan will point at the lines on a glider and say, "Look how beautiful, how aerodynamic." But I love ugly aircraft, machines that look like they shouldn't even be able to fly. The more brutal the better.

Bryan loves the poetry of flying, but I love the head-banging heavy metal of it. And that's why I'm a helicopter pilot.

After graduating from flight school, I hopped in Bryan's red Civic to head back home to Illinois. Along the way, I swung by a warehouse in Georgia to pick up a discounted wedding dress. Bryan and I had actually gotten married in a civil ceremony about a year earlier, but we'd decided to have a wedding ceremony too, to celebrate with friends and family.

We planned to get married at the Edgewood Chapel, a small redbrick church overlooking the sparkling Chesapeake Bay in Bryan's home state of Maryland. Because we were paying for the wedding ourselves, we couldn't afford a lot of bells and whistles, but there was one special tradition we both wanted: to walk through the Arch of Sabers. This is the moment when, at the end of the ceremony, the bride and groom walk underneath six raised swords held by fellow military officers.

Bryan's one task for wedding prep was to find six officers who could do this. But after three months of making calls, he was coming up blank. Finally he called the Ordnance School at Aberdeen Proving Ground and got on the phone with a Master Sergeant there. "Listen," Bryan said, "I need a detail for an Arch of Sabers, and there's a keg of beer in it for you, and one for them, if you can make that happen." Fifteen minutes later, the MSGT called back. "I've got you covered," he said. There's a reason that Master

Sergeants, some of the highest-ranking enlisted Soldiers, are nick-named "Master Blasters."

We had the ceremony in June 1994, and then settled into married life in DeKalb. But it didn't take long before our domestic bliss was interrupted by orders from the Army. In the fall of 1995, I got called up for my first overseas deployment, a NATO training exercise in Egypt called Operation Bright Star.

Bright Star was launched in 1980, following the signing of the Camp David Accords, as a way to strengthen ties between the U.S. and Egyptian military forces. Every other year, tens of thousands of military personnel convene at Cairo West Air Base for coalition training, which includes a huge field exercise with tanks rolling through the Western Desert. My job was to practice providing logistical support for the tanks and transport for troops. That might not sound too exciting, but it meant I got to fly low across the vast desert, and even past the Great Pyramid of Giza. I almost gasped the first time I got to do this—who gets to pilot an aircraft within a few thousand feet of one of the greatest wonders of the ancient world? It felt totally surreal, like flying through a dream.

Operation Bright Star lasted a month, and after that, it was back to DeKalb and my PhD program. Shortly after I returned, I learned that the Army was planning to deactivate my Reserve unit. I needed to find a way to keep flying, so I switched to the Illinois National Guard. My first position was as a Detachment Commander for Detachment 1 of Alpha Company, 106th Aviation Battalion, based out of Decatur, Illinois—aka "the Phantoms." Then, a year later, I was transferred to Bravo Company, 106th Aviation, better known as the Mad Dogs. I didn't know much about this unit, and had made the switch purely for career reasons. But the Mad Dogs would become my cherished Army family for the rest of my flying career.

In 1997, I was deployed again, this time to Guyana for Operation New Horizons. Instead of practicing battle scenarios, we'd be undertaking humanitarian missions—building hospitals, latrines, and schools for indigenous tribes in the Amazon rain forest. I was the Officer in Charge (OIC) for the aviation group, which was tasked with getting supplies into the deep reaches of the Amazon. The tribes lived in areas so remote that no roads reached them, and it took three days to ferry supplies up the Amazon River. So the best, quickest way to get there was by an hour-and-a-half-long flight.

We did a lot of sling-load missions, which meant that instead of loading supplies in the helicopter, we carried them outside in a sling attached to a cargo hook at the bottom of the aircraft's body. This kind of flying presents a real technical challenge, especially if the load is something heavy, such as pallets of bottled water or lumber. When you maneuver the helicopter, the lumber beneath you swings out, acts like a wing, and tries to fly on its own, so you've got to control the movements of not only the bird but the cargo. If anything fell out of the sling, it would disappear into the impenetrable rain forest below, never to be seen again.

Flying in Operation New Horizons was challenging—but it was also incredibly rewarding. We brought in the supplies needed to construct a mobile medical clinic, which we heard later helped save a young girl's life. She had been bitten by a venomous snake, and because her father knew there were American doctors down the river, he put her in a canoe and paddled for two days to get her to our clinic. It felt good to be providing medical resources, schools, and latrines to people who needed them. And of course, it was amazingly cool to buzz above the lush, green rain forest canopy in one of the most magical places on earth.

My third deployment was to Iceland, for Operation Northern Viking. For that one, we were tasked with cleaning up glaciers littered with old building supplies and rusting equipment left in World War II. Now I was getting to fly over sky-blue sheets of ice with deep crevasses, marveling at expanses of ice and snow that stretched to the horizon. Although I'd traveled to a lot of places as a kid, I'd never imagined that one day I would get to fly a helicopter over a glacier, feeling like I'd journeyed to some faraway frozen planet.

I loved serving during those years, though finding the time to fulfill my Reserve duties was a challenge. Throughout the late 1990s, as I worked to finish my PhD, I also had to take other jobs to pay the bills. For a while, I worked as the coordinator for the Center for Nursing Research at NIU, doing research on environmental radon exposure. Later, I took a management job at Rotary International, helping to open and support clubs in the Asia Pacific region. Serving in the Illinois National Guard was like having a second almost-full-time job, especially when I was promoted to company commander.

The Mad Dogs' home base was at Chicago Midway Airport, an hour-plus drive from DeKalb. As a pilot, I couldn't just show up for my one weekend a month, because I had to maintain proficiency in my aircraft. This meant logging an additional ninety-six flight hours per year—which may not sound like much, but when you figure in commute, prep time, and the number of weekend days you'll have to sacrifice, the extra hours add up quickly.

The training hours aren't optional, because without completing them, you lose your permission to fly. But unfortunately, a whole lot of those hours are also unpaid (though you still receive points toward retirement). The state has a finite budget for paying pilots in the National Guard, and once that pot is gone, that's it. So pilots and crew chiefs end up doing hundreds of hours of unpaid work—a practice we called "flying for God and country," or "flying for free." Thankfully, this practice has become less common after the Iraq War. And as I write this, I'm cosponsoring legislation that would give Reserve forces the same flight pay as their active duty counterparts.

When I was in command of the Mad Dogs, I'd finish up a full day at my Rotary job, then drive down to Midway and spend another four or five hours doing Guard business. Other times, I flew missions or worked extra days of duty prepping for upcoming drill weekends without getting paid. The hard truth was that when the budget ran out, it ran out—but the work still needed to be done.

Getting called up for deployments is yet another source of hardship for Reservists. When you get called up, you have to drop everything you're doing—leave your job, your family, your home—for months or even years, as long as the orders require. Many of our "weekend warriors" face pushback from their employers. By law, your employer can't fire you, but there's no real way to stop them from "downsizing" in your absence, eliminating your job or giving some other bogus reason why you shouldn't bother coming back to work.

In the Great Flood of 1993, when the Mississippi and Missouri Rivers burst their banks and left 30,000 square miles of America's heartland underwater, National Guard units were called into action for weeks on end. People had to leave their well-paying jobs as lawyers, judges, accountants, and CEOs and work full-time for the state's active duty pay of just thirty dollars a day. A lot of people lost their businesses. Some fell behind on rent or mortgage payments. But they had made a commitment to serve, and they served.

So why would anyone choose to go into the Reserve forces rather than active duty? After all, active duty troops get paid a full-time salary, and they get full retirement benefits after twenty years of service, no matter how young they are when they finish. There are several reasons people prefer the Reserve forces. Some don't want to give up civilian jobs that pay better than military service. Some don't want to commit to moving around every two or three years, which active duty servicemembers have to do. Some of them have already served on active duty and enter the Reserves after finishing their commitment.

One thing we all have in common, though, is our desire to *serve*. Being a member of the United States military is a privilege and an honor. When our country calls us to undertake a mission, we step up, even if there's a personal and professional cost to us. Citizen Soldiers do this over and over and over again—and nonmilitary people don't even know about it.

There's a real lack of appreciation for the sacrifices our Guardsmen and Reservists make. It's taxing and exhausting work, and we as a country need to take better care of those who do it. But despite the unpaid hours and challenges, I'd give anything to be able to go back in time and do it all again. Being the commander of the Mad Dogs was the best job I've ever had, bar none.

When Bryan's sister, Abigail, finished high school, we decided to give her a graduation gift she'd never forget. She had always wanted to go on a backpacking trip through Scotland, and when none of her friends could join her, Bryan and I told her we would take her ourselves.

The ten-day trip was a big financial stretch for us, and I'd never had a bucket-list urge to go to Scotland. But once we got there, we had a great time traipsing around, visiting castles, seeing the countryside, and crashing in hostels. About halfway through the trip, when we got to Glasgow, we booked a few nights in a little bed-and-breakfast—basically a pair of rooms for rent in the home of a Scottish couple. Bryan and I hit it off with them, as the husband had served in the Scottish version of the National Guard. We spent a few enjoyable evenings chatting with them about military service in our respective countries.

One morning, Bryan, Abigail, and I headed out for another day of sightseeing. When we got back to the B&B in the early afternoon, the couple were waiting for us, their faces tight with worry.

"Have you heard the news?" they asked. We hadn't heard anything, so they walked us into their kitchen, sat us down at the table, and told us that terrorists had crashed commercial airliners into the World Trade Center towers in New York.

Like people all over the world that day, we huddled together around the TV, staring in shock at the images on the screen. As I tried to take in what I was seeing, the South Tower suddenly pancaked down, right there on live TV. And as that giant cloud of gray dust enveloped lower Manhattan like a specter, I turned to Bryan. "We have to call our units," I said.

We really needed to be home, but all flights had been immediately grounded, which meant there was no possibility of getting there anytime soon. So now we had to make sure that, in our absence, our units were ready for action.

Over the next few hours, we made dozens of international calls on our hosts' home phone. I called my battalion commander to report in, and when I told him I was in Scotland, he simply said, "Get back as fast as you can." I also called my company staff to begin what's called the "grazing herd" alert process, in which everyone on the unit roster gets a call to make sure they're ready to report within twenty-four hours.

Because all flights to the States were canceled, we were stuck in the B&B for a very long night. I hardly slept, thinking, *I'm a Soldier. I should be at my post.* My unit at Midway was there, ready to serve, with all our people alerted and prepared to mobilize if called. I felt helpless and frustrated being stranded so far from home.

The next morning, Bryan, Abigail, and I decided to take our chances at the airport, in hopes of flying into at least somewhere in North America, as close as we could get to Chicago. I tried to give our hosts cash for all the phone calls we'd made, but they refused to take it. "Just go!" they said as the three of us rushed out the door.

On the way to the airport, I could see American flags hanging outside the windows of many people's homes. Some had just forty-eight stars, which meant they were probably left over from World War II, dug out of closets or attics to show solidarity in our time of need. The sight of it made me tear up then, and thinking back on it does the same now.

At the airport, we hurried to the ticket counter and showed our military IDs. "We're with the U.S. Army National Guard," I said. "We need to get home as quickly as possible." We managed to talk our way onto the first aircraft heading out, which was a flight to Toronto. We would figure out the rest later.

Arriving in Toronto on the morning of September 13, we faced more excruciating hours of waiting. But when the first flight allowed back to O'Hare was announced, we managed to get on it. And while we hadn't been able to get back in time for any immediate response to the attacks, it was obvious as soon as we flew into U.S. airspace that our military was still on high alert.

The minute our flight crossed the border, a couple of fighter jets materialized just off our wings. "Oh, look!" said a woman sitting near us. "I feel so much better that those jets are accompanying us." Several of the passengers burst into applause, clapping with joy that we were being protected.

Bryan shot me a look and subtly shook his head.

"They're here to shoot us down if we make a wrong move, aren't they?" I said under my breath. He just nodded. This was no escort—we knew those pilots would not have hesitated to shoot us out of the sky if our plane had made any strange moves. But Bryan and I kept this knowledge to ourselves, deciding to let our seatmate enjoy her feeling of "protection."

For the next several months, before restrictions were eased, the Mad Dogs had to respond to numerous airspace violations. I'd be out flying on a regular training mission and get a call from air traffic control. "We have an unidentified small plane," the controller would say. "Can you check it out?"

Americans can be pretty cavalier with their privilege, thinking their freedoms extend into breaking rules they don't happen to like. Somehow, a handful of small-aircraft general-aviation pilots thought it would be okay after 9/11 to see how far into Chicago airspace they could fly before getting in trouble. They'd refuse to answer air traffic control calls—and then, within minutes, they'd see a massive Black Hawk roar into view. We didn't have any live ammunition on board, so it's not like we were going to shoot them out of the sky. But I can guarantee you that having one or two Black Hawk helicopters suddenly appear on your wing is an intimidating sight. Those small-aircraft pilots answered air traffic control, turned tail, and scurried back to their landing fields pretty quick.

During these weeks, we knew that President Bush was planning to send U.S. forces into Afghanistan, to take out Al Qaeda and the Taliban at their roots. On October 7, U.S. and UK forces launched Operation Enduring Freedom with airstrikes on enemy training camps, marking the start of a war in Afghanistan that has now stretched on for more than two decades. Most troops deployed there in the early months were active duty and Special Forces, with Reserve units sitting tight. But in March 2003, President Bush also sent troops into Iraq, a decision that would stretch our military forces thin. I knew it was only a matter of time before our unit would be called up.

I didn't agree with the decision to invade Iraq. The enemies who had attacked us on 9/11 were in Afghanistan, so that's where we needed to go to take them out. Saddam Hussein was nothing more than a sideshow, one that would distract us from our mission to annihilate Al Qaeda. But the Commander in Chief had ordered the invasion, and the U.S. Congress had voted to support it, so I did what Soldiers are duty-bound to do: I followed a lawful order.

In May 2003, as Bryan and I were settling into the home we'd just bought in Hoffman Estates, a suburb of Chicago, we received alert orders for a potential deployment. The Mad Dogs spent two weeks preparing—getting everyone medically evaluated, inoculated, and prepared to ship out—and then we were told to stand down. For whatever reason, it looked like we wouldn't be mobilized after all, and by the fall of 2003, the Army began the process of transferring me to another unit. This was standard procedure, as I'd already been in command of the Mad Dogs for more than three years, much longer than the usual two-year period. But still, it hurt to turn over my guidon, the banner representing my command, to a new company commander.

It hurt even more a month later, when the Mad Dogs got called up. My guys—the unit I'd sweated and flown with, my military family—were going to Iraq. And because of a stupid fluke of timing, instead of going with them, I'd be sitting behind a desk at the Illinois National Guard headquarters in Springfield.

I was absolutely crushed...and then I was pissed. There was no way I'd stay home while the unit I had commanded and trained for three-plus years went off to war. It wasn't that I was thirsty to fight, but I couldn't imagine my buddies going into combat with me just waving from the sidelines. I needed to be with them. So I called Operations Officer Randy Sikowski and volunteered, telling him that I wanted to go to Iraq and was willing to do it in any capacity. I just couldn't bear to be left behind.

I couldn't get assigned to the Mad Dogs, as having a former commander taking orders from the new commander would throw a wrench into the chain of command. But the Army decided to let me deploy as an Assistant Operations Officer with the 1-106th Aviation Battalion. This would allow me to serve alongside the Mad Dogs, and even fly with them on some missions.

This was it: the combat position I had spent all those years training for. In December 2003, I shipped out to our mobilization station in Fort Knox for a couple of months of preparation.

And then, it would be on to Iraq.

Chapter 8

Iraq

I'm sitting in a C-141, shoulder-to-shoulder with guys on either side of me. We're packed in like sardines with about a hundred other Soldiers, all dressed in desert camouflage, holding our Kevlar helmets and with rucksacks at our feet. We might as well try to get comfortable, as we've got hours of flying ahead of us—from Kentucky to New England to Ireland, and then to Kuwait.

We've spent the previous two months in Fort Knox, preparing for mobilization. We've all undergone medical evaluations and physical preparedness. We've conducted convoy operations and door gunnery, revalidating our individual shooting skills. And we did all this in the depth of freezing winter, with heavy snow covering the training ranges. "Perfect training for the desert!" as the guys liked to joke.

Once we landed in Kuwait, we stayed there three weeks to acclimatize and prepare our vehicles, helicopters, and other combat equipment. And then, on March 12, 2004—my thirty-sixth birthday—I climbed into a Black Hawk for the short flight into Iraq.

Arriving at Logistical Support Area (LSA) Anaconda near the small town of Balad, Iraq, I found myself in a dusty desert outpost of metal shipping containers and heavy canvas tents. Everything was the color of sand, as far as the eye could see. And all of it baking under the desert sun, in temperatures that regularly soared above 100 degrees Fahrenheit, and sometimes as high as 125.

The base was run by the Air Force, but units from every service branch were stationed there; when we arrived, we became part of the largest deployment of an all-Reserve-forces unit since the Civil War. But despite the huge influx of personnel, the military hadn't set up any logistics beyond basic operational needs—which meant that we didn't exactly have the comforts of home.

At first, there weren't enough shower facilities, though thankfully the shower trailers arrived soon after we did. There was a very small post exchange (PX) for necessities like deodorant, soap, or chewing tobacco (a terrible product that a lot of guys got hooked on during deployment). Later, the base would swell to over 17,000 personnel and include fast-food franchises, but I never got to enjoy them. In early 2004, as Operation Iraqi Freedom was still ramping up, LSA Anaconda was little more than a dusty, hot tent city.

We lived in tents for the first few days, but soon were moved into modified Conex shipping containers, which were essentially metal boxes with room dividers and beds. Everything was powered by generators, but there weren't enough of them, and the ones we had went down all the time. So when the A/C went out, those shipping containers essentially turned into ovens, soaring to well over 100 degrees. Early on, an officer in the leadership told us, "If you get heatstroke, I'll consider it a dereliction of duty, because you didn't drink enough water." This was a crock of shit, of course, because if the generators failed while you were sleeping, you could suffer a heat injury before even waking up.

Though we were surrounded by desert, the ground inside the perimeter was covered with chunky gravel, with some rocks as big as golf balls. I walked everywhere—to the double-wide trailer that housed our Tactical Operations Center (TOC), to the flight line, to the latrines—and hoofing it across those rocks in the heat was a real workout. LSA Anaconda had been an elite Iraqi air base before the Coalition forces took control, and there was a swimming pool left over from those times, so I started swimming a mile every other day and running two miles on alternate days. We had nothing to do other than work and exercise, and as I began losing weight and tightening up, I could see the guys' faces getting leaner too.

In my eight months in Iraq, I lost thirty-eight pounds. I was in the best shape of my life, but every couple of months I had to get all-new uniforms, as I gradually shrank from size 40 to 34. I also had to get new underwear, but women's undergarments were among the "amenities" the PX didn't have. Or, to be more precise, they did eventually get some women's underwear—but only cheap nylon granny panties. First, *eww*. Second, and far more important, as a pilot you're supposed to wear cotton rather than super-flammable nylon, in case you're caught in a fire. Nylon melts into the wound, as we found out when guys started getting hit with improvised explosive devices (IEDs) while wearing synthetic Under Armour T-shirts instead of the standard-issue brown cotton ones under their battle dress uniforms.

So I was forced to order my underwear from a catalogue, and the only company I could find with halfway decent stuff that would ship to our APO address was…Victoria's Secret. That's right, I ordered matching bras and panties to wear under my flight suit—because as the old saying goes, you never know when you'll be in an accident, right? Of course, the guys running the mail room loved making fun of me when I'd walk in wearing a flight suit and dusty boots to pick up my Victoria's Secret packages.

Mail call is the bright spot of any deployed Soldier's day, and my favorite deliveries were packages of goodies from Bryan. He'd go to the little Asian market in our neighborhood, buy some of my favorite comfort foods from my childhood—cucumbers pickled in soy sauce, seaweed strips, and dried cuttlefish coated in honey and chili peppers—and then take them to a nearby Korean pack-and-ship place to mail them to me. He did this every few weeks, and then one day he noticed the woman behind the counter giving him funny looks.

"Sorry," she finally said, "but who are these *for*?" Bryan burst out laughing, suddenly realizing how confusing this must have seemed. Here was this random white guy, sending quintessentially Asian foods to some chick named Tammy Duckworth in a place called…*Anaconda*? "Oh, this is for my wife," he said. "She's a deployed Soldier and she is actually Asian! Her name just happens to be Tammy." The woman just nodded, like *Whatever, dude*.

Helicopter pilots have a dark sense of humor, and there was a little game we used to play in Iraq called "If you die, I get your gear." People would call dibs on each other's stuff, not because anyone actually wanted it, but because joking was a way to release the tension of knowing that on any mission, any one of us might not make it back. As I learned later, whoever called dibs on my stuff wasn't too pleased with what they found. Apparently, when the guys from my unit—mostly nice Midwestern boys of Irish, Polish, and German descent—saw the dried squid and fish sauce stored in my locker, nobody would touch it. Then someone had the bright idea to give my stuff to the company from Hawaii, and those guys were like, *Yeah, brah! Score!*

Life in Balad wasn't terrible, mostly because of the closeness and camaraderie that develops among deployed troops. Even so, we never forgot that we were in the middle of a war zone, surrounded by people who wanted to kill us. We wore heavy body armor and Kevlar helmets at all times, even just to walk the hundred yards from our quarters to the porta-potty latrines. We had to, because insurgents fired so many rockets and mortars into the perimeter that the base was nicknamed "Mortaritaville." Almost every day, we'd hear sirens wail, followed by a voice booming over the loudspeakers, commanding us to get down. Everyone would hustle to the nearest safe place to hunker down, and then explosives would rain from the sky, blowing up and scattering shrapnel that could kill or maim anyone caught in the wrong spot.

A few months after I arrived, three troops were killed and twenty-five more wounded when a barrage of 127mm rockets hit near the PX. One of the guys who died, a Reservist Sergeant named Arthur Mastrapa, was a mail carrier from Florida. He'd been in Iraq for nearly a year and was scheduled to ship out the very next day, returning home to his wife and two young kids. In fact, he'd reportedly just been in the Internet café near the PX, trying to book a hotel for a getaway with his wife, when the rockets hit. He was thirty-five years old.

If you had asked me during my deployment where I was most likely to be wounded, I would have said on the base, hit by a rocket blast. It never occurred to me that I might be wounded while flying and survive. Almost nobody survived helicopter mishaps—you either completed the mission and lived, or if you were hit, you died. Unlike airplanes, helicopters fly low over the terrain, leaving no time—and having no method—for bailing out safely. And even if you could bail out, you'd be deploying a parachute beneath spinning rotor blades. If you went down with your aircraft, which was much more likely, you were almost certain to die from the impact, the fire, the smoke, or some combination of all three.

During my eight months in Iraq, insurgents peppered our birds with machine-gun fire a couple of times near Abu Ghraib prison. And once, as I was flying north to the Iraqi Kurdistan capital of Erbil, a rocket-propelled grenade (RPG) exploded in a puff of black smoke just to the rear of our aircraft. We had two other, non-hostile-fire incidents: one when a Chinook went down, causing a few injuries, and another when a Black Hawk crashed because the pilots (who somehow managed to survive) were showing off like assholes.

The Chinook incident happened fairly soon after I arrived in Balad, and it became obvious that our standard operating procedures, which were written before we landed in country, were inadequate for dealing with aircraft mishaps. I wrote up a new SOP, creating tear-off sheets with checklists and contact information so nobody had to waste time looking anything up. The old SOP met the military standard, but the new one was faster and easier to use. Little did I know that the first time we'd use it would be for my own shootdown.

During my shifts as Battle Captain for the 1-106th, my job was to plan and coordinate missions for helicopter crews. But all pilots want to fly, and I was no different, so at least twice a week I made sure to get out and fly them myself. Besides, it was important to me to face the same risks as the aircrews I was sending on missions every day. I was definitely not going to be a Fobbit, a derogatory name for someone who hunkers down in the relative safety of the Forward Operating Base (FOB) instead of going outside the wire to carry out missions.

For the most part, our missions consisted of ferrying troops and supplies from one base to another, tasks we called "taxi service," "grocery runs," or "the Baghdad shuffle." Despite the mundane nicknames, they were dangerous—particularly during the First and Second Battles of Fallujah, when fighting flared up just to the southwest of Balad. These were the periods when Coalition forces went on the attack, flushing enemy combatants out of their strongholds and sending them scattering into the desert. The insurgents would then lie in wait, hoping to take their revenge on the helicopters that crisscrossed overhead. Helicopters like mine.

November 12, 2004

I remember the smell of that morning. The dry-baked, powdery dust of the Iraqi desert swirled down the flight line, mingling with the sweet smell of hydraulic fluid and sharp diesel scent of JP-8 fuel. Walking up to my Black Hawk, I breathed in the hot exhaust from other aircraft that had just taken off for their missions. And as I climbed into the cockpit, I was enveloped in a funky mix of hot metal, sweat, and body armor. There's no other smell like it in the world, and it never failed to get my blood pumping.

That day, I was scheduled to fly with three crewmembers: Chief Warrant Officer 3 (CW3) Dan Milberg, Sergeant Chris Fierce, and Specialist Kurt Hannemann. Chris, with his perfect name—*Sergeant Fierce!*—was our crew chief. Kurt, at twenty-three the youngest in our crew, was a big, friendly, wise-beyond-his-years kid from Peoria, Illinois. He was a Specialist 4, a "Speedy 4" who worked hard and was on the fast track to making Sergeant. A headquarters kid whose job was to process flight plans and other paperwork, Kurt had volunteered to be a door gunner, because we didn't have enough of them. He wanted to do his part—and he also wanted to get outside the wire.

Dan was our Pilot in Command. We hadn't flown together in a few months, ever since he'd switched to night rotations—"goggle missions," as we called them—but I always loved flying with him.

He was a solid tactical pilot, with years of wartime flying experience going back to Operation Desert Storm in the '90s. I always learned something new when I flew with Dan. And he's also just a good guy—easy to get along with, funny as hell, and willing to let me take the stick for most of the day.

I have a pretty twisted sense of humor, but Dan was the one guy who could match it. We were always talking shit during our missions, trying to top each other with the dirtiest, most sarcastic, most warped stories. We jokingly made a pact that if we knew we were going down, we'd use our final seconds to strip naked and switch places, just to fuck with the accident investigators. Other jokes were much worse, and will never be repeated outside the cockpit. We knew we could say absolutely anything to each other, and that each of us had the other's back.

The four of us climbed into aircraft serial number 83-23856, readying for the day ahead. Our bird was just over twenty years old—the 83 in its ID number indicates the year it was built—but it was one of the better helicopters our unit was flying. The dirty little secret of Army Aviation is that the best and newest equipment goes to active duty units, while the Reserve units get whatever's left over. Our Black Hawk had actually been deactivated by the Army, which meant it had been headed to the junkyard until Charlie Company of our battalion snatched it up, deeming it the best of a bad lot.

That morning, my guys knew they were in for a long one. I always assigned myself the longest mission days, sometimes up to fourteen hours, to get as much time in the air as possible. I'd happily go out for as long as the Army would let me—although there was one serious drawback to those long days.

As cool-looking as our flight suits were (as anyone who's watched *Top Gun* can attest), they had a major flaw, one that any woman who's hopped on the fashionable jumpsuit trend knows too well: You have to take off the whole damn thing just to use the bathroom. The Women in Military Service for America Memorial at Arlington National Cemetery actually put on an exhibition addressing this very topic. It was titled *To Pee or Not to Pee*.

For the guys, this was never an issue. They could just unzip the flight suit's long front zipper and do their business. And on lengthy missions, or when turnaround time on the ground was too short for us to debark, they could just pee in an empty bottle right there in the aircraft. (The bottle of choice was usually Gatorade, so if you ever planned to take a swig of Gatorade in the aircraft, it was best to reach for red, purple, or blue—never yellow—just to be safe.)

For the women, however, that long flight-suit zipper stopped just short of usefulness, if you catch my drift. Being able to pee meant taking off my holster and 9mm pistol, my aviation life-support vest packed with emergency survival gear, my body armor, and finally the flight suit itself. And even then, if there wasn't a porta-potty nearby, I might have to pop a squat right there in the desert sand, my bare butt hanging out for the enemy to target. But even in these cases, the guys were taken care of, as there were "piss tubes" positioned at regular intervals on the FOBs—PVC pipes stuck in the ground at an angle, looking like some kind of modern art installation set up for drive-by peeing.

So on these long mission days, I resorted to doing what most female troops did: I purposefully dehydrated myself and just held it in, sometimes for as long as eight hours. But months—and sometimes years—of doing this can lead to health problems, such as bladder and urinary tract infections. Years down the road, as a senator, I would use my position on the Armed Services Committee to try to ensure the Pentagon was designing body armor and clothing that was as useful to the women as to the guys. But here in Iraq, I was just another female aviator trying to keep my mind off my bladder.

I settled into the right-front cockpit seat and Dan took the left. Directly behind Dan, Kurt took up his position as door gunner, facing backward out the side door-gunner's window to aim his mounted M60 machine gun at any enemy combatants we might speed past. Chris sat behind me, also with his 7.62-caliber M60 at the ready. For safety reasons, our battalion's aircraft always traveled in pairs, so we were joined that morning by a second Black Hawk, piloted by CW3 Pat Muenks.

It had been a long, hot, dusty summer, but the heat had finally broken. A light rain was falling and the temperature was in the seventies, which felt almost chilly after the months of brutal heat. Even so, we decided to fly with our doors off, knowing the day would warm up as the sun rose and the rain tapered off. Our missions were assessed at threat level amber that day, meaning enemy engagement was possible. Per usual, we planned to fly fast and low across the desert, to minimize the amount of time the bad guys would have to spot our aircraft and open fire.

We took off for our first leg at 0730, heading from Balad to Camp Victory, near the Baghdad airport, to pick up a small group of U.S. contractors. For hours, we flew missions back and forth across central Iraq, ferrying personnel and cargo between military installations. After seven or eight missions, we finally set down in the Green Zone—the heavily guarded four-square-mile area in central Baghdad that housed international Coalition forces—in late afternoon. We were scheduled to have about an hour on the ground, then return to Balad before sunset.

Everybody was pretty stoked to be in the Green Zone, especially since we had enough time to grab a late lunch at the little café there that made stir-fry to order. Kurt and I ambled up to the counter and picked out our fresh ingredients—chicken, mush-rooms, sprouts—and on a whim I ordered another treat, a choco-late milkshake. It was the first one I'd had in almost a year, and it tasted amazing. After finishing our lunch, we still had a little bit of time, so we hustled over to a nearby bazaar that was selling Christmas ornaments. I bought a few as gifts, delicate little orna-ments with scenes of Babylon on them, and then it was time to go, after one last stop for me at the porta-potty. The TOC had radioed a request for us to divert for one additional mission—a quick run to Camp Taji, a U.S. military installation just outside Baghdad, to pick up a couple of Soldiers who needed a lift to Balad.

My guys were tired from the long day, but they were up for one last run. As we walked back to our Black Hawk, the sun finally began peeking through the clouds. The air was clean and crisp after the rain, and a bright rainbow arced across the sky. Years later, Kurt would tell me that his thought at that moment was *Wow, I can't believe they pay me extra to do this.* We were doing something we loved, in support of our country, on one of the most gorgeous days I had seen in a long time.

Given all that, we hardly minded when we arrived in Taji to find that the Soldiers had already caught a lift with another helicopter crew. But there was a stray Colonel there who needed a ride, so he climbed into our sister helicopter. We did a "hot refuel," gassing up the bird as the engines were running and the blades turning. Then, shortly after 4 P.M., our two birds took off for Balad. We were a daytime crew, and not supposed to be flying after sunset, so we'd have to hustle back. Flying time was expected to be about fifteen to twenty minutes, and then we'd be home for the night.

As our Black Hawks lifted above the dusty airfield, I could see the muddy Tigris River snaking by just to the east. I maneuvered our helicopter into Chalk 1, the lead position, with CW3 Muenks's aircraft flying just to our right as Chalk 2. Though it was possible to fly a straight line between Taji and Balad, the First Cavalry Division flight controllers dictated our departure flight path, after which we'd pick up a previously planned route, all designed so that the enemy couldn't predict our movements.

We had been in the air for about five minutes when I heard Dan's voice through my headset. "Hey, stick pig!" he said. "How about letting me get some flying time?" I smiled. Dan knew I would pilot the bird for as long as he'd let me, and he had let me do it all day. But this was our last fifteen minutes, so he wanted to take the stick. "You have the flight controls," I told him, initiating the standard three-call-and-response to ensure a smooth handover.

"I have the flight controls," Dan replied. I confirmed the transfer once more verbally, and with that, Dan was now in control of the Black Hawk.

As Dan took over, I made one last call to the flight controllers at Taji. A minute later, a grove of date palms came into view. These groves were like little oases scattered across the desert, their rows of tall palms swaying in the breeze. We were flying at about 130 miles per hour now, skimming along about ten feet above treetop level, when I heard an unmistakable *tap-tap-tap-tap*. I knew instantly what it was: small-arms fire hitting the metal fuselage outside my right door.

"Fuck," I said to Dan. "I think we've been hit." My training kicked in, and although our GPS hadn't been working that whole day—we'd been using old-fashioned printouts and paper maps—I instinctively reached forward to push TARGET STORE on the GPS to record the exact location of enemy fire.

And then the world exploded.

A rocket-propelled grenade blew through the plexiglass "chin bubble" at my feet and detonated in a violent fireball right in my lap. The explosion vaporized my right leg. It blew my left leg up into the bottom of the instrument panel, shearing off the shin below the knee and leaving my lower leg hanging by just a thin thread of flesh. And because I had leaned forward, reaching to activate the GPS, the explosion also tore through my right arm, violently shredding it into a bloody mess of muscle, sinew, and bone. In a single, shattering instant, my body was blown apart. My skin was burned and riddled with shrapnel, and blood began pumping out of my wounds.

I didn't know any of this. At the moment of the explosion, my brain went into overdrive trying to figure out what to do next. Dan hadn't responded when I said we'd been hit, so I thought he must be severely wounded. I called out to Chris and Kurt, but no one answered.

In shock and acting on pure instinct, I tried to fly the helicopter. Unaware that my legs were gone, and focused on finding a landing spot, I struggled to press the pedals. At the same time, I tried to pull on the cyclic stick between my legs, which controls the rotor and almost certainly had stopped functioning. The RPG had knocked out our avionics system, so we couldn't hear or talk to each other, and the cockpit was quickly filling with black smoke. *We're gonna get a compressor stall*, I thought, knowing the number two engine must have sucked in debris from the explosion. *We're going to have a hydraulic failure.* My mind was whirling, frantically trying to solve each new crisis.

The Black Hawk rattled and shook, not responding to anything I did with the flight controls. We had to land, but what little I could see through the cracked windshield was all palm trees. If we couldn't find an open space in a matter of seconds, we'd have to ditch in the trees, where the rotor blades would beat us up once they hit the branches. *God, we need a place to land!* my brain screamed—and just then, by some miracle, a small opening of grassy land appeared.

It came under us so fast, we'd have to make an impossibly steep approach not to overshoot. I kept trying to steer us to the opening, pissed that my pedals wouldn't work and completely unaware that Dan was controlling the bird. The helicopter went into a very steep, very fast descent. I pulled up on the collective, the stick just to my left that controls the pitch of the rotors, trying to slow our descent and cushion our landing. For a fleeting moment, I wondered why the flight instruments looked so much larger than usual. As Dan would later tell me, this was because I was slumped over in my seat, my face just inches away from the instrument panel.

Then, suddenly, we were on the ground. The rotor blades jolted to a stop not even a quarter turn into their rotation, indicating that we were close to a main transmission failure when we landed. Despite the chaos and smoke, I noticed that one of the engine power control levers (PCLs) hadn't been pulled fully back into the off position. I tried to reach up with my left arm to pull it back, but that was the last straw for my ravaged body. As I collapsed forward, I saw grass poking up through the bottom of the cockpit. *Why the fuck is there grass coming through the chin bubble?* I thought.

And then everything went black.

I have no recollection of my rescue and evacuation, though I'm told that I went in and out of consciousness while it was happening. The following details are what I've been able to learn in the years since the shootdown. Some of them I discovered only while talking to people for this book.

In the seconds after the RPG hit, Dan looked over and saw me slumped forward, hanging from my seat's shoulder harness.

My face was covered with black residue from the explosion, my eyes were closed, and my mouth was hanging open. As an EMT and police officer in civilian life back in Missouri, Dan had seen dead people, and looking at me, he thought I was gone. He was so focused on landing the aircraft that he didn't notice that I'd been coming in and out of consciousness, little flickers of life in my eyes as I fought an internal mental battle to land the aircraft.

As soon as Dan set the helicopter down, he unstrapped his harness and jumped out of the cockpit. "Get out of the aircraft!" he yelled to the crew. "Set up a perimeter!" We had landed about five hundred yards from where the RPG had hit—which meant that whoever shot us down might come charging through the trees at any moment to continue the attack. Our only saving grace was that there didn't seem to be a road between where we were hit and where we landed.

Kurt stumbled out of the aircraft, grabbed his M4, and promptly fell to the ground as his legs collapsed under him. He stood up, confused, and then felt something wet on his hand. When he looked down, his hand was covered in blood, and he twisted around to see that the whole back of his uniform was soaked crimson.

At the same time, Dan rushed around to my side of the cockpit. Looking inside, all he could see was my torso and a severed leg lying on the floor; as far as he could tell, there was nothing left of me from my waist down. I was obviously not going anywhere, so he turned his attention to Chris Fierce, who was sitting directly behind me. "Chris, get out of the aircraft!" he yelled.

"I can't," Chris told him. "My leg is broken." In fact, the explosion had torn his leg apart just below the knee, and he, too, was bleeding profusely. Despite his injury, Chris had acted quickly and courageously as we descended, picking up pieces of burning metal with his gloved hands and throwing them out the window, possibly saving the helicopter from catching fire.

"You have to get out!" Dan insisted. "I'll help you!" Leaving me for the moment, Dan reached through the door or window—he can't remember which—and managed to pull Chris out and drag him away from the aircraft.

Once he'd gotten Chris clear, Dan looked over and saw that Kurt was still standing next to the helicopter. "Set up the perimeter!" he shouted again. What was Kurt waiting for?

"I've been hit," Kurt replied, turning to show Dan the blood-soaked back of his uniform. At that moment, Dan's face just crumpled, like *How fucking bad can this get?* All three of his crewmembers were badly injured, one was possibly dead, and with no one physically able to set up a perimeter, we were potentially moments away from getting killed in an ambush.

That's when Kurt performed one of the bravest acts imaginable. Confused, woozy from blood loss, and rapidly going into shock, he picked up his M4 and stumbled toward the perimeter. Instead of running to the rear to protect himself, Kurt courageously positioned himself between us and the enemy.

Dan frantically waved down Chalk 2, our sister helicopter, and CW3 Muenks set it down near us in the field. Specialist Matt Backues, their door gunner, jumped out and ran to where Dan stood on my side of the cockpit. "Let's get her out of here," Dan said. Matt looked inside and couldn't believe what he was seeing. My visor had cracked in the explosion, and half of it had blown off. He could see one closed eye and my blackened skin, and he looked at my lips to see if I was breathing. This all happened in an instant—and then he quickly reached in to unbuckle my harness.

Matt and Dan pulled my seemingly lifeless body out of the helicopter, stumbling backward as they got me free of it. They positioned themselves on either side of me, planning to underarm-carry me to Chalk 2, but in a matter of seconds we were all slick with blood and bits of flesh, making it hard to hold on to me. On top of that, the terrain was uneven with tall grass and big clumps of dirt, so the guys couldn't stay upright. They'd fall on me, get back up, stumble a few steps, collapse to the ground. Everyone knew we had to get out of there as quickly as possible, before the insurgents came back to finish us off. Yet these men courageously took this extra time—not even to save my life, because they thought I was dead. They stayed behind, risking their own lives, to recover my body for my family. They did it for the purest of all reasons, that you *never leave a fallen comrade behind.*

Realizing that Chris was too badly hurt to make it to Chalk 2 on his own, Dan broke away to help him. Left alone to carry me, Matt grabbed the shoulder straps of my flight vest and started dragging me backward through that damned field. At one point, Colonel Hamm—an officer none of us knew, the one we'd picked up ten minutes earlier in Taji—came over to help. When Matt finally got me to the helicopter, he and the Colonel started trying to load me in, but they couldn't quite get me in the door.

In the meantime, Kurt had somehow hoisted himself into Chalk 2, and when he saw the other guys struggling to get me in, he reached down to help. He grabbed my flight vest and heaved, managing to get my upper half into the helicopter. Then he reached down to heave for a second time, to pull in my lower half. And that's when he saw that there was nothing else to pull in. As Kurt watched in shock, Matt spontaneously grabbed my lower left leg, still dangling by that thread of flesh, and chucked it into the helicopter behind me. It's a measure of what kind of man Matt is that he saved my life that day, but later all he could say was "Tammy, I'm so sorry I threw your foot like that."

"I've never seen something that traumatic, as far as human injury, in my life," Kurt told me much later. "I thought you were dead." Which is why, when Chris Fierce appeared in the doorway seconds later, needing help getting into the aircraft, an exhausted Kurt just pulled him right on top of me. There didn't seem to be much point in rearranging us, because no one in that helicopter thought I was alive.

With everyone finally on board, we took off for Taji. Sitting above me, bleeding profusely from his own wounds, Kurt kept looking down at Chris and me. Blood sloshed back and forth across the deck, and he had no idea whose it was. But Chris had managed to put a tourniquet on his own leg, so when he saw even more blood sloshing on the deck, he thought, "Shit, Tammy's still bleeding. Her heart must still be pumping." He was the first to realize that I might still be alive.

As a former medevac pilot, Pat Muenks knew instinctively that with injuries this severe, every second counted. He called ahead to Taji and requested to have a medevac bird waiting for us, to get Kurt, Chris, and me to the surgical hospital in Baghdad as quickly as possible.

As we were landing at Taji, the medevac helicopter, blades already spinning, was waiting for us in the area normally used for picking up passengers—the same area where, less than a half hour earlier, we had picked up Colonel Hamm. Later, at the debrief, one of our guys asked him, "So, how long have you been in Iraq?" The Colonel looked at his watch. He'd arrived in country *that day*, only to be thrown into this surreal scene of blood and mayhem.

"Welcome to Iraq, sir," someone said.

When Pat set the helicopter down, a couple of guys who were waiting for a lift somewhere apparently thought we were their ride. As they stood up and started sauntering to the helicopter, the door suddenly flew open and a voice roared, "Get the fuck out of here!" It was Kurt, who, for good measure, turned around so they could see the blood-soaked back of his flight suit. The guys turned tail and ran. We laugh about it now—those poor bastards thought they were hopping an easy helicopter ride up to their base, only to be confronted by our hot mess of blood and body parts.

The team at Taji quickly loaded Chris and me onto stretchers and put us into the medevac. They had a stretcher ready for Kurt too, but he just said, "No, no, let's go!" and limp-hopped into the back of the medevac bird. The Flight Medic on board approached Chris, to take care of him as the most severely injured, but Chris pushed him away, saying, "Take care of Tammy! I think she's alive." Sergeant Fierce, true to the nickname for Army non-commissioned officers (NCOs) as the "backbone of the Army," managed to render aid to a buddy even as he himself was severely wounded.

We took off for Baghdad, landing there at 5:24 P.M., less than an hour after the shootdown—within the "golden hour," as medical professionals call the crucial first sixty minutes after someone suffers catastrophic injury. That fast action—by my crew, the crew of our sister helicopter, and the medevac team—is why I'm alive today.

In 2004, the 31st Combat Support Hospital (CSH) in Baghdad took care of an average of fifteen traumas a day. On the busiest days, such as during the Second Battle of Fallujah, they took in thirty-five to forty. The helicopters would come thumping in, and the medical team would rush out to bring in the wounded. Trauma bed 2 was reserved for the most critically injured, and that's where they put me.

Where my right leg had been, there was now just a gaping, ragged wound that looked like bloody hamburger meat with jagged bones sticking out. My lower left leg was mangled beyond repair, the toes of my foot curled grotesquely and the skin on top burned black. And all of these open, bleeding wounds were contaminated with dirt, shrapnel, and burned flesh. One of the CSH surgeons who helped save my life, Dr. Adam Hamawy, described my leg injuries to me years later as "mud and blood, that's all there was."

In addition to the traumatic injuries to my lower extremities, the bones of my right arm were shattered, the skin and muscle pulverized. There was no pulse in my right hand, which was pale and lifeless. My face and torso had been pelted with hot shrapnel, and I had lost half of the blood in my body. The medical team gave me every unit of blood they had on hand. Then, as my treatment continued into the night and the CSH ran out, they started waking people up in their bunks, hustling around to find anyone who could give. In all, I would receive 40 units of blood, plasma, and platelets in Baghdad.

I have no recollection of any of this—although when the medical team rolled me in from the medevac bird, I was apparently awake. I learned that fact later from a couple of guys who were there that day, Sergeant First Class Gregory Childs, who was the NCO in charge of the emergency room, and Captain Jason Williams, one of the nurses who treated me.

According to Sergeant Childs, I was white as a sheet from blood loss as they stretchered me in, but I propped myself up on my one good elbow and kept demanding status reports on my crew. And in 2019, when I met nurse Jason Williams for the first time since the shootdown, he seemed to remember every detail from my treatment that day:

When they rolled you in, you were still awake. You were asking, *Where are my guys?* And we were like, "Just relax, we're going to take care of you. We've got people taking care of them."

We had a stationary gurney, a striker gurney, like you'd find in a hospital. They rolled you in on the mobile rickshaw, and when I reached over to pull you onto the gurney, your right hip was missing. There was nothing there. And it just, all the remaining tissue just flopped over. And I'm like, *Wow. She is significantly injured.*

I said, "You don't realize it, but you're super severely injured. Just let us take care of you." And you were looking at me and kept asking, *How's so and so? Where are they at? Are you taking care of my men?*

We were working on you to prepare you for intubation for surgery. I was about to give you the medications and what we call a rapid-sequence intubation. It's basically the medication that knocks you out and paralyzes you, so we can put the tube in your throat to go to surgery.

I didn't know your rank at the time, so I just said, "Ma'am, I'm getting ready to put you to sleep for surgery. The next time you wake up you're going to be in either Landstuhl, Germany, or back in the States."

And right before I pushed the medicine, you reached up to me. You grabbed me by the scrub and pulled me to you, and looked me dead in the eyes, and said, "You better take care of my guys."

There were a lot of heroes that day. Dan Milberg saved all our lives, landing a catastrophically damaged helicopter with extraordinary skill and nerve. Kurt Hannemann courageously went to guard our perimeter, even as he was bleeding out from wounds of his own. Matt Backues used every ounce of his strength to drag my unconscious body across the Iraqi desert, unwilling to leave any comrade behind, alive or dead.

Pat Muenks saved precious minutes by calling ahead for a medevac helicopter. Chris Fierce alerted the medevac team that they needed to check on me, as despite all appearances, he thought I might still be alive. Sergeant John Fischer from Chalk 2 helped carry Chris to safety. First Lieutenant Ura Asher kept his head as the copilot so Pat could focus on making the medevac rescue calls. Colonel Hamm, in his first few hours in country, not only tried to help carry me, he also manned a weapon when Chalk 2 got airborne in case we saw any more of the enemy on our way to Taji.

The doctors and nurses who treated me in Baghdad kept me alive, and the troops there rushed to give blood when I desperately needed more.

I didn't land the aircraft, and I didn't carry anyone on my back. I wasn't a hero that day. But that moment in the CSH ER in Baghdad is still my personal proudest moment. Because in the last breath I had before the nurse put me under, which for all anyone knew might be my last breath on this earth, I was still trying to take care of my guys. In the rawest, most traumatic moment of my life, my instinct was to check on my men.

And if those had been my last words, I'd have been fine with that.

Chapter 9

Wall of Pain

As medical teams were fighting to save my life in Baghdad, then transferring me to Landstuhl Regional Medical Center in Germany less than twelve hours later, Bryan was with his family in Maryland for his brother's wedding weekend. I had been shot down on a Friday afternoon in Iraq, and with the time difference, it was early evening that same day in Maryland when the Army started trying to reach him. Bryan had turned off his cell phone for the rehearsal dinner, and turning it back on, he saw a list of missed calls from numbers he didn't recognize—and one from my dad. His heart sank, because he knew it could only be bad news.

Sitting at his parents' kitchen table, Bryan took a deep breath and called my dad. "DA casualty has been trying to reach you all evening," Dad told him, referring to the Army Casualty Office. "Tammy's helicopter was shot down. You need to call them immediately." Dad knew that I had lost my legs, but he decided not to tell Bryan. This was a pure military instinct: As one Soldier talking to another, Dad felt it was best to allow the military process to move forward, especially since the Army would have more up-to-date information. So he and Bryan spoke for only a minute, as if conveying a casualty report over a battlefield radio.

Bryan called DA casualty, and a Sergeant there confirmed the shootdown, then informed him that I had lost my legs and would probably lose my right arm. But as bad as the news was, Bryan felt a pang of relief. *Okay, she's not dead,* he thought. *And he knows a lot about her wounds, so she must be in U.S. hands.* "You should prepare to travel to Landstuhl," the Sergeant told him, "in the event she can't be stabilized enough for transport back to the States." Bryan couldn't help but notice that the Sergeant offered no confirmation, or even encouragement, that I would survive.

Bryan told his parents what had happened, but he made a snap decision not to tell anyone else, to avoid casting a pall over his brother's wedding. The next day, he helped prepare for the wedding in a daze, not knowing whether he'd be seeing me soon at the Army's main stateside hospital, Walter Reed Army Medical Center in Washington, DC, or possibly be called to Landstuhl to say goodbye. One of his wedding duties was to pick up dozens of white roses for the venue, and he spent hours on Saturday afternoon methodically de-thorning their stems. It was a mind-numbing task he was grateful to have—a "weird blessing," as he would call it later.

Bryan stood as best man, and gave a heartfelt toast at the reception, without letting anyone know the worry that was weighing him down. It wasn't until the newlyweds left the reception that he and his parents pulled aside a few close family members. Sitting in the beautifully decorated hall, surrounded by white roses and empty tables, Bryan told them about the shootdown. One cousin who was there, Dr. Claudia Beck, would soon become a vital link between us and my doctors, translating medical jargon into terms we could understand.

By the time Bryan told his family on that Saturday night, the medical team in Landstuhl had decided that I was stable enough to be transported to the United States on the next medevac flight. (Apparently, I had awakened and even given a thumbs-up sign, though I have no memory of that.) The Army Casualty Office told Bryan I would arrive the following day, Sunday, November 14— less than seventy-two hours after the shootdown.

Medevac flights from Landstuhl to Andrews Air Force Base were marvels of military logistics and medicine. They were outfitted like flying hospitals, with different "wards" for different levels of injury. Ambulatory patients sat on benches along the sides. In front of them were the litter patients, lying on stretchers stacked two or three high, suspended one above the other. The most severely wounded, like me, were in what amounted to mobile ICU rooms, fully equipped with oxygen, monitors, and IVs. Because of the risk of dying during transport, we each had our own team of critical care doctors and nurses.

I was unconscious for all of this, but later on, Bryan would learn details of the flight from Pam Keith, the wife of fellow wounded warrior Sergeant John Keith, who lay on the litter next to mine. Sergeant Keith had been hit by an RPG, suffering a shattered femur, a traumatic brain injury, and third-degree burns to his abdomen. Pam had flown to Landstuhl to be with her husband, and she was by his side for the medevac flight. Between her husband's condition and the young children she'd had to leave at home, Pam had plenty to worry about—but she still had the presence of mind and compassion to look out for me too.

She noticed that as the medical team worked on me, they were so focused on keeping me alive that they occasionally left parts of my body uncovered. So, whenever the nurse or doctor stepped away from tending my wounds, she would reach over and pull up the sheets to cover my nakedness and, hopefully, keep me warm. Pam was the epitome of the Army spouse, serving her nation and taking care of a Soldier she didn't know, even as she faced her own worst nightmare with a grievously wounded, comatose husband.

After I arrived at Walter Reed, Bryan began keeping a journal, which he would later post online to let friends and family know what was happening. These are excerpts from those first days after I returned:

The staff in the ICU at Walter Reed got me in to see Tammy almost immediately after she got there. I did not want to go into that hospital area, and part of me still did not want to believe this was true. However, someone needed to make good decisions that would affect the rest of our lives, so there was no option but to face reality.

The emotional impact of seeing my usually tall wife (5'6") laid out on the hospital bed and chopped off to what seemed like 3 feet long was pretty severe. Her body was badly swollen, which made her face difficult to recognize. I later found out this was from lack of red blood cells, since they had used all of her blood type available and had been forced to hang bottles of pure hemoglobin to keep her heart pumping.

Though I could see the stumps of her legs, the nurses had covered the bloody mass of her right arm and the metal tinker toy contraption, which was holding it together, as if to spare me from that one particular grisly detail. The doctors were deliberately keeping her unconscious with drugs at that point. She had tubes down her throat, and sensors hooked up to show her breathing and heart rate. The emotional impact of seeing my wife, friend and fellow Soldier lying there like that felt like a body blow.

Bryan knew he had to compartmentalize his emotions, because crucial decisions had to be made about my care—and as long as the doctors were keeping me sedated, I was incapable of making them myself.

The doctors came to me while she was still unconscious and told me that I should decide to have them remove what was left of her right leg. It was a very small piece of bone, with no hamstring or quadriceps attached, and it was doubtful and unlikely that she would be able to walk on it.

They told me that I could probably save her some painful decisions later, if I made the decision then to remove what was left of that leg while the wounds were still open, and before she woke up. Very few people had ever walked with prosthetics attached to a limb that short, and her chances of doing so were very slight.

Knowing my wife well, I reasoned that the most important thing to her is self-determination, and if there was a hard decision to make, she would want to make it for herself.

In addition, what the doctors characterized as "doubtful" or "unlikely" was based on their experience with people other than Tammy. Her attitude was a factor in the equation that the doctors did not yet know about. Also, the potential upside was that she might be able to walk with prosthetics on the stump of that leg, while the potential downside, that she would have to undergo the same operation at a later date if it did not work out, was minimal.

This was a big decision. Bryan knew that if there was even a sliver of a chance I could get a prosthetic fitted and walk on it, I would want to try. But the downside would be more pain down the road if that plan didn't work out. In the end, he went against the doctors' recommendations, refusing to authorize removal of that little piece of bone. He did the right thing, because after months of recovery, multiple surgeries, the fitting of a prosthetic, and grueling physical therapy, I can walk on it today.

The eight days between when the shootdown happened and when I woke up in Walter Reed are not even a blur for me—they're nothing at all. I was heavily sedated, and have no recollection of them. But for my family, they were agony. My parents had moved back to Hawaii, and while my dad stayed there to recuperate from a recent heart attack, my mom rushed to get on a flight to Washington. In those early days, Mom and Bryan sat at my bedside for hours, taking turns so I was never alone.

The first time my mom came into my room, I apparently opened my eyes when she said my name. I wasn't aware of it, and doubt I could actually see anything, and very soon I slipped back under. From that point on I started occasionally opening my eyes, though I was still completely unresponsive to outside stimulation. But in the hopes that somehow, deep down, I could hear him, Bryan began repeating three facts to me like a mantra.

"You were injured," he'd say. "You are at Walter Reed. You are safe." Over and over he whispered these words to me, in the hopes that when I came to, I would have some understanding—even if only subconsciously—of what had happened.

When my mom was at my bedside, she recited her own kind of mantra. She had always been a Buddhist, but in recent years she had become especially devout. Like many Thai Buddhists, she believed that through shock or trauma, a person's soul can become separated from her body, and that chanting can help reunite them. So as I lay there unconscious, she sat next to me and chanted

Buddhist prayers for hours on end, calling my soul back into my body. I don't remember any of it, but the nurses later told me they found it very calming.

Mom and Bryan slept, when they could, in the tiny ICU waiting room, which they shared with family members of other wounded Soldiers. They'd sometimes go down to the cafeteria for a quick meal, but often Mom would just get food out of the vending machine in the waiting room. She had never tried Flamin' Hot Cheetos before then, but the spiciness reminded her of the Thai food she loved, so she ate bag after bag of them. (And she still loves them, to this day: After having knee replacement surgery at Walter Reed in August of 2020, Mom asked me to get her some Flamin' Hot Cheetos, bringing us full circle.) She also discovered Ensure nutritional supplement, which was sold in cans in the vending machines. "I was so hungry, I just tried it," she would tell me later. "It's good! And your stomach feels better."

Mom struggled with sadness and feelings of helplessness during those first days. She couldn't do much more than just sit and watch as I lay there hooked up to machines that beeped and wheezed and thumped all day and night. She grew to hate the sounds of those machines, even though they were keeping me alive. All these years later, she says she still sometimes hears them in her head.

There was one way she felt she could help. I had been growing my hair out while in Iraq (after cutting it short at the start of my deployment), but the doctors wanted to cut it all off again for hygiene purposes. The explosion left shrapnel embedded in my face, head, and neck, and they wanted to shave off any hair that might get in the way of treating or removing it. But when the doctors suggested this, my mom surprised them by piping up, "No no no! I will take care of it!" She braided my filthy, blood-caked hair into about eight long braids, which, stiff with dirt and dry

Age 3, in Bangkok. Mom loved to dress me in tights, even in the tropical heat. (1A)

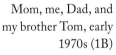

Mom, me, Dad, and my brother Tom, early 1970s (1B)

With our Christmas tree, 1971. How Dad managed to track down the perfect tree in Southeast Asia every year, I'll never know. (1C)

Tom and I pose with our home's Cambodian guard—and his automatic weapon—in Phnom Penh, 1975. (2A)

Family portrait, 1986 (2B)

At Camp Castaway, off the coast of Malaysia, age 16 (2C)

At my commissioning into the U.S. Army in 1992, age 24 (3A)

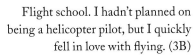

Flight school. I hadn't planned on being a helicopter pilot, but I quickly fell in love with flying. (3B)

Tom and I became part of a Duckworth family military history that stretches back to before the American Revolution. He's pictured here in a C130 aircraft during his U.S. Coast Guard service. (3C)

Bryan and me at our wedding ceremony, 1994 (4A)

At our traditional Thai ceremony, held that same day (4B)

Cleaning my helicopter in Iraq, 2004 (5A)

With fellow rotorheads in Iraq. Pat Muenks, who piloted the helicopter that evacuated my crew and me from the shootdown site, stands at right. (5B)

Our helicopter at the shootdown site, with the rocket-propelled grenade's entry and exit holes plainly visible. The RPG blew into the cockpit at bottom right, exploded in my lap, and exited over my head above the windshield. (6A)

After the shootdown, the U.S. Army destroyed our helicopter and brought the scraps back to the base. This was my side of the cockpit; the tube with wires coming out at upper left is the remains of the cyclic stick that was between my legs. (6B)

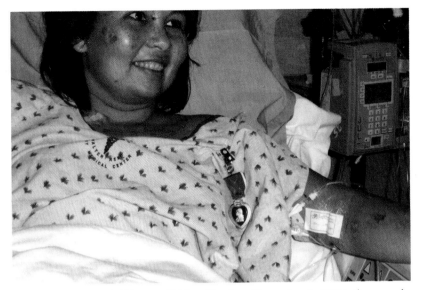

Receiving my Purple Heart at Walter Reed on December 3, 2004, three weeks after the shootdown (7A)

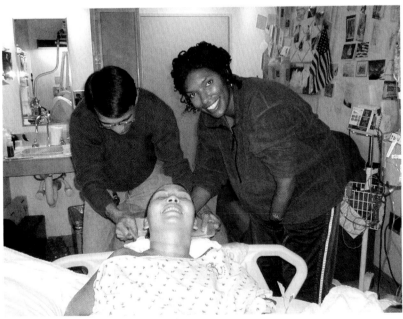

With my brother's help, Sergeant First Class Juanita Wilson—herself an amputee—washed the blood and dust out of my hair. (7B)

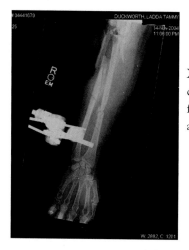

X-ray of my injured arm. You can see the multiple bone fractures and absence of flesh around my elbow. (8A)

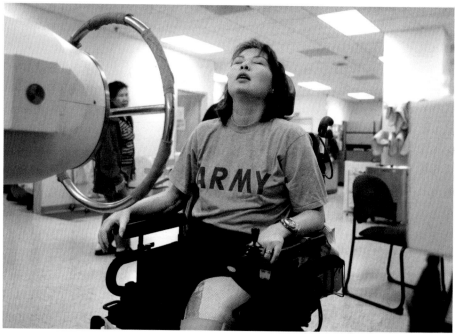

Recovery was long and arduous. Here, my mom looks on as I take a break in exhaustion. (8B)

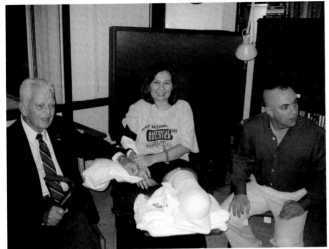

With Dad and Bryan on December 21, 2004, the day I was promoted to Major. This was my first time seeing Dad in more than a year—since before deploying to Iraq. (9A)

With Tom, Mom, and Bryan at Arlington Cemetery for my dad's funeral, March 2005 (9B)

Doing an interview as Senator Dick Durbin's guest at the 2005 State of the Union address. This was my first time meeting Dick, who became an important friend and mentor. (10A)

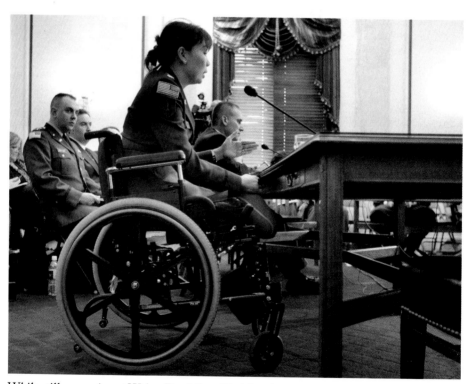

While still recovering at Walter Reed, I testified (in a borrowed uniform) in front of the U.S. Senate Veterans' Affairs Committee about conditions at the hospital. March 2005. (10B)

With Adam Sandler, Rob Schneider, and other actors at Walter Reed. Famous visitors often popped by to offer encouragement to the wounded warriors. (11A)

With one of my prosthetic legs, March 2005 (11B)

As the medical and therapy teams at Walter Reed always told us, amputees can do anything we set our minds to—including skydiving, skiing, and cycling a marathon. (12A)

(12B)

(12C)

Walking off stage after speaking at the 2012 Democratic National Convention (13A)

I never aspired to be a politician, but parts of the job—like meeting young constituents and working with fellow senators such as Cory Booker—are incredibly rewarding. (13B)

With President-elect Barack Obama on Veterans Day, 2008 (13C)

The cake served on my first Alive Day, November 12, 2005 (14A)

Celebrating my third Alive Day, November 12, 2007, with some of the guys I served with in Iraq. Four of these men—Dan, Matt, Pat, and John—helped saved my life, and the life of SGT Chris Fierce, after the shootdown. From left to right: SSG Mike McCammond, SGT (Ret) Matt Backues, CW4 (Ret) Randy Zehnder, CW5 Patrick Muenks, SGT (Ret) John Fischer, CW5 (Ret) Dan Milberg, and CW5 (Ret) Jerry Kaemmer. (14B)

Kurt Hannemann, one of our two door gunners on the day of the shootdown, later showed a reporter where the RPG had entered our Black Hawk—through the plexiglass chin bubble at my feet. (14C)

Vice President Biden jokingly swears in my daughter Abigail to the Senate, 2017. (15A)

With ten-day-old Maile, heading into the Senate for a vote (15B)

Looking down at the shootdown site in Iraq, fifteen years later, as a visiting United States Senator (16A)

Back in a cockpit after regaining my pilot's license, 2010. Though I didn't get to fly for the Army again, I will always treasure the years that I did. (16B)

shampoo, immediately stuck up at all angles from my head. At that point, with so much else to worry about, I wouldn't have cared one way or the other if the doctors had just shaved my head. But for Mom, saving my hair felt like the one thing she could do for me.

On about my fifth day at Walter Reed, the doctors started weaning me off the drugs that were keeping me unconscious. Gradually, as they lessened the doses, I entered a dreamlike state. I could see blurry images and began hearing some of what was being said around me. And just as Bryan hoped, I heard his three whispered statements, and internalized his message that I was safe.

At the same time, I could hear snippets of what the medical team was saying about my condition. Going in and out of consciousness, I heard the nurses and doctors refer to a "helicopter crash." They didn't realize it, but their use of the word "crash" would end up causing me the worst emotional trauma of the entire experience. For a couple of days after I woke up, I believed I was responsible for crashing the Black Hawk and injuring my crew. I went through forty-eight hours of pure emotional turmoil, believing that I had failed as a pilot, a Soldier, and an officer. In my darkest moments, I felt that because of that failure, I deserved to lose my legs.

When Bryan eventually figured out why I was so tormented, he told me the helicopter didn't crash at all, but had been shot down by an RPG and landed in a field. I was overwhelmed with relief. Words matter, and to this day I will correct anyone who says that my helicopter "crashed" or that I was in an "accident." It was a shootdown. The bastards took aim at us—no accident about it.

During the period when the doctors were bringing me out of my coma, they tried to prepare Bryan for what was to come. As he wrote in his journal:

Tammy had been unconscious since she had arrived at Walter Reed, and I did not know if there had been brain damage from lack of oxygen during any of the various periods when her heart had stopped beating on the operating table in theater. Though I thought I knew my wife pretty well, I was not exactly sure what her emotional state would be when she did regain consciousness after being abruptly confronted with such a life-altering situation.

During one of her many operations during this period at Walter Reed, Colonel Bill Howard, the Chief of the Occupational Therapy department, found me and took me down to the Physical Therapy department where all the amputees were walking and getting on with their lives. In retrospect, I believe he was preparing me to "sell" a positive outlook to my wife when she woke up. He was telling me it was my job to articulate a positive vision of the future when she would most need it.

Of course, Bryan would have to adjust to our new reality too. But he knew he had to set aside his own feelings, to focus on helping me understand what had happened and where we'd go from here. He steeled himself for that task, even as he waited and watched for signs that I was finally awake.

On November 20, eight days after the shootdown, I woke up slammed into a wall of pain. I don't even know how to describe it, as the words "pain" and "hurt" are inadequate to express the all-consuming agony that enveloped me. I felt like my entire body was covered in lava, or boiling water—as if every nerve ending was being seared. It was relentless, dizzying in its force, nauseating. My legs and arm were on fire, inside and out, and the rest of my body just hurt, over every square inch of me. Even my hair follicles hurt.

Opening my eyes, I could see Bryan and my mom at my bed-side. When the doctors removed my breathing tube, despite the pain, I managed to say "I love you" to them. And then I said, "Put me to work"—because as I was waking up, I had overheard a nurse explaining a respiratory exercise to Bryan. I wanted to get started on my rehab.

I had no idea at that point how badly injured I was. All I knew was that my whole body was screaming with pain, and my legs hurt the most. "Honey," I said, "I need some Tylenol for my legs." Bryan just looked at me, his hazel eyes somber. He stepped out to ask a doctor to come into the room, then sat down on my bed and took my hand in his. "Tammy," he said quietly. "That's phantom pain. You've lost your legs."

"Oh...interesting," I said. "Explain." I'm not sure whether it was because of medication or because my first response to any crisis is to try to solve it, but my reaction to this news was very matter-of-fact.

The doctor explained the phenomenon of phantom pain, in which people who've lost limbs continue to feel sensations in them. He and Bryan also described the other injuries I had suffered. I couldn't see my right arm, as the doctors were shielding it from us due to the gruesomeness of the wounds, but the doctor told me that the bones were shattered and the flesh pulverized. Bryan told me I had shrapnel wounds in my face, as well as nerve damage in my left shoulder. I also had the imprints of the Black Hawk's flight controls bruised into my hands, as I had been gripping them so tightly while trying to land the aircraft.

As Bryan and the doctor spoke, I lay there and listened, my face impassive. I was trying to take in everything I was hearing, and was still in excruciating pain. But as Bryan wrote in his journal, I still had a little bit of spark in me:

The head MD in the ICU and I told her of the extent of her injuries this morning. While that was probably the most difficult thing I have ever done, she received the news with poise and stoicism.

She listened to my rundown of all the things amputees are doing here, and my explanation of how this injury will actually not have much impact on the quality of her life (and amazingly, it really won't).

She then told me, "I love you, but you stink. Go shower." So we are in good shape.

My brother Tom also came to see me shortly after I woke up. His eyes widened as he looked at me. "Oh, Tammy," he said, shaking his head. I felt touched by his concern, until he chuckled and said, "Mom did that to you, didn't she?" *What?* Now I was *really* confused.

"Those braids," he said, with the same wide grin he's had since childhood. "You look like Coolio."

Unfortunately, these moments of lucidity were fleeting. I began throwing up, and my pain, already at five-alarm-fire levels, intensified even more. And then I began hallucinating.

Once, I saw a woman floating by wearing an iridescent, flowing sari of the most vivid blues and greens. "Bryan," I mumbled. "Go tell that angel she's beautiful." He laughed and said, "Well, I can do that. But actually, she's a middle-aged nurse in blue scrubs with a green leaf pattern."

I hallucinated entire scenarios where I was flying again, and some in which I was trying to report back to headquarters the location of the shootdown. These scenes felt absolutely real to me, and I spent a lot of time talking to people who were not in the room. Bryan said he had whole conversations with me where he was one of four or five people I thought I was talking to. "I've got to file the report!" I would say, then rattle off a series of nonsensical coordinates. "Tell the guys! They need to know where the enemy is." Once, in a throwback to our ROTC days, I instructed Bryan and the imaginary Soldiers on how to dig a hasty fighting position. He responded as if he were a cadet in my class, and later told me it was actually a pretty thorough and good lesson. He was impressed, but this hallucinatory episode confused and scared my mom, who redoubled her chanting.

Another time, a nurse was outside my room, typing information into my online charts. I thought he was communicating with me through that *tap-tap-tap*, and in my feverish fog, I believed I could conjure his computer screen in my mind. I tried to communicate back to him, saying, "Please call my battalion commander and tell him what happened!" In those first few days, I was constantly anxious about getting the information about the enemy to my command.

The doctors realized that I was having an adverse reaction to the morphine they'd been giving me. Morphine is usually a go-to in situations like mine, where a patient is severely injured and needs the strongest meds available, but with me it was doing more harm than good. Unfortunately, my condition wasn't stable enough yet for them to implant a continuous IV nerve block, so the doctors scrambled to figure out another painkiller that might work. In the meantime, they began weaning me off the morphine, and the five days that followed were the worst of my life. I was in utter agony, crushed by the rawest, most unrelenting pain imaginable.

The pain was so devastating that I could barely breathe. I was hurting so much, it took all the strength in my body just to survive, second by second. I was too weak to ask my mother to stop stroking my skin, though her gentle touch sent knife-edged stabs through my body. It was so unbearable that at some point, I realized I wasn't going to make it. I had lived through a lot, but this was too much for my body to take.

"Bryan," I whispered. He leaned close. "I have to go now. I have to circle the wagons." He sat bolt upright, his eyes wide with fear.

"No," he said. "Tammy, just hold on." He believed I was telling him I was dying. I suppose I was, but not in the way he thought. I just understood that in order to survive, I had to shut down completely and go deep inside myself. I closed my eyes. In my mind, I could see a hilltop with a ring of covered wagons, and I imagined myself sitting in the middle of it. It was like a dream state, or a meditation. I don't know how long I lay there visualizing my wagons protecting me, but I believe that's what kept me alive.

I wasn't aware of the passage of time, but after the better part of a day, I finally mustered the energy to open my eyes. On the wall across from my bed, I could see a big round clock—the kind that's ubiquitous in federal buildings, black and white with a second hand that ticked loudly. I found it weirdly comforting, as it reminded me of all the rooms I'd sat in with that same clock, marking the time of my Army service. I didn't know if I could survive a day, or even an hour. But staring at that clock, I decided I could survive one minute.

As I watched the second hand sweep around, I started counting off the seconds. "One dead insurgent, two dead insurgents, three dead insurgents…" I murmured. Even in the depth of my agony, with barely enough energy to breathe, I was filled with fury. "Four dead insurgents, five dead insurgents, six dead insurgents…" I was angry about what some random insurgent with an RPG had been able to do to me, and beginning to fantasize about revenge. But after a minute or two of this, I felt silly. So I closed my eyes, and grudgingly switched to "one-one-thousand, two-one-thousand, three-one-thousand...," just trying to make it through one minute. Then another. Then another.

At some point, I opened my eyes to find a tall African American woman standing in my room. Was this a dream? Or was she real? She walked up to my bedside, then used her right hand to pull a prosthesis off her left arm. She angled her forearm stump so I could see it, and said, "I know how much you're hurting. It will end." I just stared at her, lacking the energy to respond. And then she said, "Can I stand here for you?"

This was Sergeant First Class Juanita Wilson, and she had lost her hand to an IED explosion in Iraq just a few months earlier. The beeps, smells, and humming noises of the ICU had to have been fresh in her mind from her own ordeal, but Juanita came to my bedside anyway. There weren't many female amputees in Walter Reed, and as an Army Sergeant, she wanted to show her support for a fellow Soldier. Juanita knew that what I needed wasn't a pep talk, a smile, or a gentle touch on my skin. She knew that what I needed was to see someone else who'd made it through the hell I was enduring. Someone who had come out the other side as strong—if not stronger—than she'd gone in.

She stood next to my bed off and on for the next five days. "You can do this," she would tell me. "I have been where you are. I understand. And it *will get better.*" She would watch silently as I counted down the hours, sixty seconds at a time. Sometimes the pain was too severe, and I would pass out. But when I woke up, she was still there, radiating a peace and serenity that I clung to like a life preserver.

I honestly don't know how I would have made it through those five days without Juanita Wilson. When I think of her, the two words that come to mind are "warrior" and "compassion." She was the definition of grace and strength in my time of need, a true NCO, a Soldier. I can never thank her enough for what she did for me.

And Juanita wasn't the only Veteran to visit me in the ICU. Three other female amputees came through in those early days, some of them even before I awoke. First Lieutenant Melissa Stockwell was the first female amputee of the war. Though she lost her leg to a roadside bomb, she would later become a world-class athlete and world champion paratriathlete. Specialist Danielle Green, a former Notre Dame basketball star, lost an arm after being hit by explosives while guarding a rooftop and now works as a mental health clinician for Veterans. And First Lieutenant Dawn Halfaker, who lost her arm to an RPG, was a West Point graduate from a distinguished military family who went on to start her own national security company. These four amazing women talked with Bryan, telling him about their recovery experiences and offering suggestions for how he could help me. All of the peer visitors, who volunteered their time and energy to help their fellow wounded warriors, were a crucial part of the healing process.

Among the peer visitors at Walter Reed, two of the best known and most beloved were Tom and Eleanor Porter. Tom was a gentle giant, a tall, smiling seventy-four-year-old Veteran who showed up at my bedside while I was still comatose to talk with Bryan and my mom, and who came to visit again soon after I regained consciousness. As a young Army Lieutenant in the Korean War, Tom had lost both his legs in a landmine explosion. During his months of recuperation back in the States, Eleanor—an Army Second Lieutenant herself—had been one of his physical therapists. The couple had been married for more than fifty years, and despite their white hair and sweet demeanor, they became known among the patients at Walter Reed as the "sex-talk and cookies" couple.

This was because Tom made it his mission to talk with injured troops about love after amputation. A lot of the guys were really young, just eighteen or nineteen years old, lying in their hospital beds with limbs missing and thinking, *Who will ever love me now?* Tom would walk in, strong and smiling, and say, "Hey, I was like you. Lost my legs at twenty-two. But I courted El after that, and she and I have been married for fifty years and have wonderful kids and grandkids." He reassured them they could still have the lives they dreamed of—and his words had weight because he was living proof that it was possible. He'd wink and say, "Listen, having an amputation is better than having a puppy. Trust me, you won't have any trouble getting the ladies." And then he'd answer any questions they had about physical intimacy, bluntly and without embarrassment, because he knew these guys didn't have anyone else they could ask about it.

For years, Tom and El came into Walter Reed every Tuesday and Thursday without fail. El was known as the Cookie Lady, because she'd bring in dozens of homemade cookies to hand out. She collected them from people at her church, then loaded them into a big canvas bag with the word COOKIES stenciled on it. For those of us who were in the hospital for a long time, El knew our favorites: Bryan's were snickerdoodles; mine were oatmeal raisin. If I was at physical therapy, or in surgery, or getting my wounds debrided when El made her rounds, she'd leave a little bag of cookies on my bedside table. It was a real treat in the midst of the painful early stages of recovery, something to look forward to every week.

Of course, El wasn't handing out cookies just as a treat. They were a way of getting calories into us. All of us wounded troops had lost weight due to lack of appetite, nausea, or days spent being fed intravenously. My fellow amputees were mostly young men, between the ages of eighteen and twenty-five, who'd been in the best physical shape of their lives. Now many of them were emaciated—big, strapping guys who'd withered down to a hundred pounds. At my lowest point I weighed ninety-two pounds, and the doctors threatened to put me back on tube-feeding through my nose if I dropped below ninety. The medical teams were always looking for ways to get us to consume more calories, and El's cookies were a great way of doing that. So were the milkshakes brought by another frequent visitor, a guy named Jim Mayer—better known as the Milkshake Man.

A Vietnam Veteran in his late fifties, Jim would come to Walter Reed three or four nights a week after finishing his workday at the Department of Veterans Affairs. On the way, he'd stop at McDonald's and buy a few dozen shakes. He'd walk through the halls, poking his head into rooms and saying, "Anyone want a milkshake?" Sometimes he'd hand it off and continue on his way, but occasionally he'd come in to chat for a bit. One night, he said to me, "Mind if I sit down? I'm a little tired." As he took a chair, I could see for the first time that Jim had two prosthetic legs. He was a double amputee, like me, but if he hadn't shown me his legs, I never would have known it.

This was hugely inspiring for me, as Jim knew it would be. He walked those hallways for hours handing out his shakes. *If he can do that on two prosthetic legs, I can do it too,* I thought.

That kind of inspiration, from people who'd been through exactly what we were now facing, was priceless. In those early days, I wanted the pain to stop, and I wanted to regain the use of my right arm if that was at all possible. But what I really wanted was for my life to get back to normal again. And for me, that meant being able to get back into the cockpit—to fly again for the Army. For this too I had a peer visitor to look to for inspiration.

Lieutenant Colonel Andrew Lourake was an Air Force pilot in the late 1990s when he injured his leg in a motocross accident. When he contracted a staph infection in the hospital, his leg never really healed, and after eighteen surgeries and years of pain, he finally had it amputated above the knee. Determined to fly again, he underwent hundreds of hours of physical therapy, and in July 2004—six years after his initial accident—the Air Force cleared him to do it.

From the time I woke up in Walter Reed, I had one goal in mind: to fly again for the Army. At first, I didn't know whether that was even possible as an amputee. So when Lieutenant Colonel Lourake came to visit and told me he was back in the cockpit, that was all the confirmation I needed.

There was no way in hell I was going to let some asshole who'd gotten lucky with an RPG determine my fate. However much pain I'd have to endure, and however long it took, I was determined to get back into the cockpit of a Black Hawk.

Chapter 10

Owning the Suck

So, you want to fly again?" a nurse asked me the day after I awoke. "Yeah," I said. "I do."

"Well, then, you'd better start moving."

A wave of nausea rolled through my body, and for a moment I couldn't speak. When it passed, I said, "I can't move anything." My right arm was still pinned by the metal external fixator, or "ex-fix," which was holding my shattered bones together. I could feel the soles of my nonexistent feet burning, and phantom pain shot all the way up through the stumps of my legs, radiating into every part of my body. Everything hurt. What did this nurse expect me to do?

"Come on," she said. "Can you do anything at all? Show me." With effort, I managed to move my left hand at the wrist. "Great!" she said. "Give me ten of those." I made that small motion ten times, and she smiled. "Now three sets of ten." And that's how my recovery started, moving one hand side to side while flat on my back in the ICU. Because if making that tiny motion was all I could do, it made no sense to lie around feeling sorry for myself. I had to accept my situation, then start working to change it.

In those first days at Walter Reed, I thought a lot about a phrase I'd learned from fellow Soldiers in Iraq: "Own the suck."

When something bad happens, you can either let it own you, or *you* own *it*. It sucks to be deployed. It sucks to be sweating in 120-degree heat and have nowhere to pee. And it really sucks to lose your legs. But you know what? That's *your* suck. Your loved ones, your friends, your doctors and nurses can never really know what you're going through—only you do. So own your suck. Kick its ass! Otherwise, it owns you.

I decided to own—no, to *dominate*—my suck by taking my recovery one small step at a time. If I couldn't move my arm, I'd move my hand. If I couldn't sit up without feeling faint, I would raise my head inch by inch until I could. My situation definitely sucked, but it was what it was. If I kept my focus and worked hard, I could make it a little better tomorrow, and the next day, and the next day, until I became strong again.

By choosing to own the suck, I was able to come to grips with my situation, and what I needed to do, pretty quickly. Unfortunately, my mom was still struggling to accept what had happened to me. As a Buddhist, she believed in the concept of karma, that your fate is tied to how you've lived in the past. Essentially, you reap what you sow. So those first few weeks, Mom drove herself crazy, crying at my bedside and asking why I had to suffer like this.

"Why did this happen to you?" she would ask. "You haven't done anything bad in your life. What did you do to deserve this?"

"*Mā khaa*," I said, calling her "Mom" in Thai, "did it ever occur to you that maybe because I lived a good life, that's why I survived?" I felt terrible for making her worry so much, and it was obvious that she needed reassurance that only I could provide. "Maybe this is actually my reward," I told her. "I'm not dead." I could see in her face that my words were helping. And saying them out loud actually helped me too.

*　　*　　*

As my doctors weaned me off morphine, they tried to stabilize my condition and get my pain under control. Every day, they would take me into surgery to debride my wounds, a process that involved digging out shrapnel, washing out debris, and clearing away dead tissue in hopes of keeping infection at bay. They always put me under anesthesia for the debriding, but when I'd wake up, the gaping wounds on my leg stumps and arm hurt even worse.

I still hadn't seen my right arm, because the doctors were trying to shield both Bryan and me from how gruesome it looked. (Not that I could have seen it anyway, as I couldn't turn my head far enough to the side.) I knew it must have been bad, because even one of the nurses, Astrid Strum, had to leave the room periodically so we wouldn't see her cry. Astrid was as tough as they came. She had treated all kinds of horrific wounds, but she had never seen a female body as catastrophically injured as mine. This seemed to catch a lot of the nurses off guard, and later, when I saw photos the medical team had taken during surgery, I understood why. But she'd just take a moment to compose herself, then come back and continue caring for me with an extraordinary strength and compassion that was common among those who cared for us at Walter Reed.

My arm was such a mangled mass of shredded, raw tissue that calling it hamburger would have been a compliment. Most of the muscle and skin had been blown apart by the RPG, and all three bones—my humerus, ulna, and radius—were broken into multiple pieces. The ex-fix looked like a medieval torture tool, but it was literally the only thing holding my arm together.

The doctors still weren't sure whether the arm could be saved, but they planned to perform a complicated surgery on it as soon as I was strong enough to bear it. In an effort to relieve the most intense pain, they put in a nerve block, a device connected to a catheter tube that bathed the nerve in a constant stream of painkillers. They then spent another five days making sure I was stable enough for the surgery, which would involve not only my arm but my torso and parts of my gluteus. The entire process, which involved multiple procedures and surgeons, was expected to take eight to ten hours.

First, the doctors would piece back together the shattered bones, like a jigsaw puzzle. Then they would screw flat pieces of metal, custom made to fit my arm, into the bones to hold them in place.

The next step was to rebuild the limb with living tissue. Most of my muscle and sinew had been blown apart in the explosion, so it wasn't enough to merely repair the bones; if the doctors didn't include some new tissue, my upper arm would be just a thin stick covered with flappy skin, unprotected and virtually useless. So the plan was to create a "muscle flap," an innovative technique that would result in a fleshy, mostly functional arm.

This was a tricky, time-consuming procedure, as my doctor, Lieutenant Colonel Gerald Farber, explained on the morning of my surgery. He would make three long incisions into my belly, creating an open rectangle, and then peel back my skin and muscle wall like a trap door, opening my abdomen all the way down to my rib cage with one long horizontal side of the rectangle still attached. He would then place my arm onto the opening and sew the flap to it, affixing my arm to my side. Finally, he would remove a patch of skin from my butt, use a special machine to punch holes in it and stretch it out, and then graft it to the wound over my rib cage to seal it up.

"Don't worry, you'll be asleep through everything," he said. And then he smiled. "I've been going over the steps of this surgery all night," he told me, probably figuring I'd find that comforting.

"Well, I hope not *all* night," I said. "I mean, I hope you got some sleep."

The surgery took eleven hours, because everything didn't go quite as planned. After slicing a patch of skin off my right butt cheek, then stretching it with the special tool, the doctors discovered it wasn't big enough to graft over my rib cage. So they had to take another patch of skin, this one from my left thigh. After I woke up, I was seriously bummed to find out that in addition to all my existing wounds, I now had two brand-new ones—giant six-by-three-inch and ten-by-three-inch road-rash patches that hurt and stung like hell.

My butt was the only part of me that hadn't been injured in the explosion, and now I couldn't put any pressure on the right side of it, or on my left thigh. There was probably a joke in there somewhere about having my ass saved by my buddies only to have it literally skinned by the docs, but I wasn't laughing, because while the nerve block helped me with the pain from my amputations and my arm, it did nothing to help with these new wounds.

But despite the pain, I was happy to have the surgery finished. Now I could get out of the ICU, move into my own room, and start the recovery process.

If you lose a leg as a civilian, most insurers won't pay for a prosthetic limb until many months have passed. This is because the shape and size of your stump change over time, so every few weeks you'd have to get your equipment resized, at a cost of thousands of dollars each time. But at Walter Reed, we got our new legs within the first six weeks. The doctors wanted us to start wearing them, standing up and getting mobile as soon as possible, because the earlier you start, the smoother the recovery process tends to be.

The medical team fitted me with a clear plexiglass socket and took measurements for my new legs. "What size feet did you have?" one of the prosthetics tech assistants asked. "Eight," I told him. The new legs would need to have feet that were the same size as the ones I'd lost, so my body would be proportional and I could wear my old shoes.

Unfortunately, when my new legs came, the feet were the size of boats.

"What the hell?" I asked.

"Ahhh," the prosthetist said. "These are *men's* size eight." There were so few female leg amputees, apparently it hadn't occurred to anyone in the military supply chain to order women's feet sizes.

In fact, just about everything at Walter Reed was created with men in mind. During my first week, the Wounded Warrior Project charity brought a pre-packed "comfort kit" to me in the ICU. It had an iPod, which was nice, but the rest was stuff I had no use for: men's jockey briefs, a shaving kit, socks, and slippers. Bryan took one look and exclaimed, "Cool! Now I don't need to do laundry for another week." I just rolled my eyes.

I was especially bummed about the men's briefs, because at that point—just like in Iraq—I needed underwear and had no easy way to get it. Bryan hadn't packed a bag for me because he had traveled to Maryland before the shootdown, for his brother's wedding. So all my clothes were back in Illinois. I had no underwear and no bras, and as I started to feel strong enough for physical therapy, I couldn't do it wearing a thin hospital gown with my scabby butt hanging out the back.

Luckily, a group of Red Cross volunteers came through the hospital, asking all the patients what they needed. I requested underwear, bras, shorts, and T-shirts, and the Red Cross added them to a list. Various Veterans' groups would check in with the Red Cross and send volunteers to buy everything. But they obviously sent guys to get mine, because when my bag of goodies arrived, I pulled out a set of those damned nylon granny panties—and a couple of size DD bras. *Seriously?* I'm sure the volunteering Vets did their best, probably grabbing whatever the local Walmart had on display, but this was definitely a case of good intentions and less successful execution. I could have stuffed the granny panties into those gigantic DD cups, and they still would have had space left over. It wasn't until much later, when Air Force Colonel Pat Webb came by as a volunteer visitor and organized another shopping trip, that I got proper underwear.

By the time I got out of the ICU and into my own room, nearly three weeks had passed since the shootdown. During that time, I hadn't been able to do any of the simple daily activities we all take for granted. I hadn't eaten a meal since that stir-fry lunch in the Green Zone. Instead I had a feeding tube that snaked up my nose and down into my throat. I hadn't had a shower since Mortaritaville. And I hadn't been able to wash my hair beyond the dry shampoo powder my mom occasionally sprinkled on the crazy braids she'd given me.

But as soon as I was in a regular room, Juanita Wilson showed up. While I was in the ICU, she knew that I couldn't bear to be touched—that even having someone lean against my bed would make the sheets shift against my skin, causing unbearable pain. Now that I'd gotten the nerve block, I could withstand touch. Juanita understood all this, because she had gone through it too. So now that I could bear it, she came to give me the greatest gift I could imagine. She came to wash my hair.

"Scoot to the edge," she said. I gently shifted my weight, taking care to arrange the tubes still connected to my body, and held my head off the side of the bed. I hung on to the safety rail with my left hand while my brother gingerly poured water out of a little plastic pitcher, soaking my hair. Juanita lathered my head with shampoo, massaging it into my scalp. She washed out all the dirt and dust of Iraq, the flakes of dried blood, and the black explosive residue from my hair into the little pink plastic basin Tom was holding with his other hand. He'd empty it out, and then pour more water on my hair as she washed me, over and over again, until the water in the basin finally ran clear.

We must have been quite a sight—me with no legs, one arm stitched to my rib cage, hanging off the edge of my bed while Juanita gently washed the remnants of war out of my hair with her one remaining hand. Years later, Oprah Winfrey would bring us together in a surprise reunion on her talk show, and the minute I saw Juanita's face, I burst into tears. Even now, when I think about how tenderly she cared for me during those early weeks, I tear up all over again.

"Tammy," Bryan whispered the day after I woke up. "There are a couple of Generals waiting outside to see you."

I'm sorry . . . what? Was this real, or a hallucination? Why would Generals—plural—be coming to see me? I was a Captain at the time, an O-3, third rank from the bottom in the Army officers' seniority chart. Generals were anywhere from O-7 up to O-10, depending on how many stars they had. Having Generals come visit me was like a middle manager having the whole C-suite drop by. You normally want to be at your best when meeting with the highest-ranking officers, but I was being asked to do it in the ICU while suffering from blinding pain, vomiting, and hallucinations.

Bryan told me the names and ranks of who was waiting, then asked, "So, who do you want to see first?" I didn't know any of them, of course, and was in no shape to do a playground pick.

"Just do it by rank," I said. "Four stars first." This was the military, after all—if I had to make an impossible decision, might as well do it by protocol, right?

Bryan took my message to the waiting brass, and soon a parade of Generals came through my room, all wanting to thank me and tell me I was a good Soldier. I appreciated the sentiment, but was relieved when the visits were over. Unfortunately, I learned quickly that this wouldn't be a one-time occurrence—far from it. All day, every day, whether in the ICU or the regular hospital ward, people wanted to come to my bedside, say a word or two, get a photo taken, and then continue on their rounds to the next wounded warrior. And these weren't just military officers either. We had nonstop visits from celebrities, actors, politicians, comedians, Cabinet members—a regular who's who of high-powered strangers, dutifully filing past my hospital bed.

Visitors fell into one of two categories. The first consisted of people who really cared about the patients—guys like Gary Sinise and Adam Sandler, who visited repeatedly, offered support, and never made the visits about themselves. The second consisted of those who came for their own PR purposes, turning the wounded into props so their marketing machine could show them "supporting the troops." They'd shuffle through, offer a hello and a half-hearted handshake, flash their pearly whites for the camera, and then head out without bothering to learn our names. Feeling like exotic creatures in a cage, we patients started referring to ourselves as the Amputee Petting Zoo.

I'm not going to call these people out by name, but suffice it to say that all of the amputees who spent time recovering in Walter Reed could tell you exactly who I'm talking about. We quickly learned which celebrities would interrupt an intensive physical therapy session to snap a photo (which you'd gamely pose for, wanting to be a good sport). We knew which politicians would give you a gummy smile, their eyes glazing over as they tuned out your answers to their perfunctory questions. At one point, I was so exhausted that Bryan had to block my door with a chair to keep people out. It was hard enough summoning the energy for treatment, surgeries, physician consults, wound debriding, and physical therapy; having to paste a smile on my face to greet someone making a visit to the Amputee Petting Zoo was more than I could handle at times.

One night around nine o'clock, as I lay in my bed waiting for my evening meds, a Colonel popped his head into my room and excitedly said, "Secretary Rumsfeld is two doors down. Get ready, he's on his way!" Many military officers would be thrilled and honored to meet the Secretary of Defense in person, and that was obviously the reaction this Colonel was expecting. But I wasn't feeling it.

"Sir," I said, "is this a direct order?"

The Colonel cocked his head, his eyes narrowing. "What do you mean?" he asked.

"I mean, is this an order, that I meet with him?" I said. "He is in my chain of command, and I'll do it if so. But if not, I would like to respectfully decline."

I was trying to handle the situation politely, but it was after 9 P.M., I'd had a long and tiring day, and I just wanted to take my meds and get some sleep. I always tried to be a good Soldier, and on another day I might have just bitten my tongue and met with Rumsfeld. But in truth, there was nothing I wanted less than to meet face-to-face with one of the architects of the Iraq War. As an Army officer sworn to uphold the Constitution, I had willingly and proudly served in that war, because following orders—even ones I wasn't happy about—was what I signed up for when I joined the military. But I had never believed the war in Iraq was either necessary or wise. And at this moment, I didn't have the energy to fake-smile for the man who, as much as any other, had plunged our nation into it.

"Really?" the Colonel asked, his eyebrows raised.

"I'd prefer not to have him cross the threshold of my door, sir," I said, quietly but firmly.

The Colonel looked at Bryan, then back at me. "It's not an order," he said. "You don't have to meet with him if you don't want to." He turned abruptly and walked out of my room.

The next day, a military psychiatrist showed up at my bedside. "I heard you refused to see Secretary Rumsfeld last night," he said. "How are you feeling? Are you having any issues we should discuss?"

I shook my head. Seriously, they thought I needed a psych evaluation? For *that*? "Sir," I said, "I think my decision last night makes me the sanest person in this room." He nodded, the hint of a smile crossing his face. And after asking just a few more questions, he went on his way.

A couple of weeks later, the same Colonel who had made the rounds with Rumsfeld stopped by my room. "The USO has sent a few people over today," he said. "You want them to skip your room?" He obviously assumed that my problem wasn't with Rumsfeld specifically but with visitors in general.

"Who's here?" I asked.

"That guy from *Saturday Night Live*—Al Franken. But I can tell them if you want to be left alone."

"Oh my God!" I exclaimed. "Al Franken? He's *here*?" I thought Franken was hilarious, and I had actually been reading his new book, *Lies and the Lying Liars Who Tell Them*, while on deployment. I proceeded to completely fan-girl out, raving to this Colonel about how much I loved Franken and how excited I was to meet him in person. It was like the Beatles had come to town.

The Colonel shook his head in wonderment, then stepped out

to bring Franken in. When I saw that big smile and those little round glasses, I flipped out again. Right away he started joking and making Bryan and me laugh, like we'd all known each other forever. "I was reading your book in Iraq," I told him, "but didn't get to finish before we got shot down. And then they gave away all my gear, so I don't have it anymore."

"Well, I suppose that's a valid enough excuse," he said. He sat with us for about fifteen minutes, chatting and making jokes, and then he invited us to pose for a Polaroid. He signed it "to Tammy and Bryan, Love, Al Franken," and handed it to me. (That was the true hallmark of someone who was there for the troops: They'd take a Polaroid and give it to you right then. The ones there for the Petting Zoo would bring a professional photographer, and you'd only see the photo later in the newspapers.) And about a week after Al's visit, a USO rep dropped off a copy of his book, which he'd signed to me.

Al Franken's support for the troops was genuine, and in addition to visiting Walter Reed, he'd gone to Iraq and Afghanistan on USO tours. (I became a fan of a lot of musicians and comics that way—including the rapper 50 Cent, who came all the way to Balad to put on a concert for us troops. Anyone who voluntarily came to Mortaritaville, at the height of the war, just to entertain us became an instant favorite.)

Franken came to see me several times in Walter Reed, and I noticed he had a habit of saying, "Thank you for your service." A lot of wounded warriors hate that phrase, as it feels robotic, an empty sentiment that people say without thinking. A couple of people on the ward told him, "Al, you gotta stop saying that." So instead, he started saying, "Thank you for being grievously wounded," which cracked everybody up.

The other hallmark of those who truly cared about the troops was that they'd come visit more than once. Some came a couple of times a week, taking care to ask about your treatment or follow up on a conversation from a previous visit. Unexpected relationships developed—including, in my case, some long-term friendships with strange bedfellows.

As the Deputy Secretary of Defense, Paul Wolfowitz, like Rumsfeld, was an architect of the Iraq War. When I first met him, I didn't relish the idea of trying to make conversation. But he came through Walter Reed twice a week, checking in on the people whose lives had been upended in the war. He'd come into my room on a random weeknight, sit by my bed, and ask me questions about my treatment and rehab, or more generally about the difficulties our injured Veterans were facing. I couldn't have disagreed with him more on his policy positions, which I found reprehensible. But I could see how sincere he was in his desire to help Veterans.

I could also sense that Wolfowitz felt conflicted about the suffering the war had caused. Not only did he visit the wounded twice a week, he also went down to Section 60, the fourteen-acre area in Arlington National Cemetery where Veterans from Iraq and Afghanistan are buried. Later, I would see him there myself, quietly talking to grieving family members or just standing by a grave in silent salute. It was hard for me to reconcile how this man, who clearly cared deeply and personally for those who'd been wounded and killed in the war, could still hold on to his faulty justifications for that war.

Another Republican I became friends with during this time was former senator Bob Dole. But unlike the parade of visitors who came to see patients at Walter Reed, eighty-one-year-old Senator Dole was a patient himself. While serving in Italy during World War II, he had been struck in his back and arms by German machine-gun fire, causing physical problems that would last the rest of his life. In later years, he would always hold a pen in his right hand to mask the fact that he couldn't open his fist. Now, sixty years after he was wounded, he was back for physical rehab after falling in his apartment at the Watergate complex.

A lot of the younger guys didn't know who Senator Dole was, and he seemed to like it that way. Although he had a VIP room, and could have received private therapy sessions, he did his therapy right there in the crowded bay with the rest of us, sharing a mat with nineteen- and twenty-year-old wounded warriors.

"I'm Lieutenant Dole," he'd tell them. "Want to bet I can do more sit-ups than you?" He'd tell stories about his time in the Army, never letting on that he was one of the most famous men in American politics, who just eight years earlier had been the Republican nominee for president. Most of the young guys just thought he was a cool old Vet. The same was true of former senator Max Cleland, a triple amputee in Vietnam who was also a patient at Walter Reed while I was there. These proud Veterans from earlier generations took time to interact with their younger comrades, helping us deal with wounds both physical and psychological.

Some of the other favorites in the ward were the guys from Orange County Choppers, a custom motorcycle company run by the Teutul family. The OCC guys had a hit reality TV show at the time, and they'd come high-fiving through the therapy room like rock stars. With their tattoos and big handlebar mustaches, they had serious street cred with the younger Vets, but they weren't there just to give the guys a one-off thrill of meeting them—they also did tons of fund-raising, donating gear and motorcycles worth hundreds of thousands of dollars to support Veterans.

At first it felt weird to have celebrities and politicians roaming the halls as we went through recovery. But so many of them showed up, it soon felt normal. Barack Obama used to come through, usually late at night, without the kind of big entourage other senators traveled with. In fact, rumor had it that he took the Metro to get there. He'd pop in, ask about my family, ask how my recovery was going, and chat up my mom or Bryan if they were in the room. I didn't realize it until later, but he was on the Senate Veterans' Affairs Committee, and he was paying close attention to all of our answers, to figure out what changes needed to be made to better support the wounded.

The first time I managed to stand on a prosthetic leg, Adam Sandler was there. His movie *50 First Dates* had just come out, and every so often, he'd bring his crew or other actors around to say hello. Even though he was a huge star, he was very laid-back, and when he saw me in the therapy room fighting to get upright, he decided to hang out and watch.

Whenever someone in the therapy room accomplished a task for the first time, everybody would erupt into cheers, and I was determined to get vertical and make it happen that day. At the time, I hadn't even been able to sit up for long without getting dizzy, as I'd been lying in bed for the past six weeks, so this was a real challenge. The physical therapist strapped me to a tilt table, and bit by bit, she cranked a level that tilted the table slowly from horizontal to vertical.

"If you feel like you're going to black out, say something," she told me. I'd last about ten seconds, then go back down. Then she'd ratchet me up a little farther, for twenty seconds—and then back down. I just kept pushing, and although the dizziness was hard to take, there was no way I was going to let myself black out in front of Adam Sandler. When I finally got upright—just for a few seconds—and heard him start yelling and clapping with the rest of the Veterans in the room, I felt like I'd won a marathon.

*   *   *

On December 21, nearly six weeks after the shootdown, I rolled my wheelchair into a reception room at Walter Reed, where I was scheduled to receive the Air Medal and Army Commendation Medal and be promoted to Major. I had been notified of my promotion in Iraq just three days before my shootdown, and could never have imagined that I'd be pinning on my oak leaves in a hospital reception room instead of in the desert. But Bryan, Mom, and Tom all gathered to watch as a General pinned the decorations onto my uniform. And then, after the ceremony ended, I looked over to see a gaunt older man come limping into the room with a cane. It was my dad.

I hadn't seen him in about a year and a half, since before my deployment. I knew he'd suffered a heart attack a week before the shootdown, which is why he couldn't fly to Washington when Mom did. He'd stayed in Hawaii to recuperate, but then he'd had another heart attack in the beginning of December. Now, two weeks later, his doctors had decided he was strong enough to endure the ten-hour flight to come see me.

Dad had always been a big, sturdy guy, but at seventy-six, after two heart attacks, he was a shell of his former self. He'd also been on his own for a month, having to feed himself without Mom there to cook for him; as I learned later, he had been going to the 7-Eleven near their house for his dinners. His face was drawn, making him seem at least a decade older than I remembered. He leaned down to hug me, then held my hand as he lowered himself into a chair next to me. We chatted a little bit—I asked about his flight, and he asked about my treatment—as each of us tried to take in the physical changes the other had gone through.

I couldn't sit upright for very long, so we made our way back to my room—me in my wheelchair, Dad with his cane. I got back into my bed, and he settled into a chair at my bedside, where he soon fell asleep. He seemed so weak that I wasn't sure I'd be seeing him much in the coming days. But either way, I was glad he'd made it here.

Four days later, Mom, Dad, Tom, Bryan, and I celebrated Christmas together. The doctors had given me permission to leave the hospital for the first time, and Bryan bundled me up in a coat, blanket, and hat for the short trip to Fisher House, where he was staying. He was so nervous, and so protective, that if he could have zipped me up into a cocoon, he would have done that. I felt like a toddler in a snowsuit, swaddled nearly to the point of suffocation, as I wheeled along the snow-lined sidewalk.

Fisher House is the military version of the Ronald McDonald House, where families of the wounded can stay for free while their loved ones recover. But it's much more than just a place to sleep. Everyone is there for the same reason, which creates a real feeling of community. The American Legion stocks the pantry with milk, bread, eggs, and other necessities, and local church and Veterans' groups put on dinners and barbecues—anything to help the families as they struggle with their new reality. Fisher House was a godsend for Bryan, as it is for so many military families. I was excited to finally get out of the hospital, even if only for a short time, to be able to see it.

My family gathered in the little dining room to enjoy a meal together for the first time in years. I still didn't have much appetite, and just managed to eat some dry turkey and a roll. But sitting in that room and talking with my parents felt comforting, if a little surreal. So much had changed for all of us, but here we were together, our little family, marveling at the simple fact that we were in each other's company once again. It was a sweet holiday, relaxing and warm.

And then, the following morning, my dad had another heart attack.

Bryan was with me at my physical therapy appointment when his cell phone rang. It was my mom, calling to say that Dad was in the bathtub and couldn't get out. Bryan hurried over to their apartment at Mologne House, another residential building for families of the wounded, and as soon as he saw my dad's gray face, he called 911. EMTs rushed Dad to Walter Reed, and after the doctors managed to stabilize him, he was admitted to a room in the fourth-floor cardiac ward—one floor below my room in the amputee ward.

Now, instead of having my dad come visit me, I started visiting him. I'd roll my wheelchair down the hall to the elevator, head over to his room, and spend an hour sitting at his bedside. Sometimes I'd talk to him, but mostly I just sat nearby as he rested or slept. I'd watch as Mom snuck him saltine crackers, in defiance of the doctors' orders to cut back his salt. She knew he loved them, and not knowing how long he might last, she decided it was worth the risk of having the nurses yell at her to give him a little treat.

My relationship with my dad had always been complicated. For most of my childhood I had idolized him, totally buying into the "big man" image he tried to project. I had spent years trying to make him proud, in any way I could. But no matter how hard I tried, whether it was playing varsity sports in high school, making the honor roll, or supporting our family in Hawaii, none of it ever seemed to matter to him. I had spent a lifetime hearing how proud he was of his stepdaughter Diana, but had never once heard him say the same about me. It stung.

Even after I finally understood that Dad wasn't Superman and didn't have all the answers, I never stopped trying to earn his pride. I followed his footsteps into the military, and became one of the Army's handful of first female pilots to fly combat missions in Iraq, but no achievement ever seemed to be enough. While deployed in Iraq, I kept trying to connect with him. I called my parents, but my conversations with him were always short. "How you doing?" he'd ask. And as soon as I'd start to speak, he'd mutter, "Okay, here's your mom," and hand off the phone.

But now, as I sat at his bedside in Walter Reed, my dad finally started talking. "I'm worried about you, Tammy," he said. "How will you live, without legs?" He told me he was afraid I might never walk again, and that my life would be incomplete.

"Dad, I'm fine," I kept telling him. "I'll be able to do everything I could before the shootdown. Really!" But he'd just shake his head.

So a few days after I received my first prosthetic leg, I went straight down to show Dad, in hopes of putting him at ease. "Look," I said. "I have a foot now!" Sitting in my wheelchair, I slipped the prosthetic off my left stump to show it to him up close.

He smiled, and then said something I didn't expect. "I'm sorry you lost your legs," he told me. "You had such pretty feet." It felt strange to me that he was nostalgic about my feet, because I had actually moved past that point fairly quickly. They weren't coming back, so why focus on them? Why obsess about limbs I could never get back, when I could spend that energy focusing on using the new ones?

"Dad, look," I said, "I can stand on this one just as well." I strapped the prosthetic back on and gingerly rose out of my chair. As I stood in front of him, I saw tears welling in his eyes.

"You know," he said, "I'm so proud of you."

I heard the words, but my brain couldn't take them in. *Did he really just say that?* We looked at each other for a moment, and then I said, "Thank you, Daddy. That means a lot to me." I had waited a lifetime to hear those words come out of my father's mouth. And now that they had, I didn't know what else to say but thank you.

Two weeks later, Dad was transferred to the University of

Maryland's St. Joseph Medical Center for open-heart surgery. We knew he was weak, and that there was a high likelihood he wouldn't survive the operation, but without it he would certainly die. After we discussed it together as a family, Dad decided to go ahead with it.

The doctors were able to repair his heart, but he never woke up after the surgery. The medical team kept him sedated in hopes that he might recover, but after two weeks with no improvement, they told us that Dad was essentially brain-dead. Mom made the difficult decision to take him off life support, and on January 28, 2005, we gathered in his hospital room to say a final goodbye.

I don't remember what I said to him in that final moment. I just remember that the room was full of beeping and whirring machines, and as the nurse disconnected his life support, they all went silent, one by one. My mom bent to kiss him and say goodbye. And then, it was absolutely quiet. Dad was gone.

As I continued my recovery at Walter Reed, Mom and Tom flew back to Honolulu to go through Dad's paperwork. He had taken out an accidental-death insurance policy, for which he'd made Mom the beneficiary. But since he didn't die in an accident, there was zero payout.

He also had a regular life insurance policy. But to our shock, it was made out to someone other than Mom. The insurance company wouldn't tell us who was the beneficiary, but when I recently looked through Dad's old paperwork, I saw that fifty years earlier, he had made it out to Carol, his eldest daughter from his first marriage. Had he just forgotten to change it after marrying Mom? He'd made Mom the beneficiary of his military benefits, so that was certainly possible. We'll never know.

But that decision, plus the fact that Dad had long insisted to the

VA that he didn't have any disability, left Mom with only his basic military pension when he died. Dad hadn't even left her enough to pay for a funeral, which meant that Bryan and I would end up paying for it out of money we'd saved from my deployment. I don't believe that Dad meant to shortchange Mom; I suspect he thought for some reason that the accidental-death policy would pay out. But in some ways, it was the perfect summation of his life—the final indignity from a man who spent his life trying, and failing, to be a hero.

When I was a kid, I thought my dad could do anything. And I believed the narrative my mom's family had laid on her, that she was the uneducated one, the menial laborer, lucky to have my dad. But looking back as an adult, I see his weaknesses clearly. He never was the guy he wanted everybody to think he was. He was ill equipped to take care of us, and over and over again, my mom and I were the ones who solved the problem and got things back on track. Dad was a pretender. Mom was—still is—a survivor.

"It's okay," she said simply when we told her he hadn't left her anything. "Money comes, money goes. I have a better life now than where we've been."

Among my dad's papers was one more surprise. As it turned out, a few weeks before I had been shot down, Dad had posted a photo of me and a short essay to the website of the *Honolulu Advertiser*. He wrote that I used to live in Honolulu and was now deployed with my U.S. Army Reserve unit in Iraq. But it was the final line that got me. "We are very proud of Tammy and pray for her daily," he had written, "so long as she is involved in combat actions."

I suspect Dad knew that in coming to see me at Walter Reed, he would be making his last journey. Later, Bryan would say that when he spoke with Dad's doctors in Hawaii, it was clear that they knew he didn't have much time left. By giving him permission to travel, those doctors were helping him see his family one last time and die in his native Virginia. And that, in turn, allowed him to fulfill his final dream: having a Soldier's burial in the sacred soil of Arlington National Cemetery. If Dad had died in Hawaii, that never would have happened, as the expense of transferring his body would have been too great. But now, he would be forever laid to rest in the most hallowed cemetery in America, in the state where he was born.

Three days before my thirty-seventh birthday, on March 9, 2005, as a military band played "Nearer, My God, to Thee," a horse-drawn caisson pulled my dad's flag-draped coffin through Arlington National Cemetery. At the graveside, I sat in my wheelchair wearing my dress uniform, my right arm in a sling and a blanket pulled over my lap. Saluting with my left hand as the bugler played taps, I watched as riflemen fired a twenty-one-gun salute into the crisp air.

Military aides folded up the Stars and Stripes into a perfect triangle and handed it to my mom. And as others quietly walked away, I stayed behind, kissed my fingers, and reached out to his casket.

"Bye, Daddy," I said. Then I turned to wheel myself back to my husband and my mom, and we made our way past the rows upon rows of white gravestones as the sun sank low toward the horizon.

Chapter 11

Soldier's Creed

In late January 2005, as my dad was still lingering on life support in St. Joseph's hospital, U.S. senator Dick Durbin sent a message to Walter Reed. He wanted to know if there were any wounded warriors from Illinois who were willing, and healthy enough, to attend the State of the Union Address as his guests.

Although I wasn't a huge fan of President Bush, I definitely wanted to go. This was history in the making, an opportunity to witness in person one of the enduring rituals of our democracy. Also, I knew that whoever went would get to meet Senator Durbin, who was in the Democratic leadership as minority whip, and maybe other senators as well.

The State of the Union was scheduled for February 2, two weeks away—just twelve weeks after the shootdown. At that point, I hadn't sat upright for more than ninety minutes, and even that length of time left me dizzy and exhausted. But if I wanted to attend the address, I'd have to sit up for at least five hours, including travel to and from Capitol Hill. "I can do it," I told my doctors. "Really. I can." I had absolutely no idea if that was true, but I wasn't about to let this opportunity slip by.

There was one other Soldier from Illinois healthy enough to

attend, an Army Reserve Specialist named Jarob Walsh, and I was on the margin. If I could increase my stamina and persuade my doctors to let me go, Senator Durbin would have us both as his guests. So for the next two weeks I worked doubly hard at PT, trying to increase the length of time I could sit up. This would be my first trip off the hospital grounds, and I knew I'd have to push myself to the limit to endure it.

I would also have to find a way to get intravenous antibiotics at some point during the evening. Like most of the patients at Walter Reed who came in with open wounds from Iraq, I had developed an infection called *Acinetobacter*, sometimes nicknamed Iraqibacter. The infection was easily spread and highly drug-resistant, and the medical teams treating Iraq Vets had to fight constantly to keep it from spiraling out of control. My treatment consisted of two different maximum-strength antibiotics, administered by a drip solution directly into my veins every four hours. I had a permanent line implanted into my left arm for the IVs, but Bryan would have to find time to administer a new bag of fluids while we were in the Capitol.

Once the doctors decided I was strong enough to attend, preparations went into high gear. Not only would I need medications and an IV bag, but I also had to quickly find an Army dress uniform in my size, plus the appropriate medals and insignia. I didn't even have an engraved Duckworth name tag, but someone actually managed to track one down from another Soldier—I believe he was an Army doctor or clinician at Walter Reed—who happened to have the same last name.

The nurses prepared vials of liquid antibiotics, a medical kit for disinfecting my IV line, and little plastic baggies packed with painkillers of varying strengths—from Tylenol all the way up to methadone. They hid the IV line in my borrowed uniform jacket, snaking it up through the sleeve and out the back of my collar, where Bryan could discreetly hang the bags of fluid and connect them when needed. On the afternoon of February 2, the medical team put me on the lift of a wheelchair-accessible bus, and Bryan and I settled in for the hour-long drive to the Capitol.

With all the planning that had gone into this trip, I hadn't anticipated that the worst part would be the ride over. While the bus was wheelchair-accessible, it was far from comfortable. In fact, it was just a regular Army-issue tin-can bus, so for most of the ride, I was careening around in the back, completely unaccustomed to being in a wheelchair in a moving vehicle. In fact, I hadn't been in any kind of vehicle (while conscious) since the shootdown, so it felt bizarre and a little more thrilling than I anticipated to be zooming down the streets of Washington, DC, while fighting to stay upright.

Arriving at the Capitol, the bus dropped us off on the east side of the building, at one of only two entrances with wheelchair access. And yes, you read that right: To this day, there are only two doors in and out of the Capitol for wheelchair users, so if you happen to be in the building after those doors close, you're stuck. As a senator, I've occasionally just pushed one open after hours, setting off the alarm so I could get out (though I don't recommend that approach for everyone).

Once inside the building, we made our way to the elevators—and there again, I saw firsthand how wheelchair users are systemically inconvenienced. I was using a powered chair that night, and those suckers are *big*. I could barely fit into the elevator, much less have Bryan squeeze in beside me. This was my first significant trip out in a wheelchair, and I could already see how disabled people faced casual discrimination at every turn, particularly in the ways our buildings are designed.

Despite the inconveniences, I felt swept away by the beauty and grandeur of the Capitol: The rotunda, with its soaring dome and colorful fresco depicting George Washington flanked by angels in heaven. Life-size sculptures of great statesmen, and paintings depicting great moments in American history. Marble floors, worn down by decades' worth of footsteps. For a patriotic kid who'd grown up idolizing America from afar, it was an unbelievable feeling to be here, in this historic place, as a personal guest of my state's senior U.S. senator.

Senator Durbin welcomed us into the office of the Democratic whip, a room with a long and storied history of its own. This was the same office used by Senators Lyndon Johnson, Russell Long, and Ted Kennedy when they had served as whips, and conversations that had taken place within these walls had shaped all of our lives. From one window, I could see the Stars and Stripes waving in the wind, backlit against the Capitol dome. It was an extraordinary sight, so moving that it literally brought tears to my eyes. I had spent the past year enveloped first in the beige and tan of the Iraqi desert, then in the sterile white of Walter Reed. Seeing this much color, and sensing the sweep of history that lived in these walls, felt overwhelming.

Dick Durbin was an incredibly gracious and approachable host. He instantly made Bryan and me feel welcome, chatting with us like an old friend rather than one of the most powerful people in the country. He gave off a regular-guy vibe, speaking in a polite, straightforward way that I can only describe as Midwestern. I liked him right away, a feeling that would only grow over time.

He asked all the usual polite questions, such as where in Illinois we were from and how I had been wounded. Then he asked me how my recovery was going at Walter Reed. "Well, the medical care there is the best in the world," I told him. "But there are definitely some administrative challenges." He raised his eyebrows. I started telling him about the insufficient lodgings for family members, how our loved ones had to sleep on the ICU waiting room floor for weeks at a time when we first arrived, because there wasn't space in temporary housing—never stopping to wonder whether he really wanted to know or had asked just to be polite. The fact was, there were procedures at Walter Reed that needed improving, so I told him about them. He nodded, taking everything in.

After fifteen minutes or so, I asked Senator Durbin if there was a place where Bryan and I could have a moment of privacy. With a press availability scheduled, then a dinner, then the State of the Union Address, this was the best window of time for us to switch out my IV antibiotics. "Of course," Dick said, and he walked us to a little sitting room area attached to the main office.

As I transferred from my wheelchair onto an antique settee with blue and gold brocade upholstery, I briefly wondered how much history that particular piece of furniture had seen. (It's still there today, and every time I drop by to see Dick in that office, my heart warms when I see it.) Sitting sideways, my back against the carved mahogany armrest, I stretched my stump in front of me and settled in.

Bryan hooked up my new IV bags and asked how I was feeling. I was definitely in pain, but the truth was, I was never *not* in pain. Even though I had no feet, I could always feel the soles of my feet burning—and still do, even now. In addition to phantom pain, there was a catalogue of hurts coursing through my body, from my leg stumps, to the road-rash patches where the doctors had harvested my skin, to my still-healing arm. I popped a couple of Percocet and said, "Okay, let's get back out there," because what else was there to do? This was the new normal for me, so I had no choice but to power through.

About a dozen reporters had gathered for the press availability, and Specialist Walsh and I rolled out to meet them. This was my first experience talking to the press, and Dick kept it simple, just asking me to tell my story. I talked about the shootdown, the fact that my crew had saved my life, and a bit about my recovery. A couple of reporters asked questions, but nothing terribly hard-hitting. And then Lynn Sweet, a political reporter who worked for the *Chicago Sun-Times*, asked me about the protests at Walter Reed.

Groups of antiwar protestors had started gathering there, particularly on Friday nights, when most new patients arrived from Landstuhl. This meant that not only the wounded but their families too had to run a gauntlet of chanting, sign-waving people just to get into the hospital. Emotions regularly flared on both sides, and Lynn wanted to know what that looked like from the perspective of a wounded warrior. "How do you feel about these folks out there protesting the war, after you lost your legs fighting in it?" she asked me.

"Well," I said, "I thought that was what I was fighting for—to protect their right to protest." I didn't think before I spoke; the words just came out of my mouth, because they were the only ones that made sense to me. Later, Dick said his reaction was *Ohhh, good answer!* And much later, he would tell me that was the first moment he thought I could run for public office.

The dinner that night was like something out of a dream. Dick took me around and introduced me to other senators, including Ted Kennedy and Daniel Inouye—the longtime senator and World War II Veteran I'd met as a high school senior all those years ago in Hawaii. I felt like Alice in Wonderland, meeting people I had read about and seen on television, with so many talking to me that I didn't know which way to turn. The meal looked delicious, but I still had no appetite, because the antibiotics made me nauseous. So I sat through the traditional dinner of chicken pot pie, honey ham, and apple pie, talking with everyone while willing myself not to throw up. I had made it almost to the halfway point of the evening, but the State of the Union Address was still to come.

Rolling out onto the balcony of the House Chamber, where the address was about to take place, I was struck by how simultaneously intimate and grand the space was. The room itself isn't big, but it carries the weight of the history that has taken place there. As President Bush began speaking, I looked down to see senators, representatives, Supreme Court justices, and Cabinet members, all sitting shoulder-to-shoulder. I felt so awestruck it was almost like an out-of-body experience. It was as if I were in a movie and watching that movie at the same time.

The entire last third of President Bush's speech was about Afghanistan and Iraq. He talked about the recent Iraqi elections, quoting a young Iraqi woman as saying she had gone to vote despite mortars raining down that day. He also recognized the parents of a Marine Corps Sergeant, Byron Norwood, who had been killed during the assault on Fallujah. As much as I disagreed with the war in Iraq, I was proud to be in uniform at that moment, and still eager to return to my unit. But five hours into my trip outside Walter Reed, it was obvious that I had a long road to recovery ahead of me. By the time President Bush wrapped up, I was utterly exhausted, having sat up for so long without a break.

I must have passed out from exhaustion after the speech, because I don't remember boarding the bus, riding back, or getting into my bed at Walter Reed. But I can remember every detail before that, because being in those hallowed halls stirred something in me. I didn't know how or when it might happen, but I knew I wanted to get back there one day.

About a week after the State of the Union, I was in the occupational therapy (OT) room doing exercises for my right arm. In physical therapy, I worked mostly on my legs, learning how to walk again. OT was for learning how to accomplish everyday tasks—how to write, to make a bed, to transfer from a wheelchair to the toilet. The OT area even had a little built-in apartment, with a kitchen, bed, and bathroom, for practicing. They called it Fort Independence.

The surgeons had just detached my arm from the muscle flap on my abdomen, and despite the long scars, discolored flesh, and a bit of lumpiness, it was starting to look like an arm again. But it was still too weak to move on its own, so I had to use my left hand to lift and place it. I would have to retrain the muscles to undertake even the most basic movements.

The occupational therapist handed me a foam cylinder about an inch in diameter, sort of like a miniature pool noodle, with a pencil stuck in the middle of it. There was no way my right hand could hold on to a pencil well enough to write, so the foam noodle was intended to help me grip it. But even that was difficult, and I couldn't move my arm with anything approaching the control needed to write. So I held the noodle/pencil with my right hand, and was using my left hand to guide it into scratching out letters on a piece of paper.

My goal was to write a thank-you note to Senator Durbin, but it took some time to complete. When I finally finished, I stuck the letter into the orange apron—a highly prized item, donated by Home Depot—that was tied to the front of my wheelchair just under the seat. I was planning to mail the letter as soon as I could find out Senator Durbin's address.

Before I could do that, he showed up at one of my PT sessions. I was struggling through my exercises, sweat beading on my forehead, when he walked up and cheerily said, "Hello, Tammy!"

"Oh, hello, sir!" I responded. "I wrote you a thank-you note, although my writing looks kind of like chicken scratch. Hold on, it's in here." As I dug the envelope out of the apron, my heart sank. Creased and smeared from being stuffed in the apron pocket with various other items, it wasn't the professional-looking correspondence I had intended.

He smiled and took the envelope, then held out his business card. "I wanted to give you this. Anything you need, just let me know." I took the card with my left hand, and saw his phone number printed on it. "Seriously, call anytime," he said. "And not just if the person needing help is from Illinois. If there are problems here, I want to know. I want to help fix them."

Now, I have since learned that a lot of senators say stuff like that—but not all of them mean it. I didn't really know Senator Durbin, so I wasn't sure whether he literally meant for me to call him. But once I had that number, there was no way I wasn't gonna use it, because I had some leadership responsibility for these men and women.

The Army runs on hierarchy, no matter whether you're in battle or in a hospital ward. As a thirty-seven-year-old Major, I was for many months the oldest and highest-ranking amputee on the ward, so it was my duty to look after these younger wounded warriors, to help motivate them and address any problems that arose. Other higher-ranking amputee patients, such as Staff Sergeant Joe Bowser, also took on leadership roles. We just did what was natural for us, even in this unusual environment.

At one point, there was a spate of patients failing to show up for medical appointments. So the Army leadership at Walter Reed decided that everyone who was physically able should gather at 0700 every morning for formation, as a way of reinstating old-fashioned military discipline. But the elevator closest to the parade field could fit only one wheelchair at a time, so each morning, twenty guys in wheelchairs would be lined up for an hour, getting pissed off as they waited to ride down and go "stand" in formation. Seeing this, Staff Sergeant Bowser and I intervened on behalf of the guys, telling the admin types their plan wasn't working.

I felt a responsibility to be a voice for these young warriors when they needed help, on anything from issues at Walter Reed to problems with pay and benefits. So I started calling Senator Durbin's number. And during those times when I was swamped with rehab and medical procedures, Bryan called.

In fact, Bryan made the first contact, on behalf of someone he met one afternoon while he was waiting for me to get out of surgery. Walking down a hallway outside the waiting room, he saw a young woman crying, with a baby in her arms. "Is your husband in surgery?" Bryan asked. She shook her head, and he said, "Well, whatever is happening, you're going to be okay." He wanted to reassure her, but the woman, who looked to be about nineteen, suddenly started bawling.

She told Bryan that her husband had been in a coma for months. They had gotten married just before he'd deployed, and he'd been in Iraq for only a few days before he was wounded. "We haven't been getting his paycheck since then," she told Bryan. "We're going to lose our trailer at Fort Hood because I can't make payments. I don't even have enough money to buy formula and diapers for the baby."

Bryan was stunned. A young Soldier had sacrificed his health and well-being for our nation—and as he lay in a coma, his wife couldn't get his paychecks? Bryan put his hand on her shoulder and said, "I will help you figure this out." This was clearly an administrative snafu (an acronym for "Situation Normal All Fucked Up"—a term coined by Soldiers in World War II, proving that snafus transcend generations). But the hardship it was bringing onto this young family was real. How on earth was a nineteen-year-old woman with a baby on her hip and a husband in a coma supposed to navigate the massive military bureaucracy to solve her problem?

Bryan made some calls for her, including one to Senator Durbin's office. In the meantime, he took her to the Red Cross for supplies, then got some diapers from the stockpiles at Fisher House to give her. The woman was incredibly grateful, knowing she couldn't have sorted out the problem on her own. These wounded Soldiers and their families obviously needed advocates—and now, with our direct line to Senator Durbin, we could be those advocates.

Some of the problems at Walter Reed stemmed from the fact that the Bush administration had assumed the war in Iraq would be short, which meant the Army wasn't prepared for the administrative and logistical needs of a longer war. In November 2002, Secretary of Defense Donald Rumsfeld had declared that it would take "five days or five weeks or five months, but it certainly isn't going to last any longer than that." So when the fighting dragged on, and the wounded just kept on coming, Walter Reed was administratively unprepared to deal with the wave, even as the medical teams valiantly provided top-notch care.

Our family experienced this when I arrived in November 2004. At first, there was no place for Bryan and my mom to stay, because Mologne House was full. These were the nights when they took turns sleeping in the small ICU waiting area. About a week later, the Army finally provided them with a room there—but it was so small that Bryan and my mom had to take turns sleeping in it during some of the most stressful days and nights of their lives. And they were actually the lucky ones, because some family members were told they'd just have to pay for their own rooms in the Motel 6 across the street. In theory, the Army would reimburse them, but in practice that didn't always happen.

Over the next few months, Bryan and I called Senator Durbin's office repeatedly. We called about administrative snafus and housing problems. We called when Veterans told us they weren't receiving their proper pay. We completely abused the privilege of that phone number, but Dick Durbin didn't complain once. He assigned a staff member to be our point person, and when we would call with an issue, we never failed to get a follow-up. Dick essentially became the unofficial ombudsman for the wounded warriors at Walter Reed.

Word must have gotten around in the Illinois political sphere, because a few weeks into our barrage of calling, Barack Obama's office contacted me. The Senate Veterans' Affairs Committee, of which he was a member, had a hearing scheduled for mid-March, and Senator Obama wanted to know if I'd be willing to testify about the conditions at Walter Reed. Of course, I said yes. I'd known I wanted to get back to Capitol Hill at some point, but I couldn't have dreamed it would be this quickly, or with this degree of importance.

On March 17, 2005, I made my first appearance at a Senate committee hearing. I had about ten minutes to make my case for improving the lives of Soldiers and Veterans, so I wrote up a six-point plan for how to do that.

I started out by praising the medical teams that kept me alive:

In any previous conflict, I would not be alive today. It is a testament to the superior protective equipment that I was wearing and to the medical care pipeline from the front lines to Walter Reed that I can be here . . . There is no substitute to being treated by, and recovering with, fellow Soldiers.

I urged the senators to invest in the recovery of Soldiers, particularly through technology, job counseling, and psychological support—and not just for humanitarian reasons, but because it was ultimately cost-effective for the military to do so. As I told the committee:

> Our warriors are expensive, and indispensable. I believe we must jealously guard this resource, retaining as many as possible in the service, and sparing little in the effort to return one of them to service. For example, the cost to "make" another Military Police Captain in order to replace a wounded one is prohibitive when compared to the medical costs to fix wounded Soldiers and return them to duty . . .
>
> The frontline Soldier should not expend a moment of time to worry about a fallen comrade. We must ensure that he knows, "My buddy made it to Walter Reed; he will be OK, they have the best doctors and cutting-edge technology there." We will maintain the optimal morale and performance from our Soldiers through ensuring that these medical facilities are adequately funded.

Sixteen years after I delivered this testimony, I hold the very same Senate seat Barack Obama held then. And to this day, the fight for funding and support for our troops continues. In mid-2020, when 40,000 National Guard troops were deployed to help with COVID-19 relief work, the Trump administration randomly decided to end their deployments one day before they'd qualify for federal retirement and education benefits. It was an inhumane decision, typical of that administration, and a slap in the face to the men and women who were risking their lives to stem the pandemic.

In response, I introduced the National Guard COVID-19 Response Stability Act to ensure that all National Guard troops activated in response to the pandemic would receive additional benefits. "The Trump Administration's repeated attempts to nickel and dime members of the National Guard would be wrong under any circumstance," I said then, "but it is particularly offensive when these troops are responding to a deadly COVID-19 pandemic that has already killed more than 90,000 Americans."

Efforts to shortchange our fighting men and women angered me as a recovering Soldier in 2005 and as a U.S. senator in 2020. They go against the grain of what I believe our country stands for. As Americans, we take care of each other. As Soldiers, we never leave another behind on the battlefield. My life is a testament to these truths, and the Trump administration's efforts to undermine and dismantle them was more than a nuisance. It was an assault.

During my recovery at Walter Reed, I posted a copy of the Soldier's Creed outside my door. The creed, which I first learned at Basic Camp, consists of thirteen declarations, and it goes straight to the heart of what it means to serve in the U.S. Army.

I am an American Soldier.
I am a warrior and a member of a team.
I serve the people of the United States, and live the Army
    Values.
I will always place the mission first.
I will never accept defeat.
I will never quit.
I will never leave a fallen comrade.
I am disciplined, physically and mentally tough, trained
    and proficient in my warrior tasks and drills.
I always maintain my arms, my equipment and myself.
I am an expert and I am a professional.
I stand ready to deploy, engage, and destroy the enemies of
    the United States of America in close combat.

I am a guardian of freedom and the American way of life.
I am an American Soldier.

The four short lines in the middle are known as the "Warrior Ethos," and a couple of them never fail to choke me up. "I will always place the mission first" is one. And "I will never leave a fallen comrade" is the other. This is more than what we do as Soldiers; it is who we are, as people and as warriors.

I put the Soldier's Creed outside my door because I wanted everyone entering my hospital room to know that a Soldier—not a victim—lay in that room. I wanted people to know that I earned my wounds and my wheelchair, and that I was not someone to be pitied. When General H. Steven Blum, the chief of the National Guard Bureau, saw the creed on my door, he gave me a framed print of it. I hung that one on the wall opposite my bed so I could see it, and remember, whenever the pain got intense. In my darkest times, these words were what carried me through, and as I write this, that framed print hangs across from my desk in my Senate offices.

Recovering from devastating injuries isn't a smooth process. You have bad days, good days, and a lot of frustrating plateaus. But it's the little victories that keep you going.

During one of my early OT sessions for my right arm, my therapist, Captain Katie Yancosek, handed me a metal device that looked like a power stapler with a dial on top. This was a hydraulic hand dynamometer, used to measure how much pressure I could exert with my grip. "Squeeze it as hard as you can," she said. "*Squeeze! Squeeze! Squeeze!*" I gripped the thing with as much force as I possibly could, exerting all of my energy and focus, my whole body shaking with the effort—and the gauge still sat at zero pounds per square inch. I felt so frustrated. How would I ever be able to fly again if I couldn't even grasp the controls?

The head of the therapy department, Colonel Bill Howard, seeing the disappointment on my face, strode over. He grabbed a piece of paper and handed it to me. "Hold this," he said. I took it gently between my fingers, then looked up at him, confused.

"See?" he said. "You *do* have grip strength, no matter what that gauge tells you. Today it's one piece of paper. Tomorrow, it will be two. The next day, three, and the day after that, four. And soon, you'll be able to hold a whole stack of paper in your hand." I nodded, and he leaned in close. "Don't let this machine tell you that you don't have strength," he said. "You do, and we will get you back to where you need to be."

I knew he was right, and that my recovery would take time. I also knew that getting upset wasn't going to fix anything. Although I sometimes felt pissed off when I couldn't do something, I tried hard to tamp down those negative feelings. For the most part, I succeeded, in the sense that I managed to spend more time appreciating what I still had than obsessing over what I'd lost.

In March 2005 a reporter for KATU news in Portland, Oregon, Anna Song (now Anna Canzano), decided to profile me as one of the few female amputees in Walter Reed. Her crew filmed me doing PT exercises and telling the story of my shootdown, and as we talked, she asked me how I felt about being a double amputee.

"They're just legs," I told her. "I mean, yeah—legs are important. But I'm alive, and I have my eyesight. I was afraid I was going to lose my arm, but I didn't." I smiled, but my comments apparently shocked her, because she made special mention of them in the clip that aired. "*Just legs*," Anna intoned. "That's what she said, all right." It hadn't occurred to me that anyone would think that was weird, because that was truly how I felt. I was lucky to be alive, lucky to have my brain intact, lucky to have all five senses.

We used to play a kind of amputee poker at Walter Reed. Once, as I watched a guy who'd lost an arm slowly learning to write with his non-dominant hand, I said, "Dude, that must suck!" He looked at the stumps of my legs and said, "Seriously?" He obviously thought he'd gotten the better deal, but I couldn't imagine having to do everything one-handed. It's all a matter of perspective. "How am I doing? Oh, I'm fine—not like the guy next door, who lost both legs and four fingers!" It was like we were trying to one-up, or maybe out-limb, each other. The only ones who couldn't play were the guys who'd lost a single leg below the knee. I mean, please— that's a paper cut. You still have your knee! Quit your bitching.

So I was the Happy Warrior of Walter Reed, always trying to stay upbeat and positive. This was partly because I did feel pretty happy most of the time, and partly because I wanted to set an example as a good Soldier. Years after I finished rehab at Walter Reed, my primary medical doctor, Captain Garth Greenwell, said, "Tammy, you were the worst patient, because you would never tell the truth about how much you were hurting. I knew how bad your condition was, but you were always determined to be cheerful."

In private, though, there were moments when I felt crushed with sadness. In Iraq, I had been in the best shape of my life. At thirty-six, I was strong, healthy, and working at the best job in the world. Now, thanks to the arc of a single RPG, I was in constant pain, was fighting infection, had lost two limbs and might still lose a third, and was struggling to hold a pencil well enough to write my name.

In my darker moments, I thought about my right leg, which had been blown off in the blast. Where was it now? Were parts of it still lying in that godforsaken palm grove in Iraq? Had some dog come along and found it, taking it off to gnaw under a tree? I *hated* the fact that part of my body had been left behind in enemy territory. I tried not to think about it, but the images kept coming back to me. This felt agonizing, and deeply sad, and I didn't know how to deal with it. So, just as I'd done with the ring of covered wagons, I created a mental image to help me through.

Whenever I felt overwhelmed by dark thoughts about my leg, I imagined a lockbox. I'd visualize placing my feelings in the box, turning the key, and putting it high up on a shelf. In this way, I could at least temporarily protect myself from that sadness and frustration, allowing me to get on with the business of recovery. Still, it would be years before I managed to stop myself from thinking about whatever remained of that leg.

And it wasn't just the leg that I mourned. One night, as Bryan and I were relaxing in his room at Fisher House, we turned on the TV just as *America's Next Top Model* started. As I watched the women strut up and down the catwalk, looking gorgeous and sexy in their short skirts and high heels, a realization hit me like a slap in the face: I would never be able to dress or look like that again. Although I identified most as a helicopter pilot and Soldier, I also loved wearing pretty clothes and showing off my feminine side. But from now on, I'd have to choose clothes that were functional, outfits that I could wear comfortably with titanium legs and while sitting in a wheelchair.

I started to cry. "This *sucks*," I said to Bryan. "Everything has changed."

Bryan put his arm around me. "Yeah, it's a pain in the ass," he agreed. Then he smiled and added, "But it'll be a pain in the ass for the rest of your long, happy life." This man, who had sat for days by my bedside while I was unconscious, who had whispered the words that calmed me before I awoke, who cared for me as I recovered from surgeries and stood by me as I struggled through physical therapy—this man refused to see our situation as anything but lucky. I was alive. I was *alive*. How could I complain?

And of course, there's the fact that being a double amputee is easier in the twenty-first century than it was at any other time in history. From the moment I woke up, the medical team started telling me how amazing my prosthetic legs would be. "They'll look just like your legs," the nurses told me. "Nobody will ever know." During those first few weeks, as I tried to comfort my mom about my situation, I would tell her, "Don't worry, Mom! I'll be able to wear short dresses—nothing will look any different." I wasn't completely sure I believed this, but I wanted it to be true.

The day my cosmetic legs arrived, many months into my stay at Walter Reed, I couldn't believe how perfect they were. The flesh tone matched my skin color exactly, the freckles matched mine, and the technicians had even made sure that my second toes were longer than my big toes, the way they'd been on my real feet. These didn't look like giant weird Barbie legs. They truly looked like my legs. And when I tried them on...I hated them. Whenever I saw myself in a mirror with those legs, I felt the loss of my real ones all over again. I had such a swell of negative emotion looking at myself, I had to take them off.

But the medical team had also given me another set of legs, these ones made of titanium and shiny steel. They have feet that look like feet, but the lower legs are just narrow titanium rods, like metal sticks. The upper legs are wider, and can be decorated however you like. I have a right leg with the Stars and Stripes—a decoration that probably would have shocked twelve-year-old me when I visited the United States that first time. And on my left leg, I stuck a sticker of my Senior Army Aviator wings. A lot of Soldiers have camouflage decoration, while others have flames, or skulls, or logos like Harley-Davidson. You can customize your legs however you want. They're your legs, after all.

When I see myself with the cosmetic legs, I see loss. But with titanium legs, I see *strength*. When I wear the titanium legs, I'm not trying to get back something I lost. I'm not trying to recover anything. I'm just trying to be strong, by whatever means necessary. And I'm not alone in that choice: Most military amputees choose the mechanical limbs, for that same reason. I'm not even sure where my cosmetic legs are anymore—maybe stuffed into a closet somewhere? All I know is, the last time they made it out into the world was when the Walter Reed prosthetics team borrowed them to show the victims of the Boston Marathon bombings what cosmetic legs could look like.

Customizing our prosthetics was one way to get used to being amputees. The other—and this one is huge—was humor. I started seeing guys wearing T-shirts with funny slogans on them, like "Ask me how I lost 10 pounds overnight" and "What are you staring at, you two-legged freak?" I got a few myself, including "Dude, where's my leg?" "I do all my own stunts," and "Wanna touch it?" But my favorite one says, "Lucky for me, he's an ass man." Bryan unfortunately hates that one, and has tried to throw it away several times. I just keep digging it out and wearing it, because it cracks me up.

Being an amputee means killing it on Halloween. I've seen guys dressed as the leg lamp from *A Christmas Story*, shark-attack victims, plastic foosball players, and flamingos. Practical jokes are easy: Carrying a bloody fake limb is always popular, as is lying down next to a parked car and pretending the limb is trapped under it. A couple of years ago, I broke one of my legs during a particularly vigorous workout on the rowing machine. I posted a photo on social media showing me with a goofy smile and my titanium leg sticking out of the foot strap. "Just broke my leg rowing," I wrote in the caption. "I blame my hardcore pace. Luckily, it no longer hurts to break a leg!" There's a silver lining for you!

And there was another silver lining to losing my legs: I would never again have to go for a run. I love sports and swimming, but I've always *hated* running, and I especially hated what the Army called "fun runs." These were presented as a morale-boosting activity, where we would gather together at 0500 hours and go on a "nice" five- to ten-mile run. But I can tell you definitively, they were not good for *my* morale. So I took some comfort knowing that having no legs meant that no one could ever make me run again at zero-dark-thirty, for fun or otherwise.

That's why, when a volunteer named Mary Bryant showed up at my bedside in Walter Reed and said, "We can help you train for the New York City Marathon!" I just said, "Thanks, but *hell* no." Seriously? I had no legs! Not to mention, I had no interest in running a marathon even when I was in top physical condition. Why would I ever want to do it now?

"Oh, no," she said. "Not running. You'd be in a hand-cranked wheelchair." She was with the Achilles Freedom Team, an arm of the nonprofit Achilles International that helps wounded military get back into competitive environments. They had specialized training and equipment, and the volunteers would come by every week to get wounded warriors on a program to success.

I may hate running, but I love speed and machines that make me feel like I'm flying. I was intrigued by the hand-crank chair, and once I got my butt into one and found myself flying down the road at fifteen miles per hour, I was hooked. Since recovering, I've completed four marathons, and during every one of them, I felt strong, nimble, and free. I pushed myself to reach ever-higher speeds, sometimes up to 25 mph downhill. And no running!

This was one of the greatest benefits of recovering in Walter Reed. The medical and therapy teams always challenged us, pushing us to get out of our comfort zones. When I told my doctors I wanted to go to the State of the Union Address, they didn't say, "Well, maybe that's not a good idea" or "You're not in any shape to do that." They wanted us to do as much as we could to get stronger faster. It's a real philosophy, different from the one you might get at a civilian hospital. You weren't going to be sitting around feeling sorry for yourself, because there was always someone at your side saying, "Come on! Let's do this!"

Walter Reed had programs for swimming, ice hockey, alpine skiing, scuba diving, canoeing, skydiving, and marathons. I loved flying down the road in the hand-cranked wheelchair so much, I also tried alpine skiing, which the Department of Veterans Affairs made possible through a program they called Miracles on the Mountainside. They gave me training, then strapped me into a seat attached to a ski and gave me a push, and suddenly I was hurtling down the mountain! Well—not exactly hurtling. Tethered to my ski instructor, I was usually passed by everyone from five-year-old ski slope fiends to blind skiers and their guides. But having grown up in Southeast Asia and Hawaii, I had never snow-skied before, and even going slower than everyone else, I loved it.

I did, however, yell back at the blind wounded warrior who, upon passing me, shouted, "Get outta my way, gimpy!" with "Yeah, well, you'd slow down too if you could see what was coming!"

Wounded warrior humor at its cringeworthy best.

In the spring of 2005, these adventures were still in the future, but the volunteers and staff at Walter Reed kept pushing me to work and train harder to get myself into shape for them. Of course, they didn't have to do that, because I was already pushing myself to the limit in hopes of returning to the only activity that mattered to me. If I wanted to get back into an Army cockpit, now was the time to show them I could do it.

Chapter 12

Pandora's Box

For the first four months after the shootdown, I lived in a Walter Reed hospital room. I wanted to move into Fisher House with Bryan, but the rules stated that patients couldn't spend the night there if they were on IV meds. And I was almost always on IV meds during that time, continuing to fight the *Acinetobacter* infection.

Little by little, we began bending the rules. Sympathetic nurses taught Bryan how to hook up my IVs, inject daily blood thinners into my belly, and administer medications at the right time of day. With Bryan as my "drug master" (as he called himself), my doctors would give me a twelve-hour pass so I could spend the occasional night with him on the weekends. At first, he would bundle me into a blanket cocoon, then push me slowly in a wheelchair between Walter Reed and Fisher House, as if he were afraid any little bump in the sidewalk might break me. This was a dynamic I didn't enjoy. "Stop babying me!" I finally yelled at him. He tried not to hover, but understandably, he was eager to make sure nothing else would happen to me.

Bryan was the commander of a National Guard unit in southern

Illinois during the whole time I was at Walter Reed, which meant he had to travel there a few days every month for Guard duty. At those times, he would arrange for his cousin, Dr. Claudia Beck, to come stay with me in the hospital. Claudia, who had become an invaluable link between us and my doctors, is actually a pediatrician, so I couldn't resist the urge to needle Bryan a bit about that.

"Seriously?" I said. "Of all the relatives we have, you choose a *pediatrician* to look after me?"

"You Army Aviators always get into mischief," he replied, not even cracking a smile. "A pediatrician is exactly the kind of doctor you need."

In March, I was finally able to move into Fisher House. I was ecstatic to be out of the hospital, though I'd continue to return every day for treatments and physical therapy. All told, I would spend thirteen months recovering at Walter Reed, a length of time that made my recovery easier not only physically but mentally and emotionally as well. If I had been thrown out into the world after a month or two, I would have had to deal with people's stares, and the frustration of explaining over and over what had happened to me. Instead, I was in an environment where being an amputee was the norm, and everyone understood what everyone else was going through.

The staff knew that my number one goal was to fly again for the Army, so as soon as I was strong enough, they took me out on a field trip. They drove me to Davison Army Airfield in Fort Belvoir, Virginia, and as we pulled up on the tarmac next to a Black Hawk helicopter, my heart began to pound. I was wearing temporary artificial legs at that point, and my physical therapist, Bunnie Wyckoff, encouraged me to climb up into the cockpit. Easing into the pilot's seat felt so comfortable—like putting on an old sweatshirt. For the first time since the shootdown day, I was able to breathe in the smell of JP-8 fuel and metal that I loved so much.

Bunnie watched as I settled into the cockpit, and we talked about what it would take for me to be able to fly. Some questions were obvious: Could I work the pedals with my prosthetic legs? Was my right arm strong enough to grip the cyclic? Other questions I hadn't even thought about until I got into the seat. Helicopter pilots tend to rest their right forearms on their right thighs, an easy way to provide a little extra stability when maneuvering the controls. But with no right leg, I could no longer do that.

An even bigger question was whether I'd be able to climb on top of the helicopter to perform the required preflight inspection of the rotor, hydraulics, and other aircraft systems. I tried to hoist myself up, but my right arm was still too weak, and I didn't have enough dexterity to use the handgrips and toeholds. I watched as Bunnie climbed up, envious of her ability to do it so easily. "Just keep working on it," she said. Like all the staff at Walter Reed, whenever she saw me struggling with a task, she never said, "You're not going to be able to do this." Instead, she offered support and encouragement.

A few weeks later, Major General Jessica Wright—the adjutant general of Pennsylvania and first female helicopter pilot in the Army National Guard—gave permission for me to use the Black Hawk flight simulator at the Fort Indiantown Gap Army post. So I took a road trip up to Pennsylvania to test my skills. I figured out how to set my artificial legs to be able to work the pedals, and discovered that my right arm was both strong and dexterous enough to maneuver the cyclic. With a flight instructor sitting at my side, I took a mini "checkride" to assess my skills.

We taxied the virtual aircraft, and then I flew some traffic patterns, did some slope landings, and undertook a few emergency procedures. It was over before I knew it, and before I was ready to be done. I could've stayed in that simulator cockpit for hours, it felt so good to fly again. And when the flight instructor reported back that I met the standards for all basic flight maneuvers, I couldn't stop grinning. I hoped it meant that I could soon get into a real cockpit.

As the days grew longer and warmer, and my wounds continued to heal, I decided to tackle another task. This one was going to be difficult and potentially very unpleasant, but I knew I had to do it.

"How soon can I get off methadone?" I asked my doctors. An opioid used to treat chronic pain—and to wean addicts off of heroin—methadone was routinely prescribed to amputees at Walter Reed. But it's a very strong drug, with side effects that include dizziness, sleepiness, and nausea, which meant that no pilot could possibly fly while taking it. If I had to choose between managing my pain with methadone or suffering pain without it so I could fly, there really was no choice at all. "I want to get off it completely, as soon as possible," I told my primary care team.

Only six months had passed since I lost my legs, and the doctors thought it was too soon to start weaning me off it. They advised me that most amputees stay on methadone for at least a year, and some much longer, because not only does it help with pain, it also mitigates phantom pain, which can be as bad or worse. Staying on methadone would allow my body to focus its energy on healing, not fighting pain. But seeing how determined I was, they agreed that I could give it a try.

"Okay," said my doctor, Captain Greenwell. "Let's go ahead and cut your dosage in half." This was a drastic reduction, certain to result in horrific pain. And because methadone is itself actually an opioid, I'd also suffer from withdrawal symptoms. The doctors knew me well enough by now to understand that I wanted to forge ahead no matter what—but they probably figured that once I got a taste of these symptoms, I'd beg to get back on my regular dosage.

The effects kicked in quickly. My hands and feet started burning like hellfire, and I experienced withdrawal symptoms— shaking, sweating, vomiting. My brain felt scrambled, and the pain was intense and unrelenting. Yet as horrible as all this was, it wasn't nearly as bad as what I had endured during that first week in Walter Reed, when the doctors weaned me off morphine. So I just gritted my teeth, determined to make it through the worst days of the symptoms. And as soon as I leveled out, I said, "Okay, let's cut it in half again."

This went on for several weeks. I went from taking four pills a day to two. Then from two to one. Then Bryan started cutting my pills in half, and then into quarters. Each time we halved the dosage, I went through withdrawal all over again. But at the end of six weeks, I was no longer taking any methadone at all. I was done.

In my earliest days of recovery, one of the peer visitors who came through was Lieutenant Colonel Andrew Lourake. He was the pilot who'd lost his leg to a staph infection in the late 1990s, and then had been cleared to fly again for the Air Force after multiple surgeries and years of rehab. Talking to him had given me hope that if he could get back in a military cockpit, then so could I. But there were significant differences between his injuries and mine, and as my rehab continued, I began to realize that I had higher bars to clear.

Lieutenant Colonel Lourake had lost one leg, just above the knee. I had lost both my legs, my right one all the way up to my hip. Thanks to the tiny piece of bone that Bryan had insisted the doctors leave in my body, I could wear a prosthetic leg. But when I was flying in the simulator, I had trouble keeping it on. Sometimes when I shifted in my seat, it would slip out of place, making it hard for me to control the pedals. I was constantly fiddling with the socket, trying to get the leg to stay put. Of course, you can't be distracted like that when you're flying an actual helicopter.

This was obviously going to be a problem. And unfortunately, it wasn't the only one.

I had been learning to walk again, and was actually doing pretty well. But just being able to walk and press the pedals in a cockpit wasn't enough. If I wanted to fly for the Army, with the possibility of returning to combat, I'd have to be capable of evacuating an aircraft and carrying another crewmember to safety. After all, what if the guys in my Black Hawk had been physically unable to pull me out and carry me to the second bird? What if, in a future scenario, I was the uninjured one and the others were incapacitated? I owed it to whomever I'd be flying with to be able to rescue them in the same way Dan and Matt had rescued me.

As our flight instructors used to say, "You can teach any monkey to wiggle a stick." But it takes much more than that to be an aviator. You have to be able to carry out a mission—whatever that mission requires. As the summer days wore on, I slowly began to realize that no matter how hard I worked, and no matter how badly I wanted it, my body would never be physically capable of doing it. Which meant that I was never going to fly for the Army again.

My whole life, whenever I really wanted something, I worked my ass off until I got it. I might not be the smartest, fastest, or strongest in a given situation, but I could always outwork anyone else. When I wanted to skip a grade, I worked to make it happen. When I needed a perfect score on my instruments exam, I studied relentlessly in the face of daunting odds—and made it happen. Whether it was throwing the discus, getting my master's degree, dropping to do push-ups in a gas chamber, or willing myself to sit up for five hours so I could go to the State of the Union, working hard was my superpower.

Now, for the first time in my life, my superpower was neutralized. It didn't matter how hard I worked, how much I sweated, or how determined I was; I was never going to grow a new leg, or even a new thigh muscle needed to control an artificial leg. Because I couldn't do that, I would never fly an Army helicopter again. And that realization ripped my heart out.

Flying Black Hawks was more than my job. Being an Army aviator had become my identity, the core of who I am. It was the greatest privilege of my life. And if you told me right now that I could go back in time—go back to flight school as a butterbar (Second Lieutenant), command the Mad Dogs, fight in Iraq, and then get shot down, lose my legs, and endure the pain of recovery all over again—I would do it in a heartbeat. No hesitation. Because it would mean I'd get to fly and be with my Army buddies for another twelve years.

Nobody told me that mission in Iraq would be my last flight. Nobody gave me notice. I didn't get to say goodbye to the job that gave my life purpose and meaning for all those years. It was just stripped away from me in one violent instant. When I say, "They're only legs," I really mean it. But what that insurgent took from me was not just my legs, or full mobility in my right arm. That fucker took my identity. *That* has been what's hardest to accept.

The most painful dreams I have are not of the shootdown, or of the agonies of recovery. They're the ones in which I fall asleep, and when I open my eyes I'm lying in my bunk in Balad.

In these dreams, I get up and live an entire day in Iraq. I do all the mundane tasks, filling out flight plans, doing mission risk assessments, filing preflight paperwork. I walk across the gravel of LSA Anaconda; I smell the swirling dust. I meet up with my crew, do the pre-mission brief, and then climb into the cockpit of my Black Hawk to fly missions.

I'm in my helicopter, with my crew, roaring across the desert. I'm flying. I'm ecstatic! There are all the landing zones—LZ Duke, in the middle of the desert in southern Iraq. LZ Victory, near Saddam Hussein's old palace—a place we nicknamed Waterworld for the acres of decorative lakes filled with water sucked from this parched land. I see all the places that made up my life in Iraq, such as LZ Ironhorse and the route up north to Kirkuk and Erbil. And then, the missions end. I complete my postflight tasks, walk back to my hooch, and lie down in my rack.

And then I wake up. For an instant, I still feel exhilarated. But then I realize I'm in my bed at home, not in Iraq, and I remember. This is now, and that dream was the old me. I go through the loss and grieve all over again, because the joy I've just felt flying with my crew was a dream. It isn't real, and it never will be again.

When I awake after these dreams, I'm exhausted. I've lived a twelve-hour day through the night, and I'm physically wasted and emotionally wrecked. So even now, I do what I can to try to keep those dreams at bay. Fortunately, I know what triggers them: war stories, such as *The Hurt Locker*. I can't read books or watch movies that depict the troops' experience in the Iraq and Afghanistan wars. Interestingly, Vietnam War stories bring the dreams too, but I sleep peacefully after World War II ones.

I learned the hard way that if I allow too many of those images into my waking mind all at once, the dreams will come at night. And then I'll wake up devastated, having relived the most profound loss of my life all over again.

*   *   *

As part of the recovery process, Walter Reed offered group and individual therapy sessions. Yet although I've always encouraged Veterans to seek out mental health care, I didn't do so myself.

The main reason was that I wanted to fly again, and I knew that having therapy could jeopardize that. At the time, in 2005, the simple act of seeking out mental health treatment might cause me to lose my security clearance and not be able to get back on flight status. This practice was meant to ensure that anyone at the controls of an aircraft was mentally and emotionally fit, but in many cases, it had the opposite effect. Pilots who'd been through traumatizing experiences refused to get the help they needed, for fear of harming their careers or being seen as weak.

We build up our warriors to be physically fit and mentally strong; that's the military culture, and it runs deep. But the characteristics that make us ready for battle—mental toughness, determination to push through pain, refusal to give up the mission—are the same ones that work against us if we need help. Like so many of my fellow wounded warriors, I was hardheaded about pushing forward through the pain. *No sir, I'm fine. All good. Ready for action. When can I report back to my unit?*

When I became head of the Illinois Department of Veterans' Affairs, I decided it was time to remove the stigma of getting mental health evaluations. For years, all National Guard troops returning home from deployment automatically received medical and financial assessments as a part of their demobilization. In 2007, as IDVA director, I approached the Adjutant General of the Illinois National Guard, Major General Bill Enyart, about adding mandatory mental health screenings. No longer would troops returning home to Illinois have to actively request such screenings, which almost no one was willing to do. Now everybody would get one as part of the demobilization process—no questions asked, no stigma attached. Later, when I became an assistant secretary at the VA during the Obama administration, I also worked with the Department of Defense and Congress to stop the practice of stripping security clearances from servicemembers who choose to undergo mental health screening.

The truth is, any Veteran returning from a war zone can benefit from group or individual therapy, and that's what I always recommend. Although I didn't take advantage of professional therapy sessions myself, my long recovery at Walter Reed gave me the ability to talk about my experiences every day for thirteen months with people who understood what I was going through—other patients, my doctors, and my physical therapists. This proved to be its own kind of therapy, as it helped me to integrate my wartime experiences into everyday life. The shootdown became just one chapter of my story, rather than the whole story, and that helped tremendously in my recovery.

Part of me was still angry about what had happened, of course. So, as I'd done before, I envisioned a little box where I could put those feelings. In the early months, I chose not to dwell on them, because they didn't feel useful to my recovery. Eventually, as I grew stronger, I began cracking open the box, bit by bit. I came to think of it as my own kind of Pandora's box.

In Greek mythology, Pandora releases a catalogue of ills upon the world when she foolishly peers into a box Zeus has given her. By the time she slams it shut, the evils have escaped, and the only thing left inside is hope. Talking about my shootdown and losing my legs felt like opening my box to release the ills inside. Every time I opened it, a little more of my pain took flight, and in the end, what was left were the good things: fond memories of my service, an appreciation for what I have, and hope for the future.

I still have bad days and good days, just like anyone else. But the searing emotions I felt after the shootdown have calmed. The only time I've felt them in recent years was in 2019, and that was in a very specific situation that's not likely ever to be repeated.

It happened during a visit to my old Army unit back in Illinois. As a surprise, the crew wanted to take me up in a Black Hawk. Now, I love being in helicopters. And I especially love flying in Black Hawks. But I am a Black Hawk *pilot*. I did not want to climb in the back of that helicopter—*my* helicopter—and be ferried around as a passenger in a unit I once commanded. This wasn't resentment. It was a feeling of loss.

I didn't even realize how strongly I felt about it until the night before, when I got word of the plan. To my surprise, I broke down in tears. "No, I can't do this," I said to Bryan. "I'm a *pilot*, not some civilian getting a joyride." Black Hawks had been my life. I couldn't now pretend that they were just a diversion, or a photo op for the politician I had become. I called Randy Sikowski, my old boss from Iraq, who was (and still is) now the Downstate Director for my Senate offices in Illinois.

"I'm sorry, Randy," I said. "I really appreciate this, but I just can't do it." I knew the guys were trying to do something nice for me, and I was truly grateful. But I also understood that in that moment, it was more important to take care of myself than to try to push through that heartache. Randy understood immediately, and told me he would handle it. In the end, bad weather was forecast for the day of the intended flight, so it never even came up.

I sometimes wonder whether the bad stuff that happened to me as a child served as a kind of inoculation. For years, I lived in fear that my dad would disappear and we would end up on the streets. I knew what happened to brown and biracial people who didn't have the connection to America that we did. In my childhood, I lived through war, poverty, and discrimination. Maybe these struggles served as a vaccine of sorts, preparing me for this much bigger loss I had to go through. Or maybe they just gave me the techniques I needed to take care of myself.

Whatever the case, there's no doubt that among Veterans who've suffered trauma, I'm one of the lucky ones. Many of my fellow wounded warriors have experienced post-traumatic stress, some of them not until years after the initial event. Senator Max Cleland, who lost his legs and an arm in Vietnam, sought treatment for PTSD three decades after his injury, when he lost an election in 2002. I met Max while at Walter Reed, and talking to him helped me to truly understand that the best we can do is take life one day at a time.

In the summer of 2005, when I realized I would never fly for the Army again, that advice from Max helped save me. I was no longer sure what my purpose in life would be, but I had to just take it one day at a time, and be open to whatever came my way.

And then, in late August, Dick Durbin called me.

For six months, Bryan and I had been contacting Senator Durbin's office for help with problems and situations at Walter Reed. He never failed to respond, by either taking action in an individual case or fighting for systemic improvements. No matter how many times we contacted his office, he urged us to keep doing it. Encouraged by his desire and ability to help, we did.

When I saw that Dick was calling, I figured it was about one of the problems we'd reported. But this time, he wanted to talk about something else.

"Tammy," he said, "you've done a great job as the unofficial advocate for your fellow Soldiers. But more needs to be done. I want you to consider becoming an *official* advocate." He paused. "I think you should run for Congress."

"Uh...wow," I said. This was completely unexpected, and I wasn't sure how to respond. Even though I couldn't go back into Army Aviation, I had assumed I'd return to the full-time job I'd had before deploying. For two years, I had worked as the club and district manager of the Asia Pacific Region of Rotary International, and I loved it. Rotary is a fantastic organization, and they had let me know that no matter how long my deployment took— and then, after the shootdown, no matter how long my recovery took—my job would be waiting for me.

The congressional seat Dick was referring to was the one held for thirty years by Henry Hyde, the most powerful Republican in Illinois. Hyde had recently announced his retirement, and several Democrats were already eyeing the primary in hopes of swinging the seat. I told Dick that Bryan and I would have to talk about it. But after we hung up, I wondered if this even made sense. I had never been involved in politics, and had never wanted to be. Was I really going to start by suddenly running for the United States House of Representatives?

I asked Bryan what he thought, and he said, "Well, I don't see why you wouldn't. It makes perfect sense if we want to keep doing the work for wounded warriors."

Since attending the State of the Union Address, I'd been giving interviews, speaking to Veterans' groups, and of course I had testified in front of the Senate Committee on Veterans' Affairs in the spring. My visibility had risen over the past six months, but I still wasn't sure this was the right move.

"I mean, don't I have to run for city council or something first?" I asked Bryan. I wasn't sure I had the skills needed to run for Congress. I hadn't been in any debates since high school, and I lost every one of those. I'm also pretty introverted, and don't particularly enjoy being in front of cameras. But this was a chance to serve in a different capacity, so shouldn't I take it?

After much discussion, Bryan and I decided we needed more time to make a decision. So I called Dick to let him know.

"We're not saying no, but we're not saying yes either," I told him. "I need to do some research. Is there someone we can talk to who can give us a better idea of what we'd need to do?"

"Sure," said Dick. "I'll put you in touch with Rahm Emanuel."

A former Clinton administration official, Rahm Emanuel was a fast-talking, profanity-spewing force who was then representing Illinois's Fifth District in the U.S. House of Representatives. Rahm came to visit me at Walter Reed one afternoon, and I showed him around and introduced him to a few of my fellow wounded warriors. Later on, he called me to talk about the possibility of my getting into the race.

"Look," he said. "If you think we're not taking good care of Veterans, and you believe the war in Iraq was wrong, then you definitely should be running. Why don't you come with me to the D-triple-C, and I'll introduce you to some people."

"Okay," I said. "What's the 'D-triple-C'?" I had never heard of that abbreviation for the Democratic Congressional Campaign Committee, and barely knew anything about the committee itself. I had a lot to learn, but that didn't seem to faze either Dick or Rahm. They wanted me to run. But I still didn't know if I wanted to, and besides that, I was on active duty military status, which meant that I couldn't campaign, raise money, or do anything political beyond having these very general conversations.

After Rahm's visit, I called Dick and told him that I needed more time. On top of everything else, I was still recovering, and it was likely that I would have another surgery on my arm in the fall.

"Well, you've got to make a decision soon," Dick told me, "because the filing deadline is in December, and we'd need to gather five thousand signatures to get you on the ballot."

I was truly torn. The idea of getting into politics felt exhausting. This was a move I had never imagined for myself, and I had no interest in being in the public eye on a constant basis. The easier path would be to go back to the life I loved, working with Rotary International and serving with my National Guard unit. I had spent a year in the hospital trying to get back to that comfortable life—not to become a politician. But at the same time, I wanted to go where I could do the most good, and if politics was the best way to do that, I had to consider it seriously.

For the moment, I decided to sit tight and focus on healing my arm, hoping the next few weeks would somehow bring clarity.

In October 2005, as the sticky DC summer finally gave way to the golds and reds of autumn, the staff at Walter Reed started planning for my first Alive Day.

No one knows who started the Alive Day tradition, but it first became popular among Vietnam Vets. I learned about it from the Milkshake Man, Jim Mayer. Jim had lost both his legs to a landmine in Vietnam, and every year on the anniversary of the explosion, he celebrated having lived through it. It was too easy, and too depressing, to sit around feeling sad on the day you lost your legs—why not celebrate having survived instead?

There was a real affinity between the Vietnam guys and those of us who were in Iraq, because we both fought in unpopular wars. When the Vietnam Veterans returned home after heeding our country's call, serving honorably and being subjected to the horrors of war, they faced protests and jeers. For many, this was at least as painful as their experiences in the war, if not more so. Still haunted by the spitting and angry taunts of "baby killer," they didn't want to see the men and women who were fighting in Iraq get the same treatment. So the Vets who came through Walter Reed opened their arms wide, as if making a protective shield around us. They were determined that what happened to them should never happen to another American servicemember.

Vietnam Vets had already earned a special place in my heart, starting with the guys I'd served with back in the Bravo 2/228th, who'd let me take the stick in their OH-58 helicopters all those years ago. But teaching us all about Alive Day was their greatest gift. They also taught some of the older Vets who came through. Tom Porter had lost his legs way back in Korea, but when he learned about the Alive Day tradition, he started celebrating his too.

Some Vets mark their Alive Day quietly, with reflection. Others try to gather with their buddies who were with them that day, or who saved them. Some throw parties. Because this was my first one, we planned a big party at Mologne House, where my mom was staying. A bunch of people from Walter Reed were coming, including staff and some of my fellow wounded warriors. Most of my crew couldn't make it. But I was happy about the fact that Dan Milberg, my Pilot in Command, was planning to drive from his home in Missouri to Washington, DC, for the party. This would be our first time seeing each other since that day.

At nine thirty that morning, I was lying in my bed at Fisher House, dizzy and nauseous from yet another round of antibiotics. I was on a regimen of two different types, hanging a new IV bag every four and six hours, and as I lay there watching fluid drip into my veins, I tried to push down the feeling of dread that this time, the bacteria might actually win. If we couldn't get this infection under control, there was a chance that after all the pain, surgeries, and months of rehab, I still might lose my arm.

As I lay there feeling miserable, my phone rang. When I picked it up, I heard Dan say quietly, "Tammy, it's about to happen."

"What's about to happen?" I asked. But as soon as he said it, I knew.

"It's 1630 in Baghdad," he said, then paused. "We're getting hit right now."

Right now. This was the moment, one year ago, when the RPG blew through the cockpit floor and exploded in my lap. The moment Dan realized he had to single-handedly land a shattered helicopter or lose four lives, including his own. It was the moment my fight to survive began.

Dan and I sat on the phone together in silence, bound together by this event that had changed both our lives. We have a bond that goes beyond words, because we will always have that powerful shared memory of what happened in our cockpit at that moment.

Finally, Dan spoke. "You know," he said, "it really was a nightmare. It was like the opening of *Saving Private Ryan*." Even though I had no memory of the rescue, I knew that the horrifying images from that day were burned into his mind. During my months of recovery, Dan and Matt had described it to me in phone calls. How they pulled my broken body from the helicopter, thinking I was dead. How they carried me, the three of us slippery with my blood and flesh, across that godforsaken field. How they stumbled and got up, dropped me and lifted me, trying with every ounce of their strength to get us all to the safety of the second helicopter. "It felt like someone was ripping my heart and lungs out of my chest," Dan had told me. "It felt like we'd run a mile carrying you."

I knew all this. But then Dan told me something else.

"I honestly don't know how I would be able to handle it if you weren't doing so well," he said. And as simplistic as it might sound, those words changed everything for me. They made me realize what I had to do.

No matter what happens in my life, I will measure every day against the effort that Dan and Matt put into carrying my body to that second helicopter. Every single day, I have to live up to what he and the rest of those two aircrews went through to get me safely out of Iraq. If I spent the rest of my life feeling sorry for myself, or bemoaning the loss of my legs, that would dishonor what they did for me. I owe it to them to make something of the life that they risked their own to save. When Dan said those words to me, I understood that my success or failure in doing that would have a direct effect on him too.

I have a debt I can never repay, but I must spend my time at least trying to do so. At the very least, I owe that to the men who saved me, my brothers in arms.

I honestly don't know why I survived that day. But if you believe in miracles, I would say it's a miracle that I did.

Two weeks before the shootdown, I'd noticed that some guys had gotten lax about wearing their aviation life-support equipment—the flight helmet, survival vest, flight suit, and Darth Vader–esque maxillofacial shield designed to protect them. "It's too hot," they complained. I yelled at them to get squared away, and to set an example I made sure my visor was pulled down and gloves fully on, and I stopped rolling up the sleeves on my flight suit. On November 12, 2004, those small steps saved my life. The gloves and sleeves protected me from severe burns. And as I later learned, the RPG blast split my visor in two—which meant that if I hadn't pulled it down, the blast would have destroyed my face instead.

When I heard the machine-gun fire pinging off the aircraft, I reached for the GPS switch to mark our location. I did this instinctively, even though the GPS hadn't been working the entire day. Because I reached out at that precise moment, the explosion pulverized my arm. Otherwise, it would have pulverized my head.

We were all incredibly lucky that Dan was piloting the aircraft—the first time we had flown together in weeks, since he'd switched to flying night missions. Dan was an enormously skilled pilot, with combat experience going back to Desert Storm. Trust me when I tell you that very few pilots could have pulled off the landing that he did in such a severely damaged aircraft. Matt Backues, who watched the whole thing from the second helicopter, said later that "the fact Dan was able to land that aircraft blows my mind."

For that matter, it's a miracle Dan was actually piloting the helicopter when we were hit. If he hadn't called me a "stick pig" three minutes earlier, I would still have been in control, and it's likely we all would have died.

In the single photo that exists of our downed Black Hawk, you can see a huge entry hole in the floor and an exit hole above. When the remnants of the RPG blasted through the top of the cockpit, how on earth did they not hit the spinning rotor blades? Any strong impact would have rendered the helicopter unflyable—but somehow, by what must have been a matter of millimeters, they missed.

And what about the clearing that suddenly appeared exactly where we needed to land the helicopter? What were the chances that less than a kilometer from where the RPG tore into us, in the middle of a huge grove of palm trees, we'd suddenly see a landing spot? Yet there it was.

The fact that Pat Muenks was piloting the second aircraft also likely saved my life. A former medevac pilot, Pat knew he needed to radio ahead to Taji to have a medevac bird waiting. My survival hinged on getting me to Baghdad within the golden hour after my injury, so literally every minute counted. Even then, I barely made it, apparently coding several times on the operating table at the Combat Surgical Hospital there.

I shouldn't be here, and yet I am. I know I've been given a second chance, and every day I must try to make good use of it.

Dick Durbin called me again in mid-November, shortly after my Alive Day. I was back in the hospital, recovering after the latest surgery on my arm, nauseous and groggy from getting pumped full of antibiotics yet again. But since that conversation with Dan, my mind and heart were clear about what I had to do.

"So, what do you say?" Dick asked.

"I'm in," I said. I had no idea how to do it, but I was running for Congress.

Chapter 13

Gift from the Heavens

In all my life, I had never imagined becoming a politician. I also had never seriously considered becoming a mother. If you had told me as a young woman that one day I'd be both, I would have asked what you were smoking.

From the moment I became an Army helicopter pilot, I was laser-focused on one goal: to become the commander of an assault helicopter battalion. Knowing the competition would be fierce, I spent years hitting all the "gates," or milestones of service, taking on tours of duty as a platoon leader, a company commander, and a logistics officer. All the while, I knew that getting pregnant would derail—or at the very least, delay—my dream. Pregnancy is a medically grounding condition, meaning you can't fly. Then, after giving birth, you have to work to get back on flight status, which takes even more time. So right from the start, I told Bryan I didn't particularly want kids. I put the Army first, in hopes of meeting my goal.

By the time I was deployed to Iraq, the only box left to check was serving a tour as an S3 Operations Officer. I couldn't do this until being promoted to Major—but while in Balad, I learned that I'd be getting that promotion at the end of 2004. Everything was going exactly as planned, and my dream was finally within reach. I was thirty-six years old and exactly where I wanted to be.

And then, in the millisecond it took for that RPG to explode in my lap, all those years of planning went up in smoke.

In the beginning of my recovery, I was adamant that the asshole who shot us down would not determine my fate. At the time, that meant one thing: getting back into an Army helicopter cockpit. For so many months, I'd believed I could do it—a belief that drove me forward, and held me together, as I healed. Finally realizing that I'd never fly for the Army again was soul-crushing, but the shootdown also changed my fate in another, far better way. It opened me up to the possibility of having children.

I can't say for sure that we would never have had kids if I'd gotten my battalion command, but once that was no longer a possibility, my priorities changed. After having given everything to the Army for most of my adult life, I was ready to try to start a family.

But then, fate intervened once again.

The day after I checked out of Walter Reed in December 2005, with an IV drip still in my arm, I announced that I was running for Congress. The grueling campaign that followed, which took up all of 2006, tested not only my physical limits but our emotional limits as a couple.

Bryan and I were Soldiers, not political people, and neither of us had experience running a campaign. The learning curve was steep, and I quickly found myself consumed with fund-raising tasks, media training, and learning the ropes of local Democratic politics. There weren't enough hours in the day for me to deal with every issue, so I had to trust the professional campaign staff we had assembled. Unfortunately, Bryan disagreed with some of the choices they made, and he let me know about it.

Bryan is a student of military and American history, and he wanted my campaign to reflect sweeping historical themes. I would come home after a long, exhausting day on the campaign trail, and he'd be waiting for me with a press release he didn't agree with, saying, "This isn't your true voice." Or "This doesn't reflect Army values." He wanted to spend our evenings doing deep dives on campaign messaging, while I was just trying to keep my head above water. Though I often agreed with him, I was usually too exhausted to discuss it, and we'd end up snapping at each other, neither of us satisfied at how things were going.

Desperate not to lose Henry Hyde's seat, the Republicans threw everything they had at me during the campaign, including spending thousands of dollars on blatantly racist ads that darkened my skin, widened my already moon-shaped face, and turned my eyes into slits. The GOP's attack ads were so pervasive and nasty that my own mother, seeing them on TV when she visited us toward the end of the campaign, asked whether it was true that I'd been handing out stacks of money to violent criminals who climbed over the border wall. That whole year felt like some kind of diabolical obstacle course, with a new horror waiting around every bend.

When I lost that race in November 2006, I felt like I had failed my team, the people who had donated to my campaign, and the entire Democratic Party. It didn't matter that I'd spent five hours a day making calls to raise money, because it wasn't enough. It didn't matter how much media training I'd gotten, because I still never felt comfortable in front of cameras. It didn't matter how hard I had worked, because I had lost.

In the Army, the buck stops with the commanding officer. So, while I knew that I'd done everything in my power to win, the loss was still 100 percent my responsibility. I felt that keenly, and it was agonizing.

*　　*　　*

For three days, I sat in my bathtub, deeply depressed. I would have just stayed in bed, but the bathroom was the one place in our house where we didn't get good cell coverage. So by staying in there I could avoid the dozens of well-intentioned, but extremely painful, consolation calls that were pouring in. It seemed like everyone, from Bill and Hillary Clinton to Dick Durbin to my next-door neighbors, wanted to offer words of condolence, but I didn't want to talk to anyone. For the first time in my life, I had no idea what to do with myself. I didn't know how to move forward, past this loss.

On the fourth day, while I was in my kitchen trying to force myself to eat, my phone rang. It was John Harris, chief of staff to Illinois governor Rod Blagojevich, asking if I'd consider becoming the director of the Illinois Department of Veterans' Affairs. This would be an incredible opportunity to continue the work I'd started while in Walter Reed—a way to pursue my new mission of service to my military buddies. I eagerly accepted, and in December 2006 I became the new IDVA director. My hope was that in 2007, having my health and a steady job might mean that the whirlwind would finally slow down enough for us to focus on starting a family.

And that's when Bryan was called up for deployment to Kuwait.

Although I'd been sent on multiple Army deployments over the years, this would be Bryan's first. It felt unsettling to be the one left behind, and as I tried to prepare myself emotionally, we also had to make sure I'd be able physically to take care of everything while he was away. During my recovery at Walter Reed, some of the guys from my unit had stripped our Hoffman Estates house down to the studs, rebuilding it to be wheelchair-accessible, which was an amazing gift that enabled us to stay in our home. But even with all the retrofitting, I still couldn't shovel snow off our wheel-chair ramp, or reach items on the top shelves in the kitchen. So in the months leading up to Bryan's departure, we did even more renovation, including building a platform in the garage so I could transfer directly from my Ford F-150 into a wheelchair and roll right into the house.

We also had to deal with press attention, since the 2006 campaign had turned me into something of a public figure. Interviewers seemed fascinated by the role reversal of Bryan's deployment, while for us that was just a normal part of Army life. Michele Norris of NPR even asked whether we had considered requesting an exemption so he wouldn't have to go. We had never considered it, of course. Bryan told her, "This is what a Soldier does. When it's your time to go and serve, it's your time to go and serve."

Bryan served in Kuwait for one year in support of Operation Iraqi Freedom. He was assigned to a transportation unit, and spent his days running logistics for truck convoys going into Iraq. Most of his work hours were spent behind a desk in the relative safety of Camp Arifjan, in southern Kuwait. But like me, he wanted to share the burden of combat with his buddies. So every week, he'd press his superiors to let him go into Iraq with a convoy. They let him do it just once, entering Iraq along a road littered with IEDs. Knowing I would worry, he didn't tell me about the mission until he was already safely back in Kuwait.

During the year that Bryan was deployed, I used my new position at IDVA to continue helping Veterans in Illinois. We established a 24/7 mental health crisis hotline and mandatory mental health screening for returning Vets. We also gave tax credits to businesses that hired Veterans, and started programs to improve access to housing and health care. I was incredibly proud of the work we were doing, excited to be helping my fellow Veterans.

And I was also aware that as the months went by, my biological clock kept ticking louder and louder.

Then, in late 2008, president-elect Barack Obama offered me the position of assistant secretary of public and intergovernmental affairs in the U.S. Department of Veterans Affairs. I jumped at the chance to join the Obama-Biden administration, and in early 2009, I made the move to Washington, DC. Fortunately for us, after returning from Kuwait, Bryan was called up to work as a cybersecurity officer at the National Guard headquarters in the DC suburb of Arlington, Virginia.

After so many years of upheaval, Bryan and I were finally based in the same city with neither of us hospitalized, running ragged on the campaign trail, or deployed. We decided once again to try to start a family, figuring that this was it—now or never. I was forty-one years old.

We tried to conceive naturally, but after several months without success, I decided to bring it up at my annual women's health checkup at the Edward Hines Jr. VA Hospital, just after my forty-second birthday.

"I've been hoping to get pregnant," I told the doctor doing my physical. "But do you think it's too late at my age?"

"Ah, we professional women give up our fertility for our careers, don't we?" she said. "No, it's not too late." She urged us to try for a while longer on our own, then said, "If that doesn't work, I'll refer you to a fertility specialist." When six more months slipped away without success, I circled back, and because the VA didn't have in-house fertility services, my doctor referred me to a partner hospital outside the VA system.

It took a couple more months to get an appointment at the partner facility—which I won't name here, though it's a very well-known and respected hospital. But when I went in, the doctor didn't even examine me, instead just talking to me in a private waiting area. She told me that because I was in my early forties, I wasn't a good candidate for in vitro fertilization, or IVF.

"You're just shy of forty-three," she said, shaking her head. "The success rate for your age group is less than three percent, so I can't really refer you for IVF services." This came as a surprise—I mean, I was old, but not *that* old. But this doctor was a fertility specialist, so I figured she knew what she was talking about. Seeing the disappointment on my face, she looked at me and smiled.

"Listen," she said, "the best thing you can do is just go home, enjoy your husband, and hope for the best!" And with that, she shuffled me out the door.

So, after all that, we had our answer. We wouldn't be having children, at least not biologically, and we'd just have to be okay with that. I went home and told Bryan, who predictably smirked at the "enjoy your husband" line. We both laughed, but I couldn't help but feel sad that we had missed our window. I had waited too long.

When I deployed to Iraq in 2004, the Army issued me a year's worth of birth control patches. This was to regulate the timing of my periods: If I had a mission coming up, I'd use the patch to stop myself from menstruating that month. It was hard enough dealing with how to pee on those long mission days, but it would have been impossible to figure out where and how to change a tampon.

After checking out of Walter Reed in late 2005, I went to the VA to get more patches. "Sorry," a doctor told me. "Those aren't in our formulary." So the government had put me on a particular type of birth control for its own convenience while I was at war. But once I was home, and it was for *my* convenience rather than theirs, I was out of luck. Oh, and guess what *was* in the formulary? Viagra. Yep, any male Veteran could waltz in and get Viagra, but good luck to the female Vets who wanted some control over their own reproductive cycles.

This was so obviously unfair that I lobbied to get the formulary changed—my first time fighting for military women's rights. Four years later, upon becoming the highest-ranking female Veteran in the VA leadership, I had every intention of continuing to fight for women.

As assistant secretary, I visited dozens of VA hospitals around the country. I'd ask for a tour, and some nice administrator would take me through halls decorated with inspirational photos of recovering patients. But inevitably, the patients in those photos were male. "Where are the female Vets?" I'd ask. And they'd take me to the back corner of a rehab room, or to the end of a hallway, and show me a single photo of a woman. "Come on, let's get some women up here," I'd say, marveling anew at the fact that this seemed to be the case at every hospital I visited.

I also found that even in the women's clinics, the vast majority of Veterans on staff were male. So I advised Secretary Eric Shinseki, himself a retired Army General and Vietnam Vet, that we needed to ensure that every women's health clinic in a VA hospital had at least one female Vet working there. These were simple, commonsense steps that wouldn't have been seen as innovative in the civilian world. But for government, they were.

The VA was also behind the times in other ways. I was shocked to find that we had had no systemic organizational ties between the VA and Native American tribal governments, which hindered our ability to provide care for Native American Veterans, especially those who lived on tribal lands. This was inexcusable, so I set up an Office of Tribal Government Relations—a step that should have been taken decades earlier. Similarly, when I discovered that our primary mode of communication with Vets was—drumroll, please—newsletters sent via snail mail, I set up an Office of Online Communications in an effort to drag the VA into the twenty-first century.

But the program I'm most proud of was aimed at getting our homeless Veterans off the streets. In 2010, some 145,000 Veterans were homeless—a shockingly high figure. Many lived in shelters, but nearly half slept on the streets. These were shameful statistics, so the Obama administration launched a plan to end Veterans' homelessness in five years. As the executive sponsor of the VA's portion of that initiative, I worked with the Department of Housing and Urban Development on a program called HUD-VA Supportive Housing (HUD-VASH for short). We provided rental assistance vouchers, health care, mental health care, and substance abuse counseling, and through these measures we were able to dramatically reduce the number of homeless Vets.

But as much good as we were able to do during my two years at the VA, I got fed up pretty quickly with the bureaucratic gridlock. The VA's problems ran deep, and I soon realized that the most effective way to make the changes I wanted was through legislation. So, five years after suffering that crushing election loss in 2006, I decided to try once more for a House seat. This time, I'd be running in Illinois's newly drawn Eighth District, against a first-term Tea Party candidate named Joe Walsh.

Joe Walsh was, to put it politely, a mess. He'd been evicted from his own condo, sued by a former campaign manager, and sued by his ex-wife for failing to make six figures' worth of child support payments. He'd recently had his driver's license suspended after letting his insurance lapse, and had also been caught failing to pay taxes on a trust fund his grandfather had given him. Walsh had been elected to the House in 2010, squeaking out a win by 291 votes—about 0.1 percent of the total. Since then, he hadn't done much except run his mouth, making personal attacks on Democrats from President Obama on down.

As I expected, Walsh started disparaging me as soon as I won the primary in March 2012. That month, he told a *Politico* reporter, "I have so much respect for what she did in the fact that she sacrificed her body for this country." Then he added sarcastically, "Ehhh. Now let's move on. What else has she done? Female, wounded veteran... *ehhh*. She is nothing more than a handpicked Washington bureaucrat."

Walsh, who never served in the military, seemed to have a bee in his bonnet about my service. He kept trying to find ways to turn it against me, never seeming to realize that doing so was backfiring on him. At a campaign event in early July, he derided me for speaking publicly about it. "I'm running against a woman who, my God, it's all she talks about," he said at a town hall. "Our true heroes, the men and women who serve us—it's the last thing in the world they talk about."

Six years earlier, Walsh's attack might have upset me, but now I saw an opportunity to expose him for what he was. In an interview on MSNBC, I said, "He's just trying to shift the focus away from the fact he's done nothing in his two years in Congress other than be an extremist loudmouth for the Tea Party." Besides, his criticism made no sense. My military service was the core of my life—was I really supposed to not talk about it? The simple truth was, being an injured female Soldier helped me bring attention to the causes I cared about. If I could use it as a platform to do good, I had absolutely no qualms about that.

*   *   *

Although national Republicans had steered clear of Joe Walsh in 2010, they didn't want to lose a seat they'd just gained. So in 2012, the firehose opened, and millions of dollars came flooding into Walsh's campaign from outside Illinois. The polls that summer showed a close race, but I was lagging in two demographics that I should have sewn up.

Suburban women and women in their forties were normally strong supporters of Democratic women candidates. Although I was a forty-four-year-old suburban woman myself, my candidacy seemed to have the reverse effect on them. When my pollster Jill Normington sought feedback to find out why, she said, "What we're hearing is that while they admire your service, they can't identify with your life choices." Some women couldn't relate to the fact that I had chosen to become a helicopter pilot. Others were put off by the fact that although I was middle-aged and married, I had no kids.

"We need to show you doing more things with Bryan," Jill said. "Like going on picnics. You know, family stuff." Bryan happened to be in this meeting, so I turned to look at him.

"Yes," he said, nodding seriously. "I'm how you get in touch with your feminine side." He thought this was hilarious—that Mr. "The females at Advanced Camp are all fucked up" was now my secret weapon to win over women voters. It also, unfortunately, played into his favorite sophomoric joke. "I don't understand why guys resist being in touch with their feminine side," he liked to say. "If I had one, I'd be in touch with it *all the time*."

"Okay, smartass," I said, rolling my eyes. I mean, if I needed to talk more about Bryan on the campaign trail, I could certainly do that. I'd done it during the 2006 campaign, telling a *Washington Post* reporter that Bryan was a "true partner": "He annoys me. I annoy him. He chews gum with his mouth open. I leave my legs lying around on the floor." Maybe not your usual candidate quote, but that was our reality.

In September, I was invited to speak at the Democratic National Convention. Walsh apparently couldn't stand the fact that I was getting attention (and he wasn't), so he posted a written statement on his website mocking me.

"Ms. Duckworth has continued to show more interest in rubbing elbows with big-name party insiders, then [*sic*] staying home and tackling the tough issues facing voters in the district," he whined. "It has become abundantly clear that at this point the only debate Ms. Duckworth is actually interested in having is which outfit she'll be wearing for her big speech."

This was mildly irritating, and definitely sexist, but it wasn't worth dwelling on. Walsh must have thought his line was clever, though, because he repeated it in one of our debates the following month. At the time, polls were showing him trailing badly, 38 percent to my 52, so he apparently decided to go out swinging.

He held up a printed photo, taken at the Democratic National Convention, that showed me reaching for a red blazer someone was handing me.

"I was marching in a parade in Schaumburg Sunday, two days before the Democratic convention," he said, "when Tammy Duckworth was on a stage down in Charlotte—if you can look at the picture—*picking out a dress* for her speech Tuesday night."

If he thought he'd score points by fashion-shaming me, he was mistaken. The audience erupted in boos, apparently finding Walsh's maneuver as ridiculous as I did.

"Yes, I do sometimes look at the clothes I wear," I responded. "But for most of my adult life, I've worn one color. It's called camouflage." Enough was enough. I was done with his sexism, his criticism of my military service, and his empty posturing.

Later in the debate, I decided to address Walsh's foolishness head-on.

"My opponent has attempted to criticize me for talking about my military service," I said. "But I served, and he didn't, so you'll forgive me if I talk about it a little bit now—because I think it's important.

"My military service is key to understanding who I am as a person," I went on. "It is at the core of my life of service to this nation. You know, when you're a part of a unit, it's not about the individual; it's about the mission and banding together to get things done."

The audience, apparently as tired of Walsh as I was, broke into applause.

On November 6, 2012, I beat Walsh by more than 20,000 votes, a resounding 10-point margin. He took his sweet time conceding, but I didn't care. I had my staff pipe in ZZ Top's "Legs" and Pat Benatar's "Hit Me with Your Best Shot" during the victory party, savoring every moment and excited to start a new chapter.

Not long after the election, I was speaking on a panel at a women-in-leadership program when someone in the audience asked a question about work-life balance.

These types of questions always come up at women's events, and they're usually about how to juggle kids and a career, so I had an answer prepared.

"Well, I can't really speak to that," I said. "I'm forty-four now, so I missed my chance at motherhood."

I didn't think anything of it—and never had, during the many times I'd used the line. But after the panel, a woman named Judy

Gold (not the comic) came up to me and said, "You know, it's not too late."

Judy was a lawyer, not a doctor, but she seemed to know a lot about fertility. She told me that there were many different treatment options that might help—even something as simple as taking a pill to boost my egg production.

"I know a fantastic fertility doctor in Chicago, Dr. Confino," she told me. "He's knocked up just about every over-forty high-powered woman executive in the Chicagoland area!"

I laughed, and thanked her for the suggestion. But although I was intrigued, I didn't follow up. I had a congressional office to set up, not to mention a whole new job to learn. So I was busy. Or at least, that was the excuse I gave myself for not going.

But Judy, who became a friend, didn't let up. A month or so after that first conversation, she texted to ask if I'd contacted Dr. Confino. I replied that I hadn't, and she gently urged me to do it. I thanked her again—and still didn't go.

Another couple of months went by, and Judy texted again. "You should go," she said. "Really, Tammy—just go talk to him!"

For six months, she kept on me, periodically popping up on my phone with the same message: *Do it, do it, do it!* Finally, by the fifth or sixth time, I decided it couldn't hurt just to make an appointment. Deep down, I didn't actually believe this doctor could help me. I thought that exploring this path would most likely be a waste of time and money, but if I went in for a consultation, at least I could tell Judy I'd tried.

That evening, I brought up the subject with Bryan. I told him about this supposedly amazing fertility specialist, and said, "That other doctor told me IVF wasn't an option. But I don't know—maybe it actually is?"

"Well," Bryan said, "it can't hurt to ask, right?"

I just shrugged. I was forty-five now, and it was clear I wasn't going to get pregnant naturally. What did we have to lose? So I made an appointment in the summer of 2013. Bryan was in Washington, so on that first visit, it would be just me.

From my first meeting with Dr. Edmond Confino, at his office in the Northwestern Memorial Hospital, I could tell I was in good hands. He had a direct, no-baloney way of speaking, combined with the most caring, gentle bedside manner I had ever encountered in a physician—and I've spent a lot of time with physicians. He was also a military Veteran, having served in the Israel Defense Forces as a young doctor, so we shared that connection.

When he asked me about our efforts to get pregnant so far, I told him about my visit to the fertility specialist in 2010, three years earlier. "I was forty-two then," I said, "and the doctor informed me I wasn't a suitable candidate for fertility treatment because of my age."

He asked which hospital the doctor was affiliated with. When I told him, he nodded. "This is typical of Catholic medical institutions," he said. "They often don't inform patients of protocols that might violate the teachings of the Catholic Church."

I stared at him, feeling the blood drain from my face. "I'm sorry," I said. "Could you say that again?"

"Unfortunately, this happens a lot," Dr. Confino said. "Doctors at Catholic-affiliated hospitals don't tell women about procedures the Church frowns on."

I was dumbfounded—but only for a moment, because that feeling was instantly replaced by searing anger. How on earth could a medical doctor—a fertility specialist!—fail to inform a patient about *all* of her options? How was it legal, or ethical, for a doctor to treat a patient according to a religious doctrine the patient doesn't even believe in? I mean, it's one thing for a Catholic hospital to refuse to perform procedures that go against Church teaching. Fine. But when a woman is hoping to get pregnant, and IVF is a realistic option, how could any principled doctor simply send her home with the glib advice to "enjoy your husband"?

Not only that, but I had been referred by a federal agency, the Department of Veterans Affairs, so going to that particular institution was my only option if I wanted insurance coverage. I never could have imagined that, in following the referral of a *federal* service, I might be forced to follow the dictates of someone else's religious teachings. Whatever happened to separation of church and state?

When that doctor had told me the success rate for women my age was less than 3 percent, she was referring to the limited services offered at her hospital, which didn't include fertilizing eggs outside the body to grow embryos—one of the most common ways older women get pregnant. She could very easily have said, "There are other, more successful methods of IVF that we don't perform here, but you can explore them at other institutions." And then I would have just gone to another hospital—and not lost three years of possible fertility.

I was infuriated, but after the initial shock, I also felt dumb. I was a well-educated, high-ranking government official, and I had simply taken the word of a single doctor who hadn't even bothered to examine me. It just never occurred to me that any medical professional would withhold crucial health care information. And if it hadn't occurred to me, even with all of my experience with doctors and hospitals, it probably hadn't occurred to thousands of other women this might have happened to. How many women who wanted to become mothers had been denied their dream because of bad advice like this?

Following that conversation with Dr. Confino, I decided to take on the cause of women's right to control their own bodies. I've spoken out often on the need to abolish religious gag rules, and pushed to repeal the Hyde Amendment, which forbids federal reimbursement for abortion and abortion-related services. This law is incredibly harmful, especially for women in government service; I've learned of cases where Peace Corps volunteers and military servicewomen who've been sexually assaulted were denied access to abortion services for the resulting pregnancy.

I've also worked to change the VA's rules so that fertility services—even those opposed by Catholic institutions—will be covered. And these changes aren't just about women's rights. Many of our young, war-wounded servicemen suffered groin injuries in landmine explosions, rendering them unable to produce sperm. As long as the VA's IVF program doesn't allow for third-party donation of sperm or eggs, these young Veterans will be unable to get the medical care they need to start their own families. Considering everything that our brave Veterans, both men and women, have given to us as a nation, we at least owe them the right to pursue having a family however they choose.

A few weeks after my first visit to Dr. Confino, Bryan and I went to see him together. He talked us through the steps we could take, starting with the most minimally invasive and working up to more complex procedures. Bryan and I both liked the fact that he was methodical and very clear about what to expect. "This will be a repetitive process," he told us. "But we'll just take it step by step."

And that's what we did, for months on end. We went through all the protocols—taking fertility meds, increasing the number of eggs I was producing, harvesting those eggs, and attempting to fertilize them. We did multiple cycles at each level, but each one ended in disappointment.

At one point, Dr. Confino asked me, "Did you have a lot of X-rays at Walter Reed?"

"Oh, yeah," I said. "All the time." During the first weeks after the shootdown, I'd had my wounds debrided under general anesthesia every day, and the doctors took X-rays every time. Because I'd lost my right leg all the way up to my hip, I'd also had numerous X-rays that included my lower right abdomen. And when the doctors had sewn my right arm to my rib cage for the muscle flap surgery, they'd taken them then too.

"That's probably what's affecting your fertility," he told me. This made sense, and I knew there hadn't been any alternative to having all those X-rays. But at the same time, I couldn't help but feel sick that the bastard who shot us down might have stolen not just my Army career but my fertility too.

Thankfully, that didn't end up being the case. In February 2014, a month before my forty-sixth birthday—and nine months after I first set foot in Dr. Confino's office—I got pregnant.

I was simultaneously excited...and incredibly scared. I started obsessively checking stats on a pregnancy app, reading about what the survival rates were at different weeks. At nine weeks, I'd be "officially" pregnant, so I basically held my breath until making it to that point. At sixteen weeks, Bryan and I told our families and a handful of our closest friends. From there, I just needed to make it to twenty-four weeks, when the survival rate for premature babies jumps. I started every day with the app, devouring information about how big my baby was and how she was developing. It also offered suggestions for which foods to eat, and I remember thinking that if told to eat a bag of live frogs, I would do it. Hey, I was in the Army—I'm trained to do whatever is necessary to accomplish the mission.

Every woman has a different experience of being pregnant, so I didn't know what to expect. I had no reason to think my injuries would play any role, even though some effects lingered. Nearly ten years after the shootdown, I had phantom pain in my legs and could still feel burning on the soles of my nonexistent feet. My right arm was healed, though it had limited mobility. And although shrapnel pieces were no longer falling out of my skin, I still had dozens of metal bits embedded throughout my torso, arms, and face. But fortunately, my reproductive organs were all intact. And I was also now in my best physical shape since before the shootdown, doing Pilates three times a week, riding my hand-crank bicycle, and feeling great.

Being pregnant made me feel even better. I loved every minute of it, never suffering any morning sickness. In the spring of 2014, I launched my reelection campaign for Congress, and my pregnancy didn't slow me down at all. I did have cravings, but even those were healthy: All I wanted to eat was fruit! I'd devour a pound of persimmons, or have five pears for dinner. My mom, who moved in with us when I got pregnant, would cut up a watermelon and put it in a mixing bowl, and I'd eat the whole thing with a big smile on my face.

When the baby started kicking, I held my breath, afraid it was just a dream. Soon, I became obsessed with counting how many times she kicked, constantly checking the app for the number of kicks per hour that signified a healthy baby. Having spent so many years not wanting children, I now felt overwhelmed and grateful at the miracle that was happening in my body. But knowing the risks associated with a "geriatric" pregnancy (a term many older moms despise, but which I found hilarious), we held off on telling anyone outside our closest circle of friends and family.

I did tell one other person, though: Matt Backues. Matt was the guy who, on the day of the shootdown, had teamed up with Dan Milberg to half carry, half drag my blood-soaked body to the second helicopter. While he was fighting to save my life, he had looked up to see two other Black Hawk helicopters roar overhead. Incredibly enough, the crew chief in one of them, Specialist Judy Soto, would later become Matt's wife. Sharing the experience of that terrible day in Iraq bonded us together, and we all became friends. Matt and Judy even worked as volunteers for my 2012 campaign, and appeared in a couple of videos for me.

That summer, Matt called to tell me that Judy was pregnant. "Oh my gosh, that's so great!" I said, then blurted, "Me too!" I felt such joy in that moment—just pure elation that ten years after Matt had looked death in the face to save my life, he and I would now get to share the experience of bringing new life into this world.

In September 2014, I decided to retire from the Army after twenty-three years of service. This was an incredibly difficult decision, because I wasn't at all ready to leave. For my entire adult life, the Army had been my home, and my fellow Soldiers my family. Every day, I lived the lines of the Soldier's Creed: *I am a warrior and a member of a team. I serve the people of the United States, and live the Army Values.* These weren't just words to me; they formed the core of my being. Serving my country in peacetime and in combat, on the ground and in the air, had meant absolutely everything to me.

Since leaving Walter Reed, I had continued to serve as a drilling Guardsman, performing one weekend of service a month, plus two weeks of summer training each year. Because I had started receiving a disability pension after the shootdown, I wasn't getting paid for these days of service—and in addition, I also had to pay for my own plane tickets and hotel stays, all for the privilege of continuing to serve.

I would have continued to do so, as I wasn't ready to take off my uniform for the last time. But I knew that by staying in the Army, occupying one of a limited number of slots for Lieutenant Colonels, I was preventing some other worthy officer from attaining that rank. Over the past few years, I had seen my peers either get promoted or retire, while I was stuck in limbo. I was never going to realize my dream of commanding a battalion, and it was unlikely I'd get promoted to Colonel without career moves I couldn't realistically make. Given that, there was nothing more I could do in the Army.

These thoughts swirled in my head for a few weeks, and eventually I talked it over with Bryan, who supported my plan to retire. I didn't tell anyone else, but decided to make my move during my next scheduled drill weekend at Camp Lincoln in Springfield.

I flew back to Illinois, put on my beloved camouflage, and reported to the morning assembly, as I'd done for so many weekends over the past quarter century. The assembly always started with the First Sergeant asking the question "Who's drilling for the first time today?" I watched with envy as a fresh young Private or Lieutenant lifted a hand. Then, "Who's drilling for the *last* time today?" With a lump forming in my throat, I lifted my own. I was seven months pregnant, and the most wrenching part of this decision was knowing that my daughter would never get to see me serve in uniform. But it was time.

On October 14, 2014, I retired from the United States Army. Two weeks later, I completed a PhD in Human Services from Capella University—a goal I'd set after my doctoral studies at NIU were derailed by my deployment and the shootdown. On

November 6, I won election to a second term in the House of Representatives. And on November 12, I celebrated my ten-year Alive Day. I couldn't help but think that my younger self, climbing into my Black Hawk that long-ago morning in Iraq, could never have imagined where I'd be a decade later: a double-amputee, retired-Army, thirty-seven-weeks-pregnant member of Congress.

Less than a week later, on Monday, November 17, I went to my ob-gyn, Dr. Alan Peaceman, for a checkup. The baby wasn't due until the first week of December, and I still felt great, so I figured this would be a routine visit.

"Well," Dr. Peaceman said, after a short examination, "it's time."

"Time for what?" I asked.

"Time to induce," he told me. "The baby is quite small, stuck in the tenth percentile of size. So we need to move."

"Ah, okay," I said. "I'll have my scheduler, Kelsey, give you a call. I have to fly to DC to vote tonight, but we'll be done by Thursday. So maybe Thursday evening or Friday?"

Dr. Peaceman smiled at me kindly but with a hint of amused indulgence. "Sorry," he said. "I mean now. This is no longer a Congresswoman Tammy Duckworth scheduling question. This is 'You are leaving my clinic right now and checking into the hospital.'"

Because I'm a hyperprepared individual (and love to pack a go-bag!), I already had a duffel packed with clothes, toiletries, and all the necessary documents in my minivan. I rolled out to the parking lot, grabbed the bag, and rolled right into the hospital. On the way, I called Bryan, who was in Washington.

"Hey," I said. "They're inducing me."

"Okay," he said. "When?"

"I'm checking into the hospital now."

"Oh. Interesting," he said. "Um, I'm actually on my way to lunch." There was a pause, and then I heard him say, "Hey guys, I'm going to have to drop you off. I've gotta get to the airport." With luck, we hoped he might be able to catch a flight quickly and get to me before our daughter was born.

While planning for the birth, Dr. Peaceman had asked whether I wanted to schedule a cesarean.

I shook my head. "I'd like to try for natural childbirth," I told him.

"Okay," he said. "And by 'natural,' you mean you don't want an epidural?"

"Oh *hell no*," I said, laughing. "Give me the pain meds! I've spent enough time in hospitals in pain. Get that epidural *ready*!" I had no need to prove anything by enduring the pain. Been there, done that.

The doctors gave me the epidural an hour into my labor, and thank goodness they did, because giving birth to Abigail turned out to be an epic struggle. I pushed and I pushed, but she wouldn't budge. The doctor told me she had one arm above her head, so every time he'd check on her, he'd say, "Hey, your daughter's high-fiving me!" Too tired to smile, I just kept on pushing, a task made harder by the fact that I couldn't wear my legs, so I had no way to brace myself against the stirrups.

Bryan got to the hospital on Monday night, but as it turned out, he really didn't need to rush. After being induced on Monday morning, I went into labor that afternoon...which continued into that night...and then into Tuesday morning...to Tuesday after-noon...and still Abigail wouldn't come out. As it turned out, both of Abigail's arms were above her head, and she was wedged into my pelvis so tightly that it seemed like a cesarean was the only way she could make it into the world.

Finally, one of the doctors said, "Okay, Tammy. You're exhausted, and we can't keep trying—it's too dangerous for you and the baby. We need to do an emergency C-section." The words released a flood of emotion in me. Part of me was relieved, because I was exhausted from more than thirty hours of active labor. But I was also achingly sad. I wanted so badly to give birth naturally, which felt like the *right* way. Tired, emotionally overwrought, and desperate for it to be over so I could finally hold my baby in my arms, I managed to nod weakly through tears.

Being back in an operating room wasn't hard for me, but it was for Bryan. He sat right by my head and kept an eye on the monitors, watching intently as my vital signs fluctuated. When the doctors cut me open, my blood pressure dropped, and Bryan started to freak out. "What's going on?" he asked. "Is my wife okay?"

"She's fine," the anesthesiologist said. "You just focus on the baby." But hearing the beeping, whirring machines and seeing me lying in distress in a hospital bed were like a traumatic flashback for him. He broke into a sweat, his own heart rate rising. As magical as giving birth is, thirty-six hours into the process, we were both *so* ready for it to be over.

Finally, at 10 P.M. on Tuesday, November 18, my sweet, precious little fighter Abigail was born. She didn't cry at first, which scared me half to death. "What's wrong?" I asked. "Is she okay?" The doctors quickly suctioned her, and she took her first deep breath—and then let loose an earsplitting wail.

"Oh my God!" Bryan said, laughing. "She's *so maaaaad!*"

A nurse put Abigail on my chest, but I couldn't keep her there because my left arm was tied up with IVs and a blood pressure cuff, and my right arm wasn't stable enough to hold her. Then I started having a hard time breathing, so the team whisked her away and moved me straight into a recovery room. I'm not sure how long I lay there, but the hours felt long and agonizing, because I wasn't getting to hold my baby. When my breathing and vital signs finally stabilized, a nurse came in and handed Abigail to me.

She was a tiny thing, less than five pounds, and as she lay on my chest, she hitched up her little legs like a frog. The moment her skin touched mine, my whole body flooded with relief, love, joy—a whole universe of emotions. I couldn't believe this little girl, this tiny, precious being, was ours. She and I lay there together, breathing as one, bonding to each other. I never wanted to let her go.

Bryan and I wanted to give Abigail a Hawaiian name, but according to tradition, you can't just pick one yourself. You have to ask a Hawaiian elder to choose, and a Hawaiian priest to bless the name.

So a couple of months before Abigail was born, we had asked our friend Mark Takai for help. Mark was in the Hawaii House of Representatives, and he—like me—was campaigning for a seat in the U.S. House in 2014. We had plans to make some campaign appearances for him in Honolulu, so before flying down I gave him a call. "We want to give our daughter a Hawaiian name," I told him. "Do you know any elders and priests?"

"Sure," he said. "Let me make some calls."

After Bryan and I arrived in Hawaii, Mark invited us to meet him at Zippy's, the Hawaiian equivalent of a Denny's, for breakfast. Walking in, we were shocked to find him sitting there with Senator Daniel Akaka. Senator Akaka was a legend—a World War II Veteran and the first Native Hawaiian to serve in the U.S. Senate. "Here's your elder," Mark said with a smile. "And his son is a priest!"

As we sat down, Senator Akaka slid a piece of paper across the table. Bryan and I read the names printed on it, and we were both drawn to one in particular, Kalei Makamae Okalani. But then we exchanged a look, and I knew we were having the same thought: These were all beautiful names, but they were *loooong*. Seeing our glance, Senator Akaka laughed. "It's okay," he said. "You don't have to use the whole thing. You can just use 'Okalani' for short, as her middle name."

In the Hawaiian language, Kalei Makamae Okalani roughly means "beloved child from heaven." We were honored to have Senator Akaka bestow her Hawaiian name, but we ultimately decided to call her Abigail, after Bryan's sister—who was herself named after Abigail Adams. And so she became Abigail Okalani Duckworth Bowlsbey—our little gift from the heavens.

Nine years after we first started trying to get pregnant, Bryan and I finally had our baby girl. Now we could simply relax into family life.

Or so we thought.

Chapter 14

A Score to Settle

When Abigail was just learning to speak, Bryan loved to ask her questions. "Abigail, who's this?" he'd say, holding up her favorite teddy bear. Or "Who's that?"—and he'd point at me. She'd pipe up in her reedy little voice, and as she got older and learned more words, he kept up the game, moving on to trickier questions.

One morning, he asked, "Abigail, what's Daddy's name?"

"Bryan," she said.

"What's Mommy's name?"

"*Tammy Duckworth*," she declared in a weird, low voice. Bryan and I cracked up—what was *that* all about? Why did our toddler suddenly sound like she was channeling James Earl Jones? Then I realized: This was what Abigail heard whenever she saw my face on TV. In her first eighteen months of life, our little girl had already seen dozens of political spots, either attack ads against the terrible *Tammy Duckworth* or ads from my Senate campaign in which I'd intone, "I'm Tammy Duckworth, and I approve this message."

I had been running for the Senate since Abigail was four months old—nearly her entire life. It's the reason why I almost decided not to run.

*   *   *

For the first three months after Abigail's birth, I reveled in the joy of my new baby. She was a feisty little one, with curly hair and long eyelashes like her father's, and every time she'd reach her tiny arms toward me, my heart melted. We had decided to breastfeed her, and I couldn't get enough of those bonding moments with my precious gift from the heavens.

Having just won reelection to the House of Representatives by more than 10 percentage points, I was also in a great place politically. I liked serving in the House, and with one term under my belt, I knew its quirks and procedures. I could continue my work there and build seniority, but there was another race to consider. Republican Mark Kirk, the junior senator from Illinois, was up for reelection in 2016, and in early 2015, Democrats were already lining up to take their shot.

Although Illinois's primary vote wasn't until March 2016, the primary campaigns would start a full year before then. Already, in January 2015, donors, party chairs, and other possible candidates were calling me to find out if I was running. I wasn't even off maternity leave yet, but if I wanted to enter the race, it would be in my own best interest to announce that and hopefully clear the Democratic field.

So for the whole three months of my maternity leave, Bryan and I went back and forth about whether I should run for Kirk's seat. It was definitely tempting, as I knew I could have more impact as a senator than as one of 435 members of the House. I also loved the idea of being able to serve all the people of Illinois, as I'd done while IDVA director. I matched up well against Kirk, who like me was both a Veteran and disabled. And because Dick Durbin held our other Senate seat, I knew that if I didn't run now, I wouldn't have another chance until 2022 at the earliest—and maybe not even then, if a Democrat won the seat in 2016. From a political standpoint, if I wanted to serve in the U.S. Senate, this was the best time for me to run.

But personally, the timing wasn't ideal. Senate campaigns are long slogs, and this one promised to be particularly grueling. The Republicans desperately wanted to hold on to the seat, which meant they'd throw everything they had at the Democratic candidate. This was bound to be a nasty race. Was I really ready for a year-plus-long brawl, especially one that would take me on the road, away from my baby?

As the end of my maternity leave approached, I couldn't decide what to do. Then Senator Kirsten Gillibrand, who had campaigned throughout 2010 after giving birth to her son Henry in 2008, offered me a brutally honest piece of advice.

"Listen, spending so much time away from your baby will tear you up," she told me. "But Abigail will be too young to remember any of this. And when you're a senator, you'll only have to campaign once every six years, instead of every other year."

Kirsten's words tipped the balance, and in March 2015, I announced my candidacy. I hated the idea of being away from Abigail, but if I wanted a chance at the Senate, the time to act was now. I just hoped that what Kirsten said was true, that Abigail would be too young to remember our spending so much time apart.

I made a rule never to be away from Abigail for more than one night, and told my staff to schedule my events accordingly. This wasn't hard to do when I was in Illinois, but when I started making fund-raising trips across the country, life got complicated. I was taking a lot of long flights, and no matter where I was, I had to express breast milk every three hours, then make sure it stayed cold or frozen until I got home. I took a lot of red-eyes, stumbling bleary-eyed into the house at 7 A.M. and starting my mommy shift when Abigail woke up. Then, after a couple of hours, it was back to the office for another packed schedule of campaign events. By the end of each day, sleep-deprived and drained, I felt like there was nothing left of me.

Kirsten was right about one thing: That campaign tore me up. During my races for the House, my biggest mental and emotional challenges were the attacks from my opponents. Now the biggest challenge by far was spending so much time away from my baby. And because the Senate race was so long, the months kept piling on top of each other. I was rushing around the country, working hard to raise money and boost my polling numbers, but never making as much progress as I wanted to. Meanwhile, back at home, Abigail was growing and changing fast, and I was missing moments of her life that I could never get back.

The stress felt like water pushing against a dam. It was only a matter of time before it broke.

In March of 2016, I decisively won the primary against two other candidates. But after a solid year of campaigning, not to mention my first year of being a mom, I was exhausted. And unbeknownst to everyone except our closest circle, Bryan and I were once again trying to get pregnant.

The timing wasn't great, but we wanted Abigail to have a sibling, and at forty-eight I didn't have the luxury of waiting. We underwent several IVF procedures that didn't take, and then— success! Bryan and I were ecstatic, unable to believe our luck that another little one was on the way. Knowing the pregnancy was high-risk, we didn't tell anyone, and I just held my breath in those early weeks, eager to make it to the six-week ultrasound.

In late April, several weeks into my pregnancy, I gathered my staff for an off-site progress review to talk strategy. (Most campaigns call these "retreats," but I'm a U.S. Army Veteran. We do not *retreat*. We *progress*.) This was a big quarterly meeting, with senior staff, pollsters, and strategists from organizations such as the Democratic Senatorial Campaign Committee and EMILY's List—about twenty-five people in all.

With the whole group sitting around a conference table in downtown Chicago, people were throwing out ideas for how to get my poll numbers up. Although I had maintained a steady lead against Senator Kirk, my numbers were stagnant, so we were trying to figure out how to widen the gap. Not surprisingly, most of the suggestions involved having me do more trips, more calls, more events.

As I sat there listening, my spirits sank. I was bone tired, nervous about my pregnancy, and giving myself daily shots of blood thinners and progesterone (and those needles were *big*). I was working my butt off, spending hours of my life fulfilling a million tasks on my schedule, but it was never enough. It was like I was on a hamster wheel that never stopped going around. Whenever I worked harder on campaigning, it took me away from my baby. When I spent time trying to be a better mother, the campaign suffered. Never mind trying to get any quality time with my husband—just as in campaigns past, we were like ships passing in the night. In trying to do everything, I was doing nothing well. And somehow, even after a year on the road, there were still five months of campaigning to go.

In that moment, I realized that as much as my campaign team needed me to do this, that, or the other thing, there was only one person in the world who *actually* needed me: Abigail. I hadn't been there for her in this first year of her life, and now these people were trying to get me to spend even less time with her. *Do this, do that, go here, go there.* I was a windup doll, cranked to the straining point and doing my dance over and over.

My bad mood was evident to everyone in the room, so my chief of staff, Kaitlin Fahey, called for a snack break. Someone brought in packets of Twizzlers, pretzels, Goldfish—your usual campaign junk food. I usually like Twizzlers, but newly pregnant me was craving something sour. And that was what finally pushed me over the edge.

"Well, this is classic," I said. "Of course nobody bothers to get a single snack I actually *like*. Because nobody here gives a shit about *me*. I'm just a *commodity*."

The room fell silent as two dozen shocked faces turned toward me. "Seriously, this is ridiculous!" I snapped, the frustration of the last year now spewing out. "Everybody makes demands of me, but nobody cares what *I* need."

For an uncomfortable moment, the room was silent. Then Kaitlin spoke.

"Tammy, I'm pretty sure we're all here quite literally *for you* and your campaign, not for ourselves," she said quietly. "No one is forcing you to do anything. You hired us to tell you how to win, and now you're getting mad at us for it."

She was right, of course. But I was too wound up to be swayed by logic. I was a ball of emotion—pissed off at my team, but really at myself. What was I doing? Why had I ever agreed to spend the first year and a half of my baby's life running around, chasing some political brass ring? I was tired of being a subpar candidate and a subpar mother.

I pushed away from the conference table and rolled into a little attached kitchen area, where sandwiches had been set out for lunch. After a few minutes, Kaitlin and my pollster Jill Normington walked over. "Mind if we join you?" Jill asked. I didn't particularly want company, but I nodded, and they slid the partition doors shut to give us some privacy.

"You know," Jill said gently, "there's this idea that women can do it all, but we can't." I just looked at her. I knew Jill and her wife had a son, but we had never talked about motherhood. "This whole 'work-life balance' thing isn't real," she went on. "It's just a lie we tell women in this country over and over again. And it sucks."

Like so many working women, I'd been hearing and reading about "work-life balance" for years. I had been on panels, such as the one where I met Judy Gold, where every other question seemed to be about finding that balance. I had listened while women discussed and debated Sheryl Sandberg's *Lean In*, which had come out a few years earlier. So it's not like I'd never heard what Jill was telling me that day. But this was the first time I really *heard* it. I was tired and overwhelmed, and I felt inadequate to my tasks every day. The simple act of hearing another working mom validate those feelings filled me with relief.

"It's our job to ask you for things," Jill said. "But there's no way you can meet all the demands. You just have to pick and choose, and not drive yourself crazy trying to do the perfect thing every single time." I felt my eyes well up, because this was exactly what I'd been doing ever since Abigail was born. "Let go of the guilt," she said. "Just do the best you can."

Jill's words reminded me of a concept I learned in the Army: the 80 percent solution. As Army leaders, we were trained to recognize that the 100 percent solution—absolute perfection—isn't realistic, so the 80 percent solution was our goal: Get most things right, and get your butt moving to accomplish the mission. If you have 80 percent handled and a well-trained team, you'll be able to deal with whatever contingencies arise. But if you spend all your time planning to create the 100 percent perfect solution, the troops won't have time to prepare, train, and actually execute the mission.

I had never thought to apply the 80 percent rule to motherhood, but it made absolute sense. In fact, it was the *only* solution that made sense. I had spent my life in pursuit of that 100 percent score—and more often than not, I failed to achieve it. But the scores I did get—the mostly A's and a few B's, or the 96 percent test score—had served me well. Besides that, there's no such thing as the perfect mother, so as a new mom, I had to find a way to let that go or risk driving myself, my family, and my staff crazy.

All I could do was be the best mother, and the best candidate, that I could. And that would have to be enough.

Not long after that off-site meeting, I went in for my six-week ultrasound, and there it was—the baby's tiny heartbeat. Seeing that, I felt my own heart soar, and I beamed at Dr. Confino, who was also smiling. "It's a good sign that we can see the heartbeat this early," he said. Then he reminded me that, as we had done with Abigail, we'd wait until the nine-week ultrasound before transferring my care to the ob-gyn, Dr. Peaceman.

Three weeks later, in June 2016, I came back in for that ultrasound. I was lying in the exam room, chatting with the technician who was moving the wand over my belly, when she suddenly got very quiet. "I'm just going to get Dr. Confino," she said, and left the room. She was gone for only a moment, but that was long enough for a wave of dread to wash over me. Dr. Confino walked in, picked up the ultrasound wand, and silently moved it across my belly. I stared at the screen, desperately trying to make out anything that looked like an embryo. There was nothing.

"I'm sorry, Tammy," he said. "We've lost the pregnancy." I lay there, stunned, as the technician started wiping the jelly off my skin. Dr. Confino put his hand on my arm and said, "Come into my office when you're dressed." Then he turned and walked out of the room.

Feeling numb, I put my clothes back on and made my way down the hall. Bryan hadn't been able to come with me that day, so it was just Dr. Confino and me in his office. Gently, he said, "Often, the body will end a pregnancy that isn't viable because of a chromosomal abnormality in the embryo. Go home, get some rest. And then we'll need to schedule you for a D&C"—a dilation and curettage procedure, to clear out my uterus.

"That will tell us more about what happened, and then we can talk about your next options," he said, then reminded me that we still had more frozen embryos.

Dr. Confino and his nurse left the room so I could make phone calls in private. But I just stared at the wall for what felt like a long time, drained of thought and unable to move. It was a strange feeling, because my first reaction to challenges in my life has always been to take action. When I woke up to find out I no longer had legs, the first thing I did was ask Bryan to put me to work on my recovery. But in that little room in the fertility clinic, I just sat there, blank and immobile. *Strange*, I thought. *Shouldn't I be weeping? What's wrong with me?*

Feeling like I was outside my own body, I watched my hand pick up my phone and dial Bryan. He didn't answer. Then I dialed Kaitlin, who knew that I was seeing Dr. Confino that day.

"Hey," I said quietly. "I'm still at my appointment. Just to let you know, I've had a miscarriage." I hadn't thought about how she might respond, but I guess I expected some words of condolence followed by a discussion about scheduling. To my surprise, Kaitlin—who'd given birth to her first baby just a year earlier—burst into tears. "Oh, Tammy," she said. "I'm so, so sorry."

Kaitlin's heartfelt response shattered the numbness that had enveloped me, and I was suddenly overcome with the rawest, most painful emotion I had ever experienced. In that moment, losing this baby felt more searing than anything I'd ever felt—even worse than hearing my husband tell me I had lost my legs. It was as if a void was opening up to swallow me in that little office, and I sat there, phone in hand, and sobbed.

After a few minutes, I tried calling Bryan again. This time I got through. In a voice still thick with emotion, I told him what had happened, and he was quiet for what felt like a long time. Then, gently, he asked, "Tammy, are you all right?" I said yes, even though I felt anything but all right. We spoke only briefly, saving our longer conversation for later, when I was out of the clinic.

I took a few deep breaths, willing myself to calm down so I could make my way back to my car. As I started to roll out of the office, Dr. Confino's nurse offered to show me a private way out, so I wouldn't have to stop and talk to anyone who might recognize me. The last thing I wanted was to have someone asking me why I was here, or guessing what had happened after seeing my tear-streaked face. As bad as this news was, we had to keep it to ourselves.

No one knew. Not our Democratic allies, our campaign team (besides Kaitlin and Kelsey), or the press. Nobody. It was a very lonely feeling to have to wrap this piercing grief so tightly inside me, to pretend like everything was okay. Bryan came with me for the D&C procedure, and I allowed myself two days of bed rest afterward, but all the while the phone kept ringing, the emails kept coming, the requests for my time and energy kept pouring in. If I wanted to win that Senate seat, I would have to keep running, hustling, and working—even through the most emotionally devastating event of my life.

And so I did. Because that was the only way to move forward, and moving forward is what I've always done. It's what I *have* to do.

I ended up beating Mark Kirk by 14 percentage points in that race. You could certainly argue that winning made all the pain of that campaign worthwhile, and of course I'm incredibly proud to be a senator. But if I had known going into the race how truly agonizing that summer would be, it would have given me pause. The 2016 campaign pushed me to my limits in ways I couldn't have foreseen. And while it ended with me winning a Senate seat, it also ended with Donald Trump winning the White House. Now, more than ever, it was time to get to work.

On January 3, 2017, Vice President Joe Biden officially swore in all the newly elected and reelected senators on the Senate floor. Bryan brought Abigail, and perched up in the gallery seats above the chamber, she craned her neck to see down to where I was sitting.

Abigail had just turned two, and she'd had quite a run over the winter. With her birthday in November, then Christmas in December, she had gotten used to seeing piles of presents magically appear. So when Vice President Biden began his remarks by saying something about our "presence" in the chamber, Abigail piped up, "*Presents?*" She was too far away for me to hear, but according to Bryan, her little voice reverberated through the dome of the Senate chamber, and most of the gallery had a good laugh over it.

By tradition, the official swearing-in is followed by a smaller ceremonial one, held in the Old Senate Chamber. This is when each senator takes the oath of office individually, with family present. I stood facing the vice president, my right hand raised and my left resting on a copy of the Constitution that Bryan was holding. Mom was standing next to me, holding Abigail, who was decked out in her best pink jacket and sparkly shoes.

Vice President Biden was in full Uncle Joe mode that day, cracking dad jokes and tickling kids, and halfway through administering the oath of office to me, he leaned toward Abigail and began reciting it directly to her, asking if she would "well and faithfully discharge the duties of the office upon which you are about to enter, so help you God!" As cameras clicked, and even though he wasn't looking at me, I said, "I will." Just at that moment, Abigail decided she'd had enough, throwing her head back and uttering a groan as everybody burst into laughter.

"I guess she's not so sure," the vice president cracked—although a few people noted that he actually did seem to have sworn in my daughter instead of me.

It was a funny moment, and I was happy that Abigail was able to take part in it. But what really felt meaningful was having my mom there. This woman, who had overcome so much—losing her own mother, working as a child laborer, struggling through poverty, and raising my brother and me through every kind of crisis—was at my side as I took the oath for one of the highest elective offices in the United States. We stood there together with my daughter, three generations of Asian American women, proud to be part of this country we loved.

I entered the Senate just as Barbara Mikulski, the legendary Democrat from Maryland, retired. Senator Mikulski had the distinction of being the longest-serving woman in U.S. congressional history, having served forty years—a decade in the House, followed by five terms in the Senate.

Just under five feet tall, she was also well known for not taking crap from anybody, and for fighting relentlessly for the rights of women and minorities during her long service to this country. She was one of two senators who in 1973 bucked the rules insisting that women had to wear dresses on the Senate floor, thereby ushering in the pantsuit era.

So you can imagine how thrilled I was when I went to the Senate floor, pulled open the drawer of the desk I'd been assigned, and discovered her name among those scrawled inside. For more than a hundred years, senators have written their names on those antique mahogany desk drawers in the chamber, creating a historic record of the men and women who worked there. Having that connection to "Senator Barb," who'd served Bryan's home state of Maryland, felt really meaningful for me.

And she wasn't the only great senator who'd used my desk. Peering into the drawer, I also saw the names of Barack Obama, Paul Wellstone, Illinois's own Paul Simon, and Robert Kennedy. I'd never imagined becoming a U.S. senator, so simply being in this chamber felt amazing. But knowing I would one day be adding my name to this roster of great Americans who'd sat at this desk felt absolutely surreal.

In July 2017, six months after becoming a senator, I got pregnant once again.

This pregnancy was harder than the one I'd had with Abigail. Luckily, I still didn't have any morning sickness, but I was a lot more tired. For one thing, I was forty-nine years old. And now, with a toddler at home and a demanding job, I hadn't been able to exercise as regularly. It seemed like every day brought a new adventure in heartburn, and of course I was terrified we might lose this baby too.

But to our relief and joy, the pregnancy went to term, and Maile Pearl Bowlsbey came flying out of me in April 2018, less than a month after my fiftieth birthday. And when I say she flew out of me, I mean this spunky little girl didn't waste a minute. With Abigail, I was in labor for thirty-six agonizing hours, followed by an emergency cesarean. In comparison, I nearly gave birth to Maile in an ambulance rushing me to the hospital, less than an hour after I'd first noticed contractions.

Once again, we asked Senator Akaka to gift our baby with a Hawaiian name. He was ninety-three and very ill at the time, and in fact his own life would come to an end just two days after hers began. But he blessed her with the name Maile, which is a ceremonial lei, made from a fragrant mountain vine, that Hawaiians wear on their most auspicious occasions. Wearing leis, which represent love, respect, and blessings—the spirit of aloha—is one of my favorite Hawaiian traditions, and Bryan and I both loved the choice Senator Akaka made.

Giving our girls Hawaiian names was a way for me to honor my first U.S. home, the place where I had grown from a child to an adult. For Maile's middle name, though, we decided to honor a beloved member of Bryan's family.

Bryan's great-aunt Pearl Bowlsbey Johnson was the family rebel. She'd grown up on a farm in Maryland during the Depression years, and as a young woman in the early 1940s, instead of getting married, she enlisted in the Army. She became an Army nurse, serving on the USAHS *Frances Y. Slanger*, a hospital ship that transported wounded American troops and German prisoners of war from Europe to the United States. Pearl always wore a shawl over her uniform, but not because she liked the way it looked. She tucked an M1911 .45-caliber pistol underneath it, in case any of the German POWs acted up.

As a kid, Bryan spent his summers scampering around barefoot at Great-Aunt Pearl's Chesapeake Bay house, a ramshackle cottage with no running water and an outhouse. Pearl had hung a photo of the *Frances Y. Slanger* on the cottage wall, and she'd kept her canteen and helmet from the war years. She also bought a surplus Army jeep, which she drove like a bat out of hell, telling Bryan that "half the road is mine, and I prefer to take the half right down the middle."

Pearl was in her seventies when Bryan and I got together, and by that time she was living in a nursing home in Florida. She and

I exchanged a few letters, and we spoke on the phone, but unfortunately I never got to meet her in person. But when it came time to name Maile, Bryan and I knew we wanted to honor her. Pearl was the perfect namesake, exactly the kind of badass Army chick I hope my daughter becomes.

People like to say that I am the first sitting U.S. senator to have a baby. But I'm always quick to correct them: I'm the first ever to *give birth* while in office. The men here have been having children for generations—even if they didn't always acknowledge them.

While still pregnant, I asked Senator Amy Klobuchar, who was the ranking Democrat on the Rules and Administration Committee, to help change the Senate rules. At the time, babies and children weren't permitted on the Senate floor, and if that remained true, I wouldn't be able to vote or to introduce legislation.

I was planning to breastfeed Maile, as I had done with Abigail, so I couldn't be away from her for any real length of time. And I couldn't just hand Maile over to a staffer and race onto the floor to cast my vote—staff are federal employees, which would make even that brief moment of child care a conflict of interest. Besides, Senate votes are often scheduled in marathons, going on for hours on end. So if the rule didn't change, there was no doubt I'd end up missing votes—and with the Senate split at forty-seven Democrats to fifty-one Republicans (with two Independents), every single vote mattered.

Amy approached the Republican leadership, and almost immediately they began pushing back. Orrin Hatch, at eighty-four years old, seemed extremely worried that changing the rule for my baby might somehow unleash an army of babies. "What if there are ten babies on the floor of the Senate?" he asked, dead serious.

"That would be wonderful and a delight," said Amy.

But the Republicans remained deeply concerned. What if I

needed to change a diaper on the Senate floor? How unseemly! And what about decorum? Would babies be required to adhere to the Senate dress code? Amy tackled all these ridiculous questions with patience and good humor. She suggested that babies not be required to wear pants, skirts, ties, or shoes. "The baby is also not required to wear a Senate pin," she deadpanned, "because it would be dangerous."

As it turned out, all of this was just a smokescreen for the Republicans' most pressing concern. Eventually, they found a Republican woman who was willing to come deliver the question they really wanted to ask. Was I planning to...*breastfeed* on the Senate floor?

"Look," I said. "I have no intention of whipping out a boob in front of a bunch of seventy-year-old men, as enticing as that sounds. I really just want to be able to vote. But if the baby is hungry, I will feed her."

This didn't mollify them, and Babygate continued to rage. What if, someone suggested, instead of coming onto the Senate floor to vote, I simply carried my baby into the cloakroom off the back of the chamber? At the designated time, I could pop my head through the door that opens into the Senate chamber, and wave my hand to signal my vote! This maneuver actually had precedent: When Kirsten Gillibrand's son Henry was a toddler, that was how she had voted, to get around the no-children rule.

There was only one problem with this plan: I couldn't actually get into the cloakroom. There are two doors—one going in from the Senate floor (which wasn't an option with Maile), and another one that's a short walk from the elevator, then up a couple of steps. Meaning not wheelchair-accessible. So even if I wanted to use this workaround, just to get my vote recorded, I couldn't.

We were at an impasse. No matter how many arguments Amy

and I made to change the rule, the Republicans just weren't having it. Frustrated, I told Kaitlin to pass along a final message.

"Tell them that I *am* going to vote," I said. "And they have their choice of optics. They can either let me onto the Senate floor with my baby, and I'll just roll through, vote, and go home. Or, if I have to vote through the cloakroom, I will." Kaitlin just looked at me. She knew there was no chance I was capitulating, so she was waiting for what came next.

"But you might also remind them that the entrance to the cloakroom is next to the press gallery," I went on. "I will roll up to the steps outside the cloakroom. I will then crawl out of my wheelchair onto the floor, holding my baby in my teeth, and pull myself up the steps in order to go vote. Ask them which they'd rather have the press taking pictures of."

Kaitlin delivered my message, but incredibly, the Republicans still wouldn't consent to the apparent abomination of bringing a child onto the Senate floor. It wasn't until Republican senator Roy Blunt of Missouri became the chair of the Rules Committee, which happened the day after Maile was born, that he was finally able to persuade his colleagues to agree to change the rule. After weeks of debate and discussion, the Senate voted unanimously on April 18, 2018, to allow babies under the age of one onto the floor.

The very next day, I brought Maile to the floor for a vote. She was just ten days old, not much bigger than a doll, and in deference to the dress code, I had put a tiny green blazer over her onesie decorated with ducklings. That was the extent of my deference, though—there was no way in hell I was taking the little baby beanie off her head to comply with the "no hats in the chamber" rule.

I rolled into the chamber, my baby wrapped tightly to my chest, and quickly cast my vote—a thumbs-down against confirming an unqualified NASA appointee. I intended to turn around and roll right back out, but to my amusement, senators started flocking toward us from all sides. Chuck Schumer hurried over to see her, leaning down with a big smile on his face, and after being prodded by Amy Klobuchar, even Mitch McConnell ambled over for a look. My little Maile made history that day, as the first baby on the Senate floor. And all I—and probably many other women—could think was, *It's about time.*

A decade and a half after the shootdown, I had more blessings than I could count. I had a seat in the greatest deliberative body on earth, the U.S. Senate. I had good health, peace of mind, and a couple of kickass titanium legs. And I had my husband, who'd seen me through everything it took to make it this far, and our two beautiful girls.

Now there was just one more piece of unfinished business to take care of.

In April 2019 I returned to Iraq, not as a Soldier but as a senator. As a member of the Armed Services Committee, I led a congressional delegation (CODEL) with Senators Johnny Isakson and Angus King to receive operational and intelligence updates on the ground. I was excited to go back, because in addition to the goals of the CODEL, I had a personal goal to fulfill. Almost fifteen years earlier, I had been whisked out of Iraq unconscious and gravely injured, on a medevac aircraft. This time—for the first time—I wanted to leave Iraq under my own power. I had a score to settle.

The CODEL was scheduled to last just five days, because I didn't want to be away from Abigail and Maile for longer than that. With one day on each end for travel, that left three days to pack in meetings with Iraqi and Kurdish leadership, American diplomats, and Army personnel. We'd be staying in the U.S. Embassy compound, which was located in the Green Zone, where I'd had that beautiful stir-fry lunch and milkshake and bought those little Christmas ornaments of Babylon all those years ago.

Being in Iraq definitely stirred up old emotions. It's always hard for me to watch Soldiers going about their business, because I want nothing more than to be one of them again, enjoying the camaraderie and feeling the sense of purpose I always felt in uniform. But being a civilian among Soldiers in a combat environment was particularly unsettling. What made it even harder was that we'd be traveling around the Iraqi interior in helicopters, and I'd have to sit in the rear, rather than up in the cockpit where I belonged.

On our first morning after arriving in country, we were scheduled to fly in a Chinook helicopter from the U.S. Embassy compound in Baghdad to Taji. A Soldier handed everyone body armor, and while the other senators struggled to figure out how to get theirs on, I quickly slipped my arms through and fastened it tight. *Oh, yes*, I thought. *There it is.* This was pure muscle memory: zip, zip, zip, Velcro straps, helmet on, ready to go. I hooked my thumbs into my body armor, comforted by its familiar heft.

As we walked to the landing zone—the same LZ where I had taken off and landed hundreds of times during my deployment—I took a deep breath, and there it was: a smell so familiar, it felt like a part of me. The hot metal of the aircraft, the powdery dust, the whip of the rotor wash, the hydraulic fluid and JP-8 fuel. I heard the growl of the engine, saw the whirl of sand rise under the spinning rotor disc. When the helicopter rose into the sky, I was no longer in 2019—I was back with my crew in 2004, in the thick of the war. Lifting above the Baghdad skyline, with the Tigris to our east and the desert stretching out beyond the city, I felt the tears welling up.

Being back in a helicopter in Iraq was emotional enough. But later that day, one of the pilots informed me that they had a surprise for me. "Senator," he said, "we'd like to fly you over the spot." After researching the grid coordinates from reports filed on the day of the shootdown, they could pinpoint the location where my Black Hawk had gone down—and they wanted to take me to see it.

I had no words. I hadn't asked for this, and wouldn't have thought to. But in the seconds it took for me to get my brain around what the pilot was offering, I realized that I actually did want to go back. It took me a moment to find my voice, and when I did, I simply said, "Thank you."

The next afternoon everyone in our CODEL suited up again to fly out over the desert. The crew chief handed me a headset so I could communicate with the crew while airborne. As we zipped along at 2,000 feet—much higher than I had flown during missions—we talked about the aircraft, just general chitchat between fellow rotorheads. The Chinook has a loading ramp at the rear that can be opened in flight for a fuller view of the ground. The crew chief dropped the rear hatch so I could see out, and I watched as the familiar dusty terrain zipped by underneath us.

And then I saw the trees.

We flew right over the palm grove, and suddenly I could see the small clearing that had saved Dan, Matt, Chris, and me that day. The Black Hawk was long gone, having been blown up by U.S. forces after the shootdown so the enemy couldn't make any use of it. There was nothing in the clearing but the tall grass— the last thing I'd seen before passing out that day. Our helicopter circled the field, and as we all looked down silently, I had a fleeting thought that my foot, or perhaps just the boot, might even still be down there somewhere. Senator King snapped a photo of me, capturing that moment. I'm looking out the aircraft tail, lost in thought, wearing my prosthetic legs and holding a cane with my rebuilt arm. Though just a snapshot, it's also something more: a portrait of the person I am today, looking back in time at the events that made me who I am.

This had been a heavy moment for everyone, so heading back to the base, I joked around with the crew. "Are you sure that was the right spot?" I asked. "Because I didn't see my foot out there." The guys laughed, but they obviously knew how much it meant to me that they'd taken me there. Later that day, they presented me with a boot signed by the whole crew. "Sorry we didn't find your boot, ma'am," one of them said as he handed it to me. "But here's one for you to take home."

The next day, with that boot safely packed into my suitcase, I rolled onto an aircraft and left Iraq, fulfilling the dream I'd nurtured since waking up in Walter Reed all those years ago. I had closed the circle, leaving on my own terms. But although this was the first time I left Iraq under my own power, it won't be the last. I intend to keep going back, to work with the Iraqi people in hopes of rebuilding their country from the devastation of war. There's a piece of me there, both literally and figuratively, a tie that will bind me to that country forever.

The boot that the crew gave me now sits on a shelf in my Senate office. When I look at it, I see a reminder not of what I lost in Iraq, but of what I gained from my experiences there. That boot represents the camaraderie, the mission, and the sense of purpose I share with my fellow Soldiers. It serves as a reminder that no matter how grievous the wound, healing is always possible, and that the lowest moments can lead to the greatest heights.

It reminds me that every day is, indeed, a gift.

Acknowledgments

There are so many people to thank and simply not enough room to list all by name. Please forgive me if I do not mention you directly here, and know that I am aware of and thankful for your generosity and helping hand.

There's no way this book would have gotten written were it not for my collaborator, Lisa Dickey, who devoted so much energy to learning my voice and meeting all the remarkable individuals who have made my life possible. You have been ever patient with me and my need to cling to the security blanket of my Army identity. No one else could've made this book speak the way you have. Thank you.

Thank you also to Kaitlin Fahey, my friend and adult supervision for over a decade now. Some may call you my hammer, but without your organization, compassion, negotiation, and editorial skills, this book would never have happened. Your insights and frank assessments are precious to me, and I am forever grateful to you for never giving up on me.

To Kelsey Becker, who is rapidly reaching Kaitlin-level ability to instill fear in me, thank you for your problem-solving and continued support, no matter how much more I think I can stuff into my eternally overwhelmed schedule. Ben Garmisa, thank you for your help with my proposal and as a sounding board throughout. Sean Savett, thank you for being in my corner, and for helping me refine how I tell my story so it makes sense to a civilian audience. Randy Sikowski, you have always been my role model of an Army leader. I learned so much working for you in the ILARNG and continue to learn from you as we serve our constituents today. Thank you for being my fact-checker and my gut check on all things military.

I wouldn't be here today if it weren't for the heroism of the incredibly brave men who saved my life on November 12, 2004, putting their own lives in danger to do so: Dan Milberg, who landed our bird and, with Matt Backues, carried me out. Chris Fierce, who alerted the medics that I was still alive. Kurt Hannemann, who stood perimeter despite his own grievous wounds. Pat Muenks, who got the chain of rescue moving without a minute to spare. Thank you, my brothers in arms.

To all who were part of my rescue, care, and recovery, from that dusty field north of Taji through Baghdad, Balad, Landstuhl, Walter Reed, and up to my life today, thank you. Dan Halvachek and the rest of the medevac aircrew who fought to keep me alive. The staff at the Combat Surgical Hospital in Baghdad, including Dan Ravasio and Adam Hamawy. The Walter Reed Army Medical Center family, including Astrid Strum, Carol Gandy, Bunnie Wyckoff, Lieutenant Colonel (ret.) Bob Bahr, Harvey Naranjo, Steve and Barb Springer, John Nerges, Paul Pasquina, Gerald Farber, Benjamin Potter, and so many others. Thank you for the priceless gifts of your time, your skill, and your dedication, which you gave to me every single day of my recovery. I can never repay you, but I pledge on this day, as I do every Alive Day, to live every minute trying to be worthy of your heroism and sacrifice.

Acknowledgments

No acknowledgment would be complete without thanking my friend and mentor, Dick Durbin. When you met me in 2005, you didn't see the wounds or the wheelchair. You didn't see someone to be pitied. You looked past all that and saw my Soldier's heart that was searching for a new mission. You challenged me to serve in a new way, in public office, and have been with me at every step. You gave me the gift of this new life every bit as much as my crew and the troops who rescued me and kept me alive.

To Sean Desmond and the publishing team at Twelve, including Rachel Kambury and Stacey Reid, thank you for making this book a reality. Thank you, Bob Barnett and Deneen Howell, for your advice and wisdom. And thank you, Annie Leibovitz, for the use of your gorgeous photo on the cover.

To my mom and my brother, we've come a longer way than I ever thought imaginable. We survived and thrived, and I couldn't be prouder of where each one of us is now. Thank you for always finding ways for us to support each other.

To my husband, Bryan, my partner ever since our ROTC days, thank you for choosing to journey through life with me. Your slightly wicked smile and impossibly flirty eyes, which won me over the first time we met, still melt my heart today. We've seen some challenging and downright life-threatening times, but we have survived to enjoy so many gifts. And now I can see your smile and mischievous sense of humor reflected in our girls, both of whom are just like their Daddy in their own unique ways.

Thank you to my girls, Abigail and Maile. You are all the joy in my world. No matter what happens during my day, seeing you, hearing your voices, holding you in my arms floods my heart and soul with love and utter wonderment that I have received this priceless gift of being your mommy. You are both named for strong women, and I know you will grow into powerful, caring young ladies, capable of doing anything you set your minds to achieving. Just remember that not all children grow up with the privileges you enjoy every day. As you make your own journeys through life, I hope you will take to heart the lessons of this book, practicing empathy and sharing the gifts you've been given with others who may be laboring to survive the challenges in their own lives.

Photo Credits

1A, 1B, 1C, 2A, 2B, 2C, 3A, 3B, 3C, 4A, 4B, 7A, 7B, 8A, 9A, 10A, 11A, 12B, 14A, 16B: Duckworth family photo collection. 6A, 6B: U.S. Army. 8B, 9B, 11B: David Carson/*Post-Dispatch*/Polaris. 10B: Chip Somodevilla/Reuters. 12A: Dept. of Veterans Affairs. 12C: Saul Loeb/AFP via Getty Images. 13A: Jessica Rinaldi/Reuters. 13B: Courtesy Sen. Cory Booker. 13C: Stan Honda/AFP via Getty Images. 14B: Courtesy Pat Muenks. 14C: Dailyherald.com/Mark Welsh. 15A: AP Photo/Kevin Wolf. 15B: Alex Wong/Getty Images. 16A: Courtesy Sen. Angus King.

About the Author

Senator Tammy Duckworth is a former U.S. Army lieutenant colonel who has served as the junior United States Senator for Illinois since 2017. A proud Iraq War veteran and helicopter pilot, she represented Illinois's 8th district in the United States House of Representatives from 2013 to 2017. Before election to office, she served as Assistant Secretary for Public and Intergovernmental Affairs in the United States Department of Veterans Affairs (2009–11) and Director of the Illinois Department of Veterans Affairs (2006–09).